Praise for

An Inconvenience of Penguins

'Fascinating and funny, this book – unlike its charismatic subject – wonderfully takes flight.'
Peter Ross,
author of *Steeple Chasing*

'Jamie Lafferty has written a kind of Antarctic *Roughing It* – a wise, rude, hilarious and oddly moving account of the author's unusual quest to see all eighteen species of penguin. Like several of the birds he writes about, real travel writers are critically endangered. *An Inconvenience of Penguins* proves they are not extinct.'
Ed Caesar,
author of *The Moth and the Mountain*

'Jamie Lafferty is undoubtedly one of the best travel writers in the English language today: this brilliant debut is both a mad quest and fantastically original memoir. It reveals, in glorious technicolour, so much about these little black and white birds.'
Oliver Smith,
author of *On This Holy Island*

'Travel writer turned global birder Jamie Lafferty embarks on an epic quest – in which the journey is at least as entertaining as the end result.'
Stephen Moss,
author of *Ten Birds That Changed the World*

'Perched at the edges of our human world, penguins now find themselves at the front line in the emergency we humans have launched upon them. Jamie Laffery's epic adventures in search of these charismatic avians is highly entertaining and gloriously obsessional in equal degrees. A very enjoyable read.'
Philip Hoare,
author of *Leviathan*

'A brilliantly vivid, ice-blasted account of one travel-writer's determination to see all 18 species of penguin. Jamie is funny, bluntly truthful and so skilled in making us feel as if we're there among the fluffy Adélie chicks. Bombastic, adventurous fun.'
Lizzie Pook,
author of *Maude Horton's Glorious Revenge*

'Every page has lyrical and witty words about travel, penguins and penguin people. I've read many books about penguins, this is the best!'
Nigel Marven,
wildlife filmmaker

'Came here for the penguins; stayed for the stories of their fried eggs, gossip about the love lives of Antarctic explorers, etymological trivia and witty footnotes. An eclectic and delightful whirlwind of a book.'
Joanna Bagniewska,
author of *The Modern Bestiary*

An Inconvenience *of* Penguins

An Inconvenience *of* Penguins

JAMIE LAFFERTY

Epic voyages in pursuit of the
world's most beloved bird

Copyright © 2025 Jamie Lafferty

The right of Jamie Lafferty to be identified as the Author of the Work has been asserted by him in accordance with the Copyright, Designs and Patents Act 1988.

First published in 2025 by Wildfire
An imprint of Headline Publishing Group Limited

1

Apart from any use permitted under UK copyright law, this publication may only be reproduced, stored, or transmitted, in any form, or by any means, with prior permission in writing of the publishers or, in the case of reprographic production, in accordance with the terms of licences issued by the Copyright Licensing Agency.

Cataloguing in Publication Data is available from the British Library.

Hardback ISBN 978 1 0354 1312 6
Trade Paperback ISBN 978 1 0354 1313 3

Designed and typeset by EM&EN
Printed and bound in Great Britain by Clays Ltd, Elcograf S.p.A.

Headline's policy is to use papers that are natural, renewable and recyclable products and made from wood grown in well-managed forests and other controlled sources. The logging and manufacturing processes are expected to conform to the environmental regulations of the country of origin.

Headline Publishing Group Limited
An Hachette UK Company
Carmelite House
50 Victoria Embankment
London EC4Y 0DZ

The authorised representative in the EEA is Hachette Ireland,
8 Castlecourt Centre, Dublin 15, D15 XTP3, Ireland (email: info@hbgi.ie)

www.headline.co.uk
www.hachette.co.uk

For Wheelsie, obviously.

And KHMS.

Contents

Author's Note xi

Prologue xiii

1. Spark Bird 1

2. Penguin Supper 25

3. Love in a Cold Climate 45

4. Penguins in the Shit 60

5. Think of the Children 77

6. 'And then we heard the Emperors calling' 98

7. Requiem for a Penguin 117

8. Out of Reach 130

9. Extinction Events 146

10. Fear and Loathing in Las Malvinas 165

11. War and Penguin 182

12. Feathered, Untethered 192

13. A Troubled Kingdom 210

14. All at Sea 228

15. A Town Called Penguin *or*
The Little Penguin That Could 249

16. Does a Penguin Shit in the Woods? 269

17. Macca Attacker 282

18. Bingo Bird 297

Epilogue 315

Acknowledgements 317

Author's Note

I have capitalised every penguin name in this book, chiefly because it looked tidier than mixing ordinary and proper nouns. Also, because all penguins are created equal.*

The footnotes have not been used for citation or reference. This is not an academic text, and certainly not a guidebook. In fact, I would advise against attempting to see every penguin species in the world.

Population estimates mostly come from BirdLife. Many are years out of date.

---

* Except the Kings, which are just a bit better than the others.

Prologue

> But, I have to smile, for the salt of the sea is in my blood, and there may be ten thousand roads over the land, but they shall never confuse me, for my heart's blood will ever return to its beautiful source.
> – John Fante, *Ask the Dust*, 1939

Ahead there was nothing but penguins. A writhing wall of Kings filled the air with noise and colour and stench. Over 60,000 of the birds stood in front of me at Gold Harbour, their high trumpeting calls competing in the gloaming of South Georgia. An expedition cruise ship patiently waited at anchor while the penguins continued urgently about their penguin business.

The din was incredible. The polar regions can be deeply silent places, but this avian city was cacophonous. A hanging glacier framed this congregation of birds, which have colonised the southern section of Gold Harbour's sweeping beach for decades. The penguins appeared in such numbers and confusion that they looked like snow on a broken television. As we transferred to shore we had first smelled them, then heard them, then finally saw them.

The penguins were not solely responsible for the atrocious reek. The colony was interspersed with pinnipeds – colossal southern elephant seals, gigantic jiggling monsters which heaped on top of each other, moulting and belching throughout

Prologue

the afternoon. They were joined by belligerent fur seals, which bluff-charged penguins and people alike and were beloved by neither.

While some passengers panicked, the birds mostly just tottered away disgusted. Though also prone to violent outbursts, the Kings typically carry themselves with comparative dignity and almost noble bearing. I only really saw them lose their tempers when a neighbour got too close, or a villainous Antarctic skua attempted to snatch a young chick.

Running between these taller, more self-conscious birds were Gentoo penguins, their white head flashes and fiery orange feet catching the eye as they dashed through the colony. Flippers held back, they looked like carefree children running around pretending to be airplanes. Snowy sheathbills and giant petrels flew above, as did the occasional South Georgia pintail duck. In the air and on the ground, everything appeared to be in motion.

I stood with my notebook trying to work out what to write. It was January 2020 and I was on a travel writing assignment; somehow, I'd managed to get another Antarctic trip hosted to facilitate a newspaper article.* It was, improbably, the fifth time I'd succeeded in this – editors at home were beginning to regard me as some kind of polar specialist. Even as the primal scenes unfolded in front of me, I wanted more; if I could keep it up, I could become the go-to correspondent for the Antarctic region. It was a place I didn't want to share, especially as any time I read

---

* Virtually all modern travel writing is facilitated by media being hosted in exchange for guaranteed coverage. The write-up will almost always be positive. For the cruise company, hotel, airline, tourist board, etc., this is much cheaper than buying traditional adverts.

Prologue

a piece by a contemporary or rival, I was left disappointed and sometimes irritated.

Their problem, in part, was the penguins. The writers would inevitably come down here and be overwhelmed by the birds, then spend 1,999 words of a 2,000-word article screaming, 'I LOVE PENGUINS!' On the first few trips, that had been my impulse too – only now was a broader picture starting to settle in my mind. As Antarctic tourism grew, the more ambitious editors wanted to know what lay beyond the birds.

Still, this was just my second visit to South Georgia, one of the world's great penguin epicentres, and it was again hard to stay calm. They amass here with far greater densities than even continental Antarctica, and standing in front of that regal wall, there was no point in fighting the bedlam, the joy. As I looked across the beach, twinkling black and white and gold, a young expedition guide walked past me. It was her first-ever time in South Georgia and she was struggling to remain professional; when I asked what she thought of it all, she grabbed the thick cuff of my thermal jacket and stared back with wet eyes, saying nothing.

I remembered a line from Sir Ernest Shackleton, who failed in his endeavours every time he came to the Antarctic region but is still cherished as a polar hero. 'Tongue and pen fail in attempting to describe the magic,' wrote the man they called The Boss. I'd learned a bit about Shackleton on the trip – we'd even visited his grave in the old whaling station of Grytviken the previous day – and while I was sceptical about his beatification, I thought that line at least sounded relatable. How to describe all this and even get close to sufficiency? I took some photographs and opted to worry about it later.

The travelling year ahead felt as full as the beach, a long

Prologue

road of golden possibilities: after this voyage I'd have a month in India, three weeks in British Columbia, a month switching between nations in West Africa. I knew nothing about Guinea-Bissau but I was eager to learn. I'd been freelance for four years and this felt like it was finally going to be the one when everything would click into place.

Yet I couldn't help wonder when I'd get back here – South Georgia, Antarctica; all of it was so vast and chaotic and profound, as magnetic as the pole itself. The other places might be genuinely transcendent and fascinating and all the other adjectives I'd use to write about them, but I knew they wouldn't be able to trump *this*. Shackleton echoed again: 'We were now revelling in the indescribable freshness of the Antarctic that seems to permeate one's being, and which must be responsible for that longing to go again which assails each returned explorer from polar regions.'

What part the penguins played in that deep southerly current was harder to define. This cold world could be punishing and merciless, but the birds brought levity. Though their brethren often fell around them, they waddled on, appearing soft in a hard landscape, amusing when surrounded by gravitas. Without them here, the place would be a grey void. No penguins, no party.

We reboarded the ship in time for dinner and cocktails, and the Australian passengers all rushed online. On previous trips I'd regarded the internet as a pollution in this otherwise prehistoric place – all it ever did was provide distractions when there were plenty outside. Plus, the news was always of something up north on fire: a government, a city, an idea. In early 2020, Australia was literally aflame, with wildfires engulfing almost every state. The passengers wanted to check that their families

Prologue

and property were safe before allowing themselves to get back to the bar. This, finally, seemed like a reasonable use of the internet in the Antarctic region.

I'd taken the decision not to connect at all, but little bits of news were still discussed around me. Harry and Meghan had stepped down as active members of the royal family. Some earnest Americans asked what I thought but I couldn't even pretend to care. Someone else mentioned a novel disease rapidly emerging in Asia, which sounded like science fiction, tinged with a hint of racism. I thought little of it. Instead, I ordered another drink, reviewed some penguin photos, then stood back while other passengers turned up the music and danced like it was the end of the world.

1

Spark Bird*

> What outlandish beings are these? . . . Their bodies are grotesquely misshapen; their bills short; their feet seemingly legless; while the members at their sides are neither fin, wing, nor arm. And truly neither fish, flesh, nor fowl is the penguin . . . without exception the most ambiguous and least lovely creature yet discovered by man . . . As if ashamed of her failure, Nature keeps this ungainly child hidden away at the ends of the earth.
>
> – Herman Melville, *The Encantadas*, 1854

I was just over 11,000 km away from the penguin in question, Italian wine tickling the edges of my thoughts, when an idea arrived. I didn't want to leave Sorrento – or at least I didn't want to go back home to Scotland. It was now mid-September 2020, and though this sliver of European travel had been possible, a new wave of the disease was about to break. Another lockdown already felt inevitable, and I would soon be back in solitary confinement, eating porridge for every breakfast and lentil stew for every dinner, then sad-drinking whatever money was left.

---

* 'For a birder, a spark bird is the one you see, usually in some kind of unexpected situation, that grabs you in a way that you haven't been grabbed before by birds, and turns you on to a wavelength that you haven't been turned on to before.' – Noah Strycker, *This American Life*, 2021.

An Inconvenience of Penguins

By comparison, the scene in front of me was one of civility and calm. On the table a carafe of Pinot Grigio was perspiring next to a bowl of perfect olives. The temperature in Sorrento had hit the absolute optimum for shorts and t-shirts.[*] Everyone looked beautiful, even if they weren't. When I focused, I could hear the blissful sounds of the Tyrrhenian Sea.

Earlier that day I'd been in Pompeii, which, owing to the Covid pandemic, had 85 per cent fewer tourists than usual. That had been blissful in a way too. Without all the people I could feel just how huge and tragic the place was, without fear of being decapitated by a selfie stick or accidentally trampling a child to death. Without those distractions, it was possible to remember that the petrified city is a mass grave.

My guide, Lino Davide, admitted that his job was easier now, too. 'When Napoli had seven or eight cruise ships, it would get so busy here we couldn't see the stones,' he said, theatrically casting a hand across the ancient Roman city. Financially it was a disaster, and no one knew how or when things would get better, but Lino could at least appreciate the quiet.

I was on assignment in Italy for *The Times*, my first real work in seven months. All the grand globetrotting plans for 2020 had fallen away with such violent haste that this unimaginative trip to a country I don't particularly like felt exotic and thrilling.

Back home, the future had never felt less certain. On the face of it, I had very little – I'd been a travel writer for over a decade and now there was no travel. I similarly had no pets, no children, no income, no guarantees. It all felt like a terrible trap, a tight snare around my ankles.

---

[*]   23°C.

Spark Bird

But what if, the Italian wine asked, what if there was a way to escape all that? What if there was a chance to abscond? What if while on the run I could see penguins once more? The last time things had felt uncomplicated was on that feral beach at Gold Harbour. Seeing those demented little fun machines again in this wretched year felt like it could turn things around – clouds would part, gloom would lift. Or I'd sicken, run out of money and get stuck abroad somewhere sinister, but at least I wouldn't be locked down in that dismal little flat.

There was nowhere else quite like South Georgia, but surely there was a substitute somewhere. I opened Google Maps and spun the globe like a bored Greek deity, looking for the birds' territories. Australia and New Zealand were firmly shut. Little information was coming out of South Africa. No ships were going back to the Antarctic regions. I spun the world again, an idea formed, and I stopped my finger on Ecuador.

I texted a friend working in travel PR.

> On a scale of suicidal–10, how would you rate my great idea to go to the Galapagos?

The reply came four minutes later.

> I'd go if I could. Haven't they set up some kind of safe corridor from Quito?

I had no idea. I was half drunk at the gateway to the Amalfi Coast – until five minutes earlier I hadn't thought about the Galapagos, or its endemic penguins, in a very long time. But now it seemed clear: if this could happen, then it must.

Since April I'd mostly been focused on how to stretch my £904.89 monthly welfare payment cleverly enough to avoid getting evicted. The money I was earning from *The Times* would

An Inconvenience of Penguins

be a mirage – £400 that would get deducted from the next Universal Credit payment. I'd only really start 'earning' if I got over the £904.89, a lesson I'd learned the hard way. When a surprise payment from a magazine I'd assumed was deceased arrived, I indulgently had a photobook printed.* This was all very jolly until I saw that my benefit payment had been slashed owing to my earnings.

I was more careful now, plus I'd recently received the first of the Self-Employed Income Support Scheme payments, which wasn't the great act of generosity it was purported to be but gave me just about enough money to pay for the flights to Ecuador.† Some travel editors hinted that I might be able to pitch stories once there – they just weren't willing to commit to anything ahead of time.

Nonetheless, at least one tour company said they'd be able to get me on a cruise ship if I made it as far as the islands. And so, like Ishmael on the dole, 'having little or no money in my purse, and nothing particular to interest me on shore, I thought I would sail about a little and see the watery part of the world'.

Twelve days later I was on a flight from Edinburgh to Madrid, then another to Quito.

My friend, the writer Stephen Phelan, lives in Madrid and agreed to meet me at the airport during the layover. The bars weren't open inside and he couldn't come into the building

---

* This was supposed to cover the last 10 years of travel for me but ended up mostly being pictures of the penguin species I'd seen on various trips in that time.

† The SEISS money wiped out my Universal Credit payment; it was also taxable.

without a ticket of his own, so we met by the taxi rank. He'd brought a bag of beer; I felt it hit my back when we hugged. Both of us held our breath during the embrace, then nervously crept along to a bench and surreptitiously opened a couple of cans like naughty teenagers, fully expecting to be moved along by the police. We were hardly Hemingway and Fitzgerald, but the sun was shining, Madrid's malicious summer heat had faded, and my pal and I were having a beer together for the first time in more than a year.

'I don't really know how long I'll be away, or what it'll be like when I get there,' I said, taking a sip of a strange blueberry IPA. 'But I don't see that there's much to lose.'

'So long as you stay healthy,' said Stephen, with justifiable concern.

I explained that Ecuador was coming out of an exceptionally bleak period of the pandemic, but with austral spring breaking, case rates were far lower than in darkening Europe. Mask-wearing was compulsory inside and out. Social distancing was mandatory. The South Americans had learned the hard way – but unlike the British, they had at least learned.

A *New York Times* report from Guayaquil described the nadir as seen by a doctor: 'There were corpses in wheelchairs, in stretchers and on the floor in the emergency area. The smell was such that the staff refused to enter. Several colleagues fell sick and waited in wheelchairs for patients to die, hoping it would give them a chance to use a ventilator.'

'Look after yourself,' said Stephen when we parted. I promised I would, as though I had any control over an ungovernable and invisible disease.

The 11-hour flight from Madrid to Quito was mostly empty. No booze was served, but almost every passenger could luxuriate in a row of their own. I spent my conscious hours doing my taxes from the previous year, sorting an unruly bag of receipts. I flicked through the chaotically busy months of 2019, smiling at some of the memories, guessing at some of the handwritten chitties, all the while building towards the sudden and complete stop of March 2020.

Landing in the Andes, we were shepherded in front of Ecuadorians in hazmat suits who were wholly disguised by their protective gear and not in the mood for small talk. Some of the new arrivals, dizzy with jetlag and Quito's altitude, looked miserable in the face of all the fuss. I waved around proof of my disease-free status that I'd paid £100 for in Glasgow and made a note to include it on my work expenses in the next round of tax calculations. A clean bill of health had got me into the country, but I was told I'd need another to fly to the Galapagos.

The following morning, I went for a walk around the city, the altitude placing rubber bands around my lungs. I'd had fantasies of reading a book in a bar, or picking at a meal in a plaza, but most places hadn't reopened even though they were now legally permitted to do so. Quito had the feeling of being locked in a long, hungover Sunday.

Covid-19 was clinging to every surface, even when it wasn't. Masks never came off. Hand sanitiser was thrown around in the fashion of sumo wrestlers with salt. Some buildings, including my hotel, had their visitors walk through ozone chambers which apparently helped sterilise clothes, then disquietingly greeted guests by putting a temperature gun to their heads. The local market sprayed entrants with disinfectant, while in some shops, tellers wearing medical gloves misted individual notes with antibacterial spray. It was impossible to know if these measures were worthwhile, but the Ecuadorians had not forgotten their Covid dead.

Back at the hotel that night, two short nurses came to my room for the next Covid test, burrowing deep inside my skull to search for a disease that wasn't there. '*¿Listo?*' asked Gabriela, who was decked from head to toe in PPE. *Listo* means 'ready' in Spanish, but it can also mean 'clever'. I wasn't the former before the test began and felt less of the latter by the time it ended. Through watering eyes and between fits of sneezing, I was at least grateful that they'd brought a card machine – and that they'd charged half as much as at home.

By breakfast there was confirmation of what I'd already suspected: I was still fit to travel.

It takes a little over two hours to fly to the Galapagos from Quito, the pilots dropping off the Andes like seabirds from cliffs. I'd visited the islands almost a decade earlier as a filthy backpacker but had never had the chance to return. It can be a difficult destination to sell to British travel titles – a little too niche for some, too distant for others. In my years of pitching it, at least one editor said that they weren't comfortable promoting a destination that was already being ruined by over-tourism.*

That was of course not going to be a problem this time round – along with the penguins, it was the sudden emptiness that had brought me all the way from the restaurant in Sorrento. The marketing machine around the Galapagos had been relentless in the years I'd been away, and the number of tourist boats had swollen to a fleet of over 100. Since the pandemic began, tour companies that had cynically claimed to be offering

---

* It's also the sort of trip some travel editors keep for themselves.

An Inconvenience of Penguins

'small-ship' cruises with 'just 100' passengers – the maximum allowed by local authorities – had mostly sailed their vessels elsewhere to be dry-docked.* Now, the handful that were nervously returning were going with the line that this was a chance to 'see the Galapagos like they were 30 years ago'.

I was just glad to see them at all. Our plane looped around the northern islands, black volcanic bodies in the glittering Pacific, then landed smoothly into a warm headwind on Baltra Island, on an airstrip originally built by American forces during the Second World War. Guides waited for us under face masks and sunglasses, identifiable only by the boards they were holding.

A dozen or so of us were herded together under a Metropolitan Touring banner, then transferred to our ship for the next few days: *La Pinta*. As we shuffled off the tarmac, I noticed a handful of Darwin's finches fluttering nearby.

The great scientist's presence on the islands is never forgotten, nor undersold, and his visage is used to promote everything from coffee to diving tours. It is true he came here in 1835, though not as the wizened old man with a waterfall beard, nor even as the stocky, balding 40-something with impressive sideburns. Darwin was just 26 when he visited the Galapagos, and though he gathered samples and data that would, much later, help form his theories of evolution, he had no epiphany while on the archipelago. He never came back, either.

He made no mention of penguins specifically, but he was presumably referring to them and endemic flightless cormorants when he described 'aquatic birds', some of which were

---

* Meaning they're lifted out of the water and kept dry, either for repairs or to avoid the endless gnawing of the salty ocean.

'peculiar to these islands, and some common to North and South America'.

Here he was possibly confused by the endemic Galapagos penguin looking much like its cousin, the Humboldt, which he would have seen in Peru, and the Magellanic, which he saw when visiting the Falklands on the same epic voyage. Along with the African species, this family of four are collectively known as banded penguins. The Galapagos bird is the smallest in the genus and looks distinct, the clear black and white lines common to the other three instead smudged across its chest and face.

By far the northernmost species, *Spheniscus mendiculus* is perhaps the least penguiny penguin.* Far removed from the icy homes of so many better-known species, they nest on lava rock, endure heat few of their brethren could survive, and share the ocean with sharks, rays and usually no small number of tourists. They are highly endangered, and were they to go extinct, it seems unlikely that any other penguin would migrate to this equatorial archipelago to fill their niche.

To be described inaccurately or even ignored by young Darwin was a mercy. His diary has repeated mentions of tormenting the local animals, at one point knocking a Galapagos hawk off its perch with the end of his rifle. Several other animals had it worse, and none were abused more than the giant tortoise – today the islands' chief mascot and symbol of ecological fragility, but to the crew of HMS *Beagle*, a lumbering packed lunch.

---

* I promise I'm not going to bore you with Latin names throughout this book, but this one translates as Wedged Little Beggar, which is at least pretty funny.

An Inconvenience of Penguins

Like most visitors in the 19th century, Darwin feasted on these huge animals, remarking that the 'breastplate roasted, with the flesh attached to it, is very good; and the young tortoises make excellent soup'. By 1835, sailors had been coming to the islands for 300 years, though few had successfully managed to settle. Just as they'd done with penguins around the coasts of South America, buccaneers, whalers and survivors of shipwrecks all ate giant tortoises. It is estimated that as many as 200,000 were harvested, with some ships taking hundreds at a time.*

The reptiles made for an ideal takeaway meal: able to be stored for months on their backs without food or water, they provided meat and fat, which according to US Navy Captain David Porter was 'as yellow as our best butter, and of a sweeter flavour than a hog's lard'. It's said that the poor, delicious tortoises could even be boiled directly in their shells when the time came. At some point, it was also discovered that you could drink straight from a sac near their necks if you couldn't find water elsewhere. Intrepid Charlie gave it a go, merrily reporting that it had 'only a very slightly bitter taste'. Porter was more effusive, insisting it was 'perfectly fresh and sweet'.

Darwin was also gleeful when annoying the tortoises:

> I was always amused, when overtaking one of these great monsters as it was quietly pacing along . . . I frequently got on their backs, and then, upon giving a few raps on the hinder part of their shell, they would rise up and walk away, but I found it very difficult to keep my balance.

---

* For its part, the *Beagle* took 30 before making its trans-Pacific crossing.

Spark Bird

Young Charles may have been, as one of his uncles put it, a 'man of enlarged curiosity', but the Galapagos penguin should be glad it too wasn't regarded as one of his edible playthings.

I spent four days on *La Pinta* touring the eastern islands. A tentative enquiry about the chance of seeing the local penguins was waved off – their small colonies are mostly found in the west of the archipelago. The Galapagos penguin is the second smallest in the world and, owing to its endemism, one of the rarest, with no more than 2,000 believed alive. In the aftermath of the catastrophic 1982–83 El Niño, their numbers were thought to have dropped by almost 80 per cent. Annual populations go up and down depending on the temperature of the Humboldt Current, the cold waters of which run north along the western side of South America. The chillier the sea, the more abundant the penguins' food, but El Niños disrupt this complex system and effectively starve the birds. Even without that, recent estimates suggest that they are losing 100 individuals a year, giving them less than two decades before functional extinction.

And yet everywhere across the islands, there was a seductive sense that for many species, the Galapagos is still a wild place, near perfect and thriving. One morning at Punta Pitt we walked across a beach, the soft sand interlaced with olivine crystals, glinting in the sun like tiny emeralds. The guides gave us an hour in the water there, and I spent most of it flirting with a sea lion, crushing my lungs as I tried to swim with it, watching it copy my somersaults, then trying not to panic when it lurched directly towards me, only to bank away at the last moment.

I came up for air, keeping an eye on my playmate while I took in as much oxygen as I could, then swam back to the sandy bottom where we both floated for a moment, watching each other. Down there, the weight of the world was simultaneously bearing down on me and entirely forgotten. Down there, there wasn't a pandemic or squabbling politicians or a climate emergency – or anything, really, beyond another curious mammal and some inscrutable starfish. But there wasn't any air either, so I righted myself and kicked for the surface.

The cruise continued south to Española, thought to be the oldest of the Galapagos's 13 major islands. I hadn't seen any penguins, but I was drinking free cocktails, trying to convince my stubborn Celtic skin to take a tan, and no longer worried about, well, everything. I still had no money and wouldn't be able to tip the lovely staff at the end, but this was nonetheless fine make-believe.

The guides explained that new land is born when lava is ejected from a volcanic hotspot on the ocean floor, then carried away by the movement of the continental plate. Eventually, as it shifts east, room is made for new islands. The theory is that this process finally leads to them being dragged under the South American plate. I imagined it was like little puffs of cloud coming out of a chimney, only to drift away on a gentle breeze before fading, then disappearing. It was like that, only with billions of tonnes of lava over several million years. In any case, the islands in the west are the youngest and those in the east are the oldest, one day fated to vanish under the waves, assuming sea levels haven't already risen to drown them. One way or another, low-lying Española will likely be the first to go. It seemed wise of the already endangered penguins to primarily nest on the opposite side of the island chain.

The cruise ended in Puerto Ayora, the largest town on the Galapagos, home to the majority of its 30,000 human residents. It had grown and become gaudier in the decade since I'd visited as a backpacker, necessarily augmented to cater for large numbers of tourists, all now suddenly banished by the pandemic. Alongside Charles Darwin, images of penguins adorned mugs and t-shirts, though both were outnumbered by doodles of blue-footed boobies.

Many of the businesses were still shuttered, some permanently.* As the largest and most developed settlement on the archipelago, lockdown had been strictest here. The economic impact was most keenly felt, too – around 300,000 visitors had been forecast for 2020, though in the end just 75,000 made it, with almost the entirety coming in the first couple of months before Covid-19 could no longer be ignored. Since the 1960s, more and more of the Galapagos had turned towards tourism, and by the time of the 2020 collapse, 90 per cent of the $800 million economy relied on it.

With the weak government in Quito unable or unwilling to ease the islanders' plight, many of those who remained entered a barter system. I heard of fruit being traded for meat, milk for English lessons. Clothes were handed down, not just within families but through the community. A farmer I spoke to said he'd swapped 50 oranges for some dental work. Elsewhere, Brett Peters and Maria Ayala, the affable owners of the Galapagos Deli in Puerto Ayora, traded produce they couldn't use in their restaurant for houseplants to decorate their new home. Realising she wasn't going to be aboard any cruise ships for the foreseeable future, naturalist Lola Villacreses did a crash course online

---

* This including the old brothel, a multi-storey hovel that was on the market for $750,000, a high price no matter how much cleaning had taken place.

and began growing fruits and vegetables on her smallholding in the fertile Santa Cruz highlands. Whenever I bumped into her, she gave me a bucket of tomatoes.

'Things have been changing very fast. All the money used to be in the town, but not now,' said Matías Espinosa, a dive master and naturalist whose businesses had also been crippled by the pandemic. We'd been introduced in the Galapagos Deli and spent a couple of hours fretting about our futures, as well as that of the island. Half German, half Ecuadorian, Matías was intense and likeable and had a habit of laughing so hard with his head flung back that he dislodged his glasses. At other times, he spoke with such resignation I couldn't meet his eye.

'Covid froze all our enterprise,' he said while sipping a coffee and pushing his glasses back up his nose. 'Instead, we have this trading now, so the farmers are the kings of the island.' He explained that cash hadn't been abandoned entirely – even during the most stringent lockdown locals had paid for fuel for fishing boats that brought in catch on behalf of the community. Upon returning, the day's haul was announced over megaphones, and fish that would ordinarily be exported to the US at great expense were taken door to door and given away.

At times, I thought this sounded Edenic – calamity bonding a community at the very edge of the map, allowing it to eschew money in favour of organic trade and kindness. Inevitably, it was more complicated than that. Matías explained that most businesses had been founded on loans at egregious rates, which were almost tolerable when the islands were awash with tourists but now felt like they were squeezing the last of the life out of the residents. He worried not only for himself and for his young family, but for the animals of the Galapagos, too.

Spark Bird

'We have shown that tourism can directly support conservation, but now we have no tourism,' he said, looking out on to a quiet road. 'If 30,000 people cannot find a way to live with nature in this paradise, then you can take that as an example for the human species. If we can't make it work, then maybe we need to prepare our backpacks and find a way to live on the moon.'

Matías suggested I do the Galapagoan equivalent of this anyway by heading to Isabela, in the west of the archipelago. It is the most sparsely populated of the islands for one thing, but a home of the Galapagos penguin for another. I could easily have stayed in Puerto Ayora and relaxed some more, but I'd travelled so far it seemed like a ridiculous waste not to try and see the birds. At this point in the whole adventure, I was penguin-curious rather than obsessed. It felt like I still had some free will, and yet even with that, I chose to chase the birds.

I asked Brett Peters to help with the logistics – as well as the deli, he owned a small tour company that he'd set up just months before the industry fell apart. Despite the obvious challenges, he was endlessly generous with his time and support, and, thanks to him, just a couple of days later I was on a bumpy speedboat careening across the waves towards a new island and its penguins.

Larger than all the other islands combined, Isabela is comprised of five volcanoes fused together by eruptions and time. Despite its enormousness, just 2,000 people live there, though in late 2020 many – afraid that their distant home might become a jail cell where they'd be locked in with the virus – had retreated to places they could get access to a ventilator.

An Inconvenience of Penguins

When I met guide Pablo Valladares by the island's main dock, Isabela had only just been declared Covid-free. Pablo, who ordinarily led nature tours across the island, explained that I was his first guest since February, and that after our time together in late October, he didn't have anything else booked for the rest of the year.

His ample availability was virtually unprecedented – the last time Sir David Attenborough and his BBC crew came to Isabela, Pablo was their local fixer. His day rate was high, his calendar full, and then the planet shut down. For several months, he'd been spending his time surfing and tending to a small farm, grateful he had some savings. It wasn't ideal, but things had been a lot worse.

When the pandemic broke out, Pablo had been on a trip of his own, to Nicaragua's Corn Islands. As news of a national lockdown arrived, he found himself in a frantic dash to get back to Ecuador. With his wife and son, he made it as far as his sister's place in the plague-ridden city of Guayaquil before the planes stopped. There they spent three months cooped up in her apartment. From the window Pablo would occasionally see fires on a hillside outside a hospital. He thought they were burning the possessions of the dead. He hoped it was only their possessions.

On arriving back in Isabela, the guide found that his neighbour had dropped off a basket of fruit collected from his garden. These care packages continued to arrive every day while the family quarantined until Pablo could finally cross the street and shake the man's hand. 'We weren't even close friends before *la pandemia*,' he said as we walked up a sandy road towards the village of Puerto Villamil. 'Now I'm teaching his son to surf, to show my gratitude.'

Spark Bird

While the bartering had eased in Puerto Ayora, it was still a vital part of life on Isabela. Without anything to trade, I had brought all the cash I could with me – it wasn't much but I hoped it would at least be enough to get me through a week on the island. Still, I felt guilty when walking down the dusty main street, where vendors would stand at their doors and wave or just stare. Even if I'd had the Spanish to explain that I was waiting for my next Universal Credit payment, I'm not sure I could have brought myself to tell them that the disease had stolen my livelihood too.

One day I asked how the bartering worked, and Pablo told me that while the internet connection on the island is notoriously unreliable, there was enough bandwidth for a huge and sometimes unruly WhatsApp group of 256 members, the maximum allowed by the app. This ramshackle marketplace was being supplemented by the hunting of feral animals. The buccaneers who'd been here before Darwin's time had brought pigs, goats, donkeys and cattle with them, presumably to break up their tortoise-heavy diet.

As so often happens with introduced species, the livestock quickly broke loose and started causing havoc for endemic animals, trampling on birds' nests, eating young tortoises and spreading seeds of invasive flora. For decades, the progeny of these original invaders have been persecuted, though many still roam freely on massive Isabela. At the start of the pandemic, residents negotiated with national park rangers and revived organised hunting, heading out of town on horseback and returning with feral cattle or pigs slung on the back. When Pablo told me this story it was easy to imagine these *casadores* camping in the thick bush, exhausted after a successful hunt,

An Inconvenience of Penguins

their knives slick with blood, their dogs drooling expectantly in the shadows, flames dancing in their eyes.

'Hunting has been happening on the Galapagos since the first settlers were here,' he told me the following day as we hiked up the Sierra Negra volcano, a blasted, blackened peak that rises above Puerto Villamil. 'Back then they were going after the giant tortoises, too, but it wasn't really a hunt, more like a collection. Hunting the pigs, though, it's . . .' He shook his hand as though he was trying to get rid of a piece of sticky tape, Latino sign language for 'too much'. When I asked if penguins are ever on the menu, he looked at me as though I was insane.

I really liked Pablo. I really liked all the locals I met on the Galapagos. This man from Isabela had excellent stories about watching volcanoes erupt, of a prison break from the old penitentiary on the island's southern shore, and of buried treasure seemingly looted by a mysterious ship under a French flag. The only time I didn't care for one of his stories was when he patiently explained to me that the Galapagos penguins, of which there were several hundred on Isabela, all nested on the north shore – and were completely inaccessible to anyone not on a cruise ship.

I retreated again to the main island of Santa Cruz to spend a couple of weeks in a rented room in Puerto Ayora. I found some feral goat meat on sale at a local butcher, decided that buying it would represent conservation through consumption, and spent $15 on enough for a curry that I ate for six days in a row.* Only

---

* Monotonous, absolutely, but significantly better than the porridge-and-lentil diet I'd been forced into at home.

once or twice did I wonder what giant tortoise might taste like instead.

When I could find a bench not already occupied by flatulent sea lions, I spent my days on the pier reading Douglas Stuart's new Booker winner, *Shuggie Bain*, though it made me so homesick I had to take breaks. For these I'd walk to the flawless beach at Tortuga Bay to take photos of brown pelicans, sally lightfoot crabs and gangs of marine iguanas lying in foetid heaps to keep warm in the unseasonably cool afternoons. I'd have traded them all for a penguin, but they were beyond my reach.

After four weeks or so on the islands, some PR agencies back in London had seen where I was on social media. There were so few writers on the road that I had become a novelty. With no flights to cover, it took only a perfunctory negotiation to be back on another ship, this time Ecoventura's laughably opulent yacht *Theory*. I was grateful to be getting on board, for the chance to get back in the water and to take a break from the goat curry, but there was still a problem – the ship's plan was to sail back to the same islands I'd visited at the start of the trip. There were alternative itineraries taking in Isabela and other penguin-populated islands, but those cruises were for choosers, and I was still very much part of the begging fraternity.

In the days before setting sail, I moved to the island of San Cristóbal and got a room in the town of Puerto Baquerizo Moreno, the second largest settlement in the Galapagos and the archipelago's administrative capital. Here, environmental and governmental decisions are made for all the islanders, including their conservation policies.

Coincidentally, on my second day in town, the 2020 US election result became clear – Trump, the repugnant anti-scientist, had been voted out. I was upstairs in the Midori Bar when the result came in. There would of course be riots and conspiracies and killings to come in Washington, but in that moment the world's air felt looser, and along with three others hunched behind laptops, I ordered a mid-morning beer to toast the result.

The next day it was time to board the new ship. Much smaller and fancier than *La Pinta*, *Theory* placed all her passengers and crew in a bubble, meaning we wouldn't visit any settlements around the archipelago. There was just a dozen or so passengers on board: a Korean-American mother and son from San Francisco; a cantankerous and largely joyless couple from England; and three generations of a wealthy Cuban-American family from Southern California, who had come close to booking out the whole ship for themselves.

The cruise passed more or less as before, with the Galapagos throwing up miracles of dolphins, sea lions that greeted us with the familiarity of relatives, and shivers of sharks resting in volcanic fissures. We circumnavigated San Cristóbal, then returned to Española. After that, we set a course for Floreana, the smallest of the inhabited islands, which, even by Galapagoan standards, has a peculiar history.

In the 1930s it had been inhabited by eccentric Germans who'd come to create a utopia, a society free from the inter-war chaos of their homeland. Predictably, it didn't work out, and though they had what is thought to be the first human birth on the island, they eventually realised they had created a purgatory of their own – one presided over by a self-styled baroness, and plagued with scandal, hunger and death.

That grim slice of Floreana's history doesn't get much airtime on luxury cruise ships – it's too odd and perhaps too regrettable. A much more palatable bit of varnished tourism can be found at the Post Office Bay, where a purportedly ancient barrel stands as a curious sort of post box. The lore holds that whalers, pirates and other villains on the margins of society would come here on their years-long voyages and leave messages in the hope that someone returning to their homeland could deliver whatever news they had. How their scurvy was coming along, perhaps, which harlots they'd fallen in love with, or maybe their favourite recipe for giant tortoise meat.

Today, tourists are encouraged to do a kitsch version of the same – to leave an unstamped postcard in the box, then to sift through the pile to see if there is anything left for someone from their home country. If there is, tradition states that they should deliver it by hand. In 2011, I'd written one to my future self and remarkably it turned up three years later, a very slow boomerang.[*] My perennially dreadful handwriting on that card reads:

Dear Future Me,

I hope by the time this card reaches you, you've paid off your bloody credit card. Still, don't forget that this trip was certainly worth it, problems and all.[†] *I know you'll eulogise it, but please don't exaggerate the size of the sharks, and don't forget to be a bit humble, you stupid, lucky bastard.*

Take care of yourself.

J xx

•

---

[*] Sadly, the coward who'd brought it to Scotland decided to post it the last few miles rather than deliver it in person.

[†] This included my first ship breaking down when a drunk crewmember destroyed the engine, leaving us stuck at anchor for days before being transferred to a somehow inferior alternative.

An Inconvenience of Penguins

Theory was repositioned for a final excursion off Floreana. The following morning we would return to land and be swiftly transferred to the airport, then back to the noise and comparative sterility of the Ecuadorian mainland. Had the sun not been shining with such golden insistence that everything was going to be OK, I might have believed otherwise.

As during most stops, snorkelling was an option, so I took my gear and headed out on a Zodiac. Like in Antarctica, these motorised dinghies are launched from the larger vessel and used to efficiently transport people into the realm of penguins. Unlike in Antarctica, it is not lethally cold if you fall into the water.

Once the guide waved me in, I plopped over the side and swam away from the rest of the group, kicking hard and clearing my snorkel. Below, great schools of surgeonfish shimmered away from me, while close to the seabed I noticed the blunt head of a spotted eagle ray. In five weeks of being in the Galapagos, I'd seen these species several times, so paid them little attention and instead swam to an outcrop of lava rock.

A couple of juvenile white-tipped reef sharks tried to hide under a shelf, perhaps 3m or so below the surface. (Some years earlier while on assignment in Indonesia's Komodo National Park, I'd been taught the rudiments of free-diving and at one point got down to 16m.) The sharks were well within range, so I guzzled as much air as I could manage, then went down to see them.

That was when I got the fright, a jolt of surprise that blew all the air out of my lungs as I shouted underwater: 'PENGUINS!'

There were two of them, something I could only gather after I'd panicked and rushed back to the surface to grab more air. I shouted for my shipmates and wasn't sure if they'd heard, but I honestly didn't care. I set off after the little birds, swimming as fast as I could, trying to keep an eye on them.

Their attention was focused on a ball of black-striped salema, which the penguins herded and harassed with balletic style. It's often said that penguins fly when underwater, their aquatic propulsion working much the same as it would for other birds in the air. Over my years of visiting Antarctica, I'd seen hundreds of thousands of the birds on land, but this was the first time I'd seen them like this, flapping and gliding, banking and diving. All of their terrestrial idiocy was gone, replaced with efficiency as graceful as it was lethal.

The fish attempted to keep 20cm away from their pursuers, giving the impression that the birds were emitting some kind of force field as they flew through the shoal. This more or less worked until one of the penguins swooped around and disrupted the fish's hard-won organisation. In the chaos, both birds snatched some lunch.

Too soon, they grew bored of this game and shot off into the infinite blue. I worried I hadn't made the most of the moment so swam after them, calmer now, and after a while looked above the water to see how far I'd drifted from the ship. I checked the horizon then looked the other way, where, on a rough rock, I saw the scaly black feet of a Galapagos penguin.

A sole representative of this rare penguin species stood looking at me through one eye, then it turned its little head and examined me with the other. All the elegance it had shown in the water was gone and it looked like it might fall over if the breeze got up. Nonetheless, to me its gaze felt like something significant, a meaningful event in a year where so much meaning had been stripped away, a year of online calls and offline despair, of squalor and alcohol. A year of fear.

An Inconvenience of Penguins

The bird knew nothing of it but, somehow, I wanted it to. 'Hello,' I said, stupidly.

When the world stopped, I'd grown certain I'd never see another penguin – here or anywhere. I had wondered what dull, safe existence I'd have to build when life got going again. Instead, here I was, floating in warm Galapagoan water, metres away from an ugly little miracle.

I wanted more of this feeling. If I could regain control of my travel writing career, I could perhaps manipulate it to see more penguins, generate more of this glee. I'd already seen 12 species by this point in my life, but now I'd wipe the slate and start again. The Galapagos animals would be penguin number one, my spark bird.

There was a chance of addiction, certainly, but I'd done pretty well to get through lockdown without one already. The logistics would be baffling, the practicalities non-existent. Every penguin seemed to live on the edge of the known world, so far from home; in that moment there were still species I didn't even know existed, living in places I'd never heard of. I would have no finances to draw on and would have to work with a moribund travel industry, and yet there now seemed to be a path towards something better. Plus, this elephantine dose of dopamine felt so incredibly moreish.

I reached for some bigger words, something to convey gratitude to the bird, but only managed 'hello' again.

The penguin shook the water from its sleek feathers, sending droplets of the Pacific into the gilded air, and said nothing in reply.

2

Penguin Supper

> One day, it happened that four of us pursued one, who was courageous to the point of heroism. The hunt lasted more than an hour, and when the poor creature finally fell, it had endured three bullets from a revolver, two bullets from a rifle, without counting numerous blows with a cudgel. We were, ourselves, exhausted.
>
> – Georges Lecointe, aboard the *Belgica*, 1898

Despite what had felt like salvation in the Galapagos, the ongoing grind of the pandemic meant it took almost a year and a half before I could truly begin my penguin voyages. I returned from South America at the end of 2020, spent all of 2021 penguinless and eventually resumed the chase in the austral autumn of 2022, when my travel writing work flickered back into life.

There were 18 species to see, spread globally around the southern hemisphere, from coastal deserts to island rainforests. Partly because of this, the only people likely to have seen all the world's penguin species were scientists with niche fields of study and gnarled birders with deep pockets. Several of the birds were endemic on archipelagos so remote and unexplored they didn't appear on most maps, but rather than worry too much about those semi-mythic places yet, I started with what I knew. Two years since I had last visited, I was sailing to Antarctica.

An Inconvenience of Penguins

When the time came, the departure of Aurora Expeditions' *Greg Mortimer* from Punta Arenas in the south of Chile was mourned by no one. Flat and industrial, Punta Arenas was a difficult place to love. Grass yellowed under abandoned trucks and dry-docked boats. Ramshackle gardens were populated by smashed wooden pallets, half-disassembled engines and wild-looking dogs, which at these ungenerous latitudes maintained their winter coats and surliness all year long. At the fringes of town there were signs of long-extinct industry. Everything was slowly devoured by ravenous Patagonian winds and sea spray. Everywhere there was rust.

The colossal grey sky offered little hope that things would improve in the capital of Chile's far south. The highly amended 2021–22 Antarctic cruise season had only opted to engage with this old staging post because working with the traditional Argentinian departure point of Ushuaia had become overly complicated by Covid restrictions and local incompetence. Aurora Expeditions' weird-looking X-bow ship,* *Greg Mortimer*, had brought in a bit of business, as had Norwegian cruise giants Hurtigruten, but there were no plans to return the following season. Punta Arenas was only being used as a port in an economic storm.

Over a century ago, the majority of the great Antarctic explorers passed through Punta Arenas at one time or another. While those associations have waned, the city's relationship with the white continent continued in some form, even before the pandemic. It's from Punta Arenas's Presidente Carlos Ibáñez del

---

* Weird in that its inverted bow has been variously compared to a bird, a jumbo jet and an iron. In fact, its distracting design is based on the lethally efficient nose of an orca.

Penguin Supper

Campo Airport that most commercial Antarctic flights depart and return, scrambling to take tourists to King George Island when narrow weather windows allow. When medical emergencies occur – as they do every Antarctic tourism season – it's to this Chilean city patients are typically evacuated by the same planes.

The newly elected socialist president of Chile, Gabriel Boric, was born down here.* Looking at his decaying city, it was understandable that a person raised in Punta Arenas would want to try and fix the world. Things were once very different. In the late 1800s the town was awash with bars and brothels lying in wait for sailors and prospectors to spend money they'd scarcely earned. A bacchanalian port, it had evolved from a notorious penal colony to become a riotous stopover for seamen as they swapped the Atlantic for the Pacific or, in rare cases, the Southern Ocean. Wool and coal industries brought prosperity to the region before the gold rush; vice migrated south to absorb the cash, no matter its provenance.

President Boric's great-grandfather was drawn here by the chance to get rich quick, too, one of thousands of Croats who travelled to the end of the world in search of gold. Whatever the purpose of the men arriving here, hedonism was never far away. 'Alcohol is at the base of all the crimes and most of the pleasures in Punta Arenas,' wrote Frederick Cook, the bombastic American doctor aboard Adrien de Gerlache's *Belgica* in 1897. Great-grandaddy Boric may well have seen that ship coming into port before it sailed south in the name of scientific discovery and glory for the Belgian Empire.

Aged just 24, the eventual maestro of the poles, Roald Amundsen, was also aboard the *Belgica* that year. Employed as

---

* Upsettingly, Boric is three years younger than me.

An Inconvenience of Penguins

first mate, the Norwegian was about to embark on a years-long lesson on what not to do ahead of his triumphant expedition to the South Pole in 1911. Isolated among Belgians with whom he could hardly communicate, much less understand, he formed an unlikely friendship with the eccentric Dr Cook.

The pair soon found themselves struggling to keep the inept de Gerlache in control of a ship he often nearly lost. The Belgian leader's ultimate goal was to strike further south than any ship had reached to secure a place in world history, but while still in this port, he had to sack a few already drunk and unruly crew, then only narrowly avoided a shoot-out with the would-be mutineers. Amundsen supported the captain as best he could but made sure to write long notes about what was going wrong.

The *Belgica* almost didn't get out of the Beagle Channel, the vast estuary which divides Argentinian and Chilean territories as they braid at the end of South America.* It is one of the most generous stretches of water en route to Antarctica, yet de Gerlache managed to run aground in a storm before he had even reached the Southern Ocean.

Almost 125 years later, the *Greg Mortimer* began following the *Belgica*'s route, traversing waters that bear the names of some of history's greatest sailors – the Magellan Strait and the Drake Passage – with no such trouble. In the Beagle we watched glaciers racing up mountains, bleeding water as they went. Expedition staff pointed out that they weren't 'retreating' but more accurately diminishing from all sides.†

---

* The Beagle Channel is named after the ship which had carried young Charles Darwin 60 years earlier.

† And anyway, to retreat sounds somewhat voluntary.

Penguin Supper

Dark, wet hills surrounded us while bus-sized knots of kelp bobbed past, visited by swooping birds and incurious seals. Once out in open sea, passengers rushed to attach seasickness patches and swallow fistfuls of antiemetics. I decided not to join them. I was last seasick in 1987 when I was four years old and returning from Germany on the *Dana Anglia*, a monstrous ferry sailing back to the UK from Hamburg. Ours was apparently the last ship to sail before the arrival of the Great Storm of that year, later dubbed the Michael Fish Hurricane in dishonour of the bumbling weather presenter who confidently predicted that Britain was in no danger of facing cyclone-strength winds. Anyway, the *Dana Anglia* got rocked around, I spewed, didn't like it, and so retired from the practice immediately afterwards. Though I have vomited in many places for many reasons since, seasickness has never again been the cause. I remind myself and anyone who'll listen of this in every port before setting sail. It seems to work as well as any medication.

In the end, the bravado wasn't necessary. The Drake Passage is often described as notorious in much the same way ice is described as treacherous – it is defamatory and not always true. As we passed out into the sliver of ocean that lies between South America and Antarctica, it was as docile as we could have wished for. Worse seas would come on our 23-day voyage, tumult so strong it would knock older passengers off chairs and hold them down like high school bullies, but in that first stretch of ocean there was no drama, and only a little puking.

Aurora's 'Antarctica Complete' itinerary had us racing to cross the Antarctic Circle as one of its main goals, an arbitrary bit of tourism designed to please the box-ticking set. For many of the 79 passengers on board, penguins were a higher priority. This of course included me. Having long thought something like this would never happen again, my stomach fluttered

An Inconvenience of Penguins

knowing that ahead of us lay hundreds of thousands of penguins, covering perhaps as many as six species.

The Antarctic Peninsula is home to all three of the family known as brushtailed penguins – Adélies, Chinstraps and Gentoos – many thousands of which nest at sites now named after men associated with de Gerlache's tragicomic expedition.* Then, as now, people were delighted by the sight of the birds going about their ridiculous business, and none offered more levity than the Gentoos. 'The decent and honest Gentoo is a shrewd communist having nothing to defend against its fellow citizens, having shared the land, and having simplified the task of childrearing by establishing a communal nursery,' wrote Emil Racoviță, the ship's zoologist, in the relatively happy early days of the *Belgica*'s voyage.

By the time Racoviță and others were observing the penguins, things had grown tense thanks to animals the sailors had brought with them. The ship had a considerable rat infestation, yet in a fit of rage, a crewmember threw one of the ship's cats overboard, handing an even bigger advantage to the rodents. Seemingly hating their fellow mammals, the crew instead fell in love with the Gentoos – so much so that they took three on board as pets. Two quickly died, but the other was dubbed Bébé and lived for a few months as a sort of mascot, offering a rare bit of comic relief as ice, scurvy and insanity began to envelop the ship when it became trapped in sea ice.

Gentoos, with their shocking orange beaks and flash of white above the eyes, have long been among the most beloved

---

* The brushtailed penguins have very different markings but are united by their stiff tail feathers, which they sometimes use for resting.

Penguin Supper

penguins. They have none of the stuffiness of Kings or Emperors, nor the viciousness of the crested penguins, but bags of perceived personality and an objectively amusing call during which they throw back their necks and honk like someone playing out-of-tune bagpipes. This rasping song sees the tops of their little chests rise and fall, reminiscent of depressions on tamper-proof bottle lids. When I think of the sounds of Antarctica, this is the first that comes to mind.

Their nesting habits often seem amusing, too, with penguins waddling around gathering rocks from the shore or, just as readily, stealing from any unguarded nests nearby. The Australian explorer and scientific pioneer Douglas Mawson endured as much as anyone to survive Antarctic disaster, but when he wasn't desperately trying to stay alive he took time to delight in the Gentoos' kleptomaniacal nesting habits. He closely observed their mating patterns, too, noting that 'partners are selected and the pairs, united in matrimonial bliss, settle down for a short honeymoon at their nests'; eventually, 'two eggs are laid which are defended from the depredations of marauding skua gulls throughout the succeeding weeks, as the hatching proceeds in blizzard and in sunshine.'

Much is known about the Gentoo,* yet bizarrely there is scant agreement on the etymology of its name. The best guess is that it's based on an archaic and insulting term for Hindus, perhaps derived from the white marking on the head looking like a turban.†

---

* For example, despite being the third largest penguin, it is the fastest swimmer, with a top speed of 36kph.

† Which it doesn't, and even if it did, a turban would more commonly be worn by Sikhs. You can never rely on racists for accuracy.

An Inconvenience of Penguins

Something less in doubt is that Gentoos are what scientists call 'climate change winners'. Unlike true Antarctic species such as the Emperors and Adélies, Gentoos are adaptable and have already begun to alter their diets and nesting habits to cope with warming seas and scarcer supplies of krill, the small crustaceans which form the bedrock of the entire Antarctic ecosystem. Consequently, their population and ranges can extend while those of their nominal rivals diminish. Their expansion into new territories has been excellently termed gentoofication, a good pun but perhaps not enough to offset the grinding climate apocalypse.*

The Gentoos' penchant for vagrancy also creates a false impression of abundance. Over the years, I have seen them in the Falkland Islands, in South Georgia and in parts of Patagonia, too. Down on the Antarctic Peninsula, they assemble in significant colonies along some of the most popular stops for cruise ships carrying polar tourists. They also have a funny habit of turning up in the colonies of other species, seemingly without an invite, suggesting that they are skilled gatecrashers, or perhaps opportunistic surveyors spying on potential new homes for their growing population.

All the human eyes on the Gentoo and its extraordinary orange lipstick leave many visitors thinking that it is an already thriving species. In fact, of the three brushtailed penguins, it is currently the rarest by a distance – there are an estimated 10 million mature Adélie penguins and 8 million Chinstraps, while there aren't yet even a million Gentoos. For now, they are

---

* It's admittedly better than my best penguin joke, which is: As much as I like the Gentoos, I really can't wait for the Gen-threes . . . It sounds better if you say it aloud. Sorry. Please keep reading.

Penguin Supper

bronze medallists, though climate change is fast hobbling the others on the podium.

The de Gerlache expedition is now remembered for the squalor, madness and death on board the *Belgica*, but many of the places named after the mission are extraordinarily beautiful, even by the lofty standards of Antarctica. The vast Gerlache Strait is one of the bonniest in the region, only outdone by the Lemaire Channel, an outrageous frozen corridor of sheer mountains and fjords, first traversed by the Belgian ship and named after one of its compatriots.

Reminders of tragedies from the expedition also abound. There's Danco Island, christened after de Gerlache's doomed friend Emile Danco, who died with a whimper on board; there's Wiencke Island, named in tribute to Carl August Wiencke, a teenage sailor who was swept overboard and almost rescued, only to die in frozen terror as he was carried away by the icy sea.

Similarly popular is Neko Harbour, which was also discovered – though not named – by the de Gerlache expedition. So much as anything can be typical in Antarctica, Neko is a typical stop for most cruise ships, with a sheltered bay, a dramatic glacier and a short hike available to passengers who want soaring views back out to open water. When our expedition leader knew it was available, she booked it for us immediately.* It's often visited by humpback whales, too, and their saline reports echoing off the glacier are another polar sound that lives in my memory.

---

* Booked it so that no other ship would be there at the same time. As much as Antarctic tourism has grown, landings are never shared by vessels so that they may offer passengers the conceit of exclusivity.

An Inconvenience of Penguins

As with almost all the places discovered by the Belgians, there are also Gentoo penguins.* The Neko rookery hosts several hundred birds, the majority of which know to run up the beach any time they hear the nearby glacier calving, lest they be swept away by a following tsunami. Younger penguins in the colony are likely to face this ignominy at least once, but they have harsher lessons to learn.

After the snowy hike and a brief visit with three dozing Weddell seals on the cold beach, I made my way over to the Gentoos' shambolic rookery, which thanks to recent snowfall was less guano-blasted than usual. Immediately I noticed that a lone downy chick was having a miserable morning. Every time it tried to cower back towards the heart of the colony, an adult – presumably not a relative – would wickedly peck at it, nudging the baby perilously out towards the edge of the group. It seemed confused: hurt emotionally as much as physically by the rejection.

In truth the chick's prospects were bleak beyond that morning anyway. It was mid-March, the onset of austral autumn, and the baby Gentoo had too much growing to do before the Antarctic winter closed around its soft feathers. Most of its would-be peers were already fed and grown, assuming they hadn't been ripped to pieces by leopard seals when venturing into the sea. Ahead of that potential trauma, however, this Gentoo baby had some more pressing survival goals.

Part of the uncanniness of penguin rookeries lies in their immediateness. When did you last see a crow's egg? Or a sparrow's chick? Where so many other birds' life cycles are invisible, the penguin shares it all. Nothing is clandestine, nothing dis-

---

* This includes Danco and Wiencke Islands.

Penguin Supper

creet – life, death and defecation happen on top of each other. They are animals without cunning, though not unburdened from drama.

Lolloping around the corner came a giant southern petrel, its huge, webbed feet slapping on the snow, its conspiratorial shoulders bouncing as though it were laughing. The giant petrel has approximately the same wingspan as a mute swan, the sort found benignly gliding along British rivers. Unlike the swans, they have a killer instinct and a pitilessness that can appear downright cruel. Giant petrels will feed on dead whales and seals – and no doubt on dead sailors if they ever found any.* Not content with scavenging, however, they're also keen predators and nothing delights them more than dining on penguin chicks.

The petrel in Neko Harbour had been stalking the rookery for around 20 minutes, dwarfing the adult Gentoos but unwilling or unable to stab at any of them. The target was instead the baby, grey and cute, which peeped in distress each time it saw a flash of the petrel's awful beak.

The giant petrel is not a true bird of prey, and its clownish feet are more useful for swimming than crushing skulls. Its beak, however, is a baleful weapon. A nasty barb at the end is designed to pick apart flesh, while a large exhaust running along the top appears industrial. All petrels have this salt nostril, allowing them to filter seawater as they endlessly glide on ocean winds, but none have anything quite as pronounced as that of the giants. Often the gutters running underneath are clogged

---

* A guide on the trip told me a story of working on a subantarctic island on which one of the staff decided to play dead on a beach. Giant petrels and skuas circled only briefly before coming to have a peck at them. They attempted to start with the eyes; wisely the scientist had worn protective goggles.

with old blood and other ugliness from previous meals, calling to mind an unsanitary butcher.

The infant penguin knew that terrible beak meant danger – even without the loud objections of a nearby adult which had nervously made its way forward. The penguins opened their pathetic little flippers and tried to make themselves appear bigger to the hulking predator. Their orange beaks, neon carrots glowing inside and out, offered a rare bit of fire in the Antarctic palette. The adult opened its mouth, revealing a spiky tongue ordinarily used for grabbing krill and fish, then slowly bowed, up and down, emitting a strangely sinister-sounding hiss in a bid to deter the petrel. Improbably, this tactic worked – the standoff lasted for a couple of minutes before the aggressor decided to retreat.

For a time after that, things calmed down. In the surf, healthy adult Gentoos returned from the sea, or tarried in the water to preen and play, shooting themselves through the shallows, leaping from the surface, then stumbling ashore, droplets wicking from their feathery wetsuits. They studiously ignored three Antarctic skuas that were disassembling a former friend or relative into breakfast items, then returned to the reassuring chaos of the rookery.

On their way home, some penguins paused, squawked in alarm, then shuffled back. Ahead, Death moved like a marionette. The giant petrel had returned, its focus once again on the chick. This time it made a running start, blasting past any chance of confrontation. Panic rippled through the penguins, many fleeing in noisy disarray. With the barrier of adults scattered, the chick – small and fluffy and so soft – was exposed once more. This time, the petrel did not hesitate.

Penguin Supper

It snatched the baby behind the head, yanking it along the beach, the chick's pale pink feet scrabbling uselessly, unable to find any purchase on the frozen ground. Time simultaneously sped up and slowed down. The petrel didn't have to kill the chick outright – a sufficient maiming would guarantee the meal at some point – but the grip behind the head wouldn't be enough on its own. Worse would have to follow.

Dozens of Gentoos honked in alarm, while the condemned chick squeaked in terror. Many wings flapped without flying. As it hauled the youngster away from the group, the petrel had never looked more giant.

Gentoos are not the penguin world's most skilled parents. Douglas Mawson was particularly fond of eating their eggs, and he occasionally hung around to watch the aftermath of his theft. 'The penguin makes a great fuss on returning to find that the eggs are gone, but generally finishes up by sitting on the empty nest,' he wrote in *The Home of the Blizzard*. 'We have frequently put ten or a dozen eggs into one nest and watched the proprietress on her return look about very doubtfully and then squat down and try to tuck the whole lot under herself with her beak.'

With hatchlings, they are rarely much better guardians. Gentoos, like all penguins, have grown to hate the sky, as though resenting the genetic path that has left them earthbound. There is another, more immediate reason to detest the firmament: it is the domain of the skua and the giant petrel.

The most upsetting animal attack I have ever seen was on Cuverville Island in 2017, when two Antarctic skuas savaged a Gentoo chick. Like the giant petrel, this 'wanton and relentless

An Inconvenience of Penguins

ogre' has not evolved claws to deliver an effective coup de grâce, making every murder a protracted process. They first removed its face, then stabbed under the soft wings and up its backside to vivisect the screaming baby. This seems like an evolutionary cruelty – why not give the skuas proper tools for their repugnant job?

Some witnesses cried. Another wanted to vomit. A group of ridiculous, macho firefighters from Arizona pleaded with the stoic expedition leader to end the suffering with a rock, a case that was flatly and correctly dismissed. What if other skuas were learning from this behaviour? Perhaps more importantly: what if other penguins were? Meanwhile, none of the nearby Gentoos attempted to interject, and the chick slowly died in nauseating agony.

No one likes to see penguins suffer. In a preamble to several penguin recipes, British Antarctic Survey chef Gerald T. Cutland wrote in his 1957 cookbook *Fit for a FID*:

> When cooking Penguin, I have an awful feeling inside of me that I am cooking little men who are just that little too curious and stupid. I never got to the stage of dreaming about them . . . but I did have one pop into the kitchen once to see what was going on. At first I thought how nice to have your meal come to the pot in such a fresh state but, alas, I never had the heart to do it in.

On board the *Belgica* there was similar reluctance. Not least because of their affection for their cherished Bébé, there was a general view – especially among the officers – that eating penguin was uncivilised. Even when Amundsen and his friend Dr Cook seemed to prove that eating it as close to raw as possible

Penguin Supper

helped alleviate scurvy, many of the Belgians still resisted, then sickened and came close to death.*

In fairness, the meat is hardly renowned as being delicious. Even as he was encouraging his shipmates to eat penguins, Cook wrote in his diary:

> It is rather difficult to describe its taste and appearance; we have absolutely no meat with which to compare it. The penguin, as an animal, seems to be made up of an equal proportion of mammal, fish, and fowl. If it is possible to imagine a piece of beef, an odoriferous codfish, and a canvas-back duck, roasted in a pot, with blood and cod-liver oil for sauce, the illustration will be complete.

It's unlikely that flavour was on the mind of the giant petrel in Neko Harbour, but as it dragged its prey away from the rookery, it could have been forgiven for salivating. And yet, just as the meal seemed inevitable, a hero emerged.

Unable to abide the murder, an adult Gentoo charged forward. Wailing as it ran, looking every bit like a parent witnessing their child being kidnapped, the penguin made an ungainly sprint towards the molester.† Perhaps the attacker had to adjust its grip, perhaps it caught a flipper in the eye, but whatever the reason, it let go of the chick, ran off and attempted to take to the air.

The giant petrel is a superlative glider but like many large birds requires a long running start to get airborne. Pilots call

---

* Perhaps the most upsetting symptom of scurvy sees old wounds reopen, effectively un-healing, sometimes years after the initial trauma.

† As adult Gentoos are virtually identical, it was impossible to know if this really was a parent or simply a bird compelled by instinct to *do something*.

this take-off roll. On water it can be a satisfying thing to photograph when great splashes are left behind by the bird's huge feet, its take-off roll lasting sometimes over 50m. Chastened, the giant petrel in front of me felt the need to escape as quickly as possible and did so without proper clearance from ground control, in this instance the three skuas feasting nearby. The petrel's flight plan took it right through their breakfast, a decision to which the skuas reacted in their usual manner, which is to say with little hesitation and maximum violence.

As the petrel ran over the top of them and out to the water, all three skuas flew after it in a flash, pecking from above and the side, screeching furiously at the larger bird's transgression. By the time the petrel had disappeared around an iceberg, it still hadn't managed to properly take off – or shake the skuas.

Back on the beach, the penguins trembled together while passengers giggled in nervous relief. Later, Aurora staff reminded us that a chick so young at this time of year had no chance of surviving winter anyway.

Towards the end of our time on the Antarctic Peninsula, the *Greg Mortimer* anchored in sunshine off the Argentine Islands. Before Zodiacs had even been launched, we could see dozens of Gentoo penguins athletically leaping from the sea as they returned to their rookeries around Ukraine's Vernadsky Base on Galindez Island in the heart of the archipelago. Photographers sent out thousands of shots trying to catch them as they porpoised unpredictably out of the water.

In an ordinary year, we'd have visited the Ukrainians and their sprawling home, but Covid restrictions made that impossible. In many ways Antarctica had been immune from the pandemic, but not here. Adding to the grim novelty was the

Penguin Supper

knowledge that our ship was partially crewed by Ukrainians – including the captain, Oleg Klaptenko – whose country had recently been invaded by Russia.*

I'd read that 25-year-old scientist Yan Bakhmat was stranded on base, knowing that his home had been destroyed, waiting for the Antarctic season to end and who-knew-what to follow. 'It's impossible to describe, you can only live through it when you are thousands of kilometres away from everything and everyone you know and love, when you can't influence anything,' he told the *Guardian*. 'You just realise that you have nowhere to return, and all you can do is turn yourself to a new reality. Your life has divided into "before" and "after".' Puttering past Vernadsky, I thought of Bakhmat, simultaneously right there and a million miles away.

Back on the *Belgica* in 1899, the crew were finally moving towards their own 'after'. Though it was never de Gerlache's intention, the crew of the *Belgica* became the first people to ever overwinter in Antarctica. Penguins had saved their lives – the pioneering and later much disgraced Dr Cook had proven that their consumption helped fend off scurvy.† He and Amundsen ate great quantities and thrived as a result.

They weren't quite done with the birds though – they had a final, grim calling to help the ship escape north, which it eventually did on 14 March 1899, with two men dead, one insane and several suffering from what would now be called post-traumatic

---

* Later that year, I met Russians who were avoiding being drafted into a war they disagreed with by working long stints in Antarctica.

† Cook would go on to falsely claim to have been the first person to summit Mount Denali. Later still, he claimed to have also been the first to reach the North Pole – an honour which almost certainly belongs to his *Belgica* shipmate and friend Roald Amundsen.

stress disorder. With sea ice in danger of tearing the ship apart, they formed a plan to put the penguins to use once more, a striking piece of grotesquery detailed in Julian Sancton's excellent book on the expedition, Madhouse at the End of the Earth. As with many of the innovations on the ship, Cook's bloody hands were all over it: 'He hung penguin carcasses from the gunwales and dangled them in front of spots where the ice was striking the wood. The fleshy fenders helped blunt the impact of the floes until they were crushed to a pulp.'

After five days sailing in the Belgica's waters, our own ship turned north for Elephant Island, unencumbered by ice or anything other than the passengers' expanding waistlines. Later, as we swapped de Gerlache's wake for Ernest Shackleton's, we'd see more Gentoos, but not in the same abundance as on the Antarctic Peninsula. Shooting through the water like errant torpedoes, their numbers increasing, their prospects bright, and without a single Belgian trying to take a bite out of them, they looked happier than ever.

More than a year later I found myself in the Falkland Islands with a rare and totally legal opportunity to eat a Gentoo penguin egg. The eating of penguin flesh or eggs in Antarctica has been illegal since 1959, but a limited amount of traditional egg-collecting still happens on the British archipelago. Having seen so many on the ground in Antarctica and beyond – and having taken so many precautions to avoid touching or disturbing them – it felt more than a little transgressive to hold an egg in my hand. About four times the size of a chicken egg, it felt solid, like it could survive being thrown through a double-glazed window. The chef invited me to crack it into a sizzling pan.

Penguin Supper

Right before I did, I girded myself with the knowledge that these days egging in the Falklands is a sustainable, licensed business. The islanders harvest only the first of a Gentoo's two eggs, which the penguin will always replace by laying a third.* This collection happens at the same time each year, meaning the birds re-lay at the same time. Because of this inorganic process, the chicks all hatch concurrently, and so crèches are larger. This is better for protection against villains like the skua and the giant petrel and so the Falkland Island population of Gentoos is increasing, not despite the egg collection but partly because of it.

I tentatively hit the egg against the rim of the pan. Nothing happened. I tried again with a bit more force, but the egg remained unblemished. I looked at the chef, who regarded me with undisguised disappointment. Skuas and giant petrels really had to slam these eggs around to get them open, and so would I.

I drove the thing against the pan and its armour finally cracked, revealing a thick inner lining which tore like old skin to let the albumen slide into the oil. There followed an indescribable oddness of not seeing this turn white in the heat. Instead, it stayed translucent, appearing plastic, artificial like cling film. There was no noticeable smell. The yolk was a ferocious African sunset, while inside the broken shell, there was a light blue lining, not unlike that of a glacier.

The chef told me it'd take a bit longer than a regular egg, but that the white would never become so, no matter how long

---

* Older islanders told me they used to also take King and Magellanic eggs, and that the former is far too much for a single person to eat while the latter isn't worth collecting because of all the fleas in Magellanic burrows.

An Inconvenience of Penguins

it was cooked. He preferred to eat them with a little Worcestershire sauce but, he insisted, the absolute best way to enjoy them was as a meringue. For now, though, I should try mine plain. I nodded solemnly, pulling at the plastic non-white with a fork and making sure to take a piece of the yolk, too.

When I raised it to my mouth, horrors appeared in my mind. For a second all the death and decay of a festering penguin colony was present in my mouth, a world of guano and eyeless chicks, of mummified adults and exposed ribcages. I saw that peeping baby with its face ripped off; I saw snowy sheathbills pecking at fresh penguin droppings. Faintly I could smell that rank, distant odour of ammonia and fish, so peculiar to large rookeries – shit and death, death and shit. A retch formed in my throat and my chest started to pop in and out like a calling Gentoo.

And then, in a second, these images were gone, and I was chewing the fried penguin egg. The albumen was fine, as bland as any bird's – the problems lay in the yolk, not quite congealed, somehow agricultural, and tasting like it had come from a pan that'd just been used to cook kippers. I did not agree with the assessment of Mawson's crew that they were 'the best eggs we ever tasted' nor that it had 'a flavour that goes straight to the heart'.

For the next mouthful, I asked for the Worcestershire sauce, but I didn't come close to finishing the whole thing.

3

Love in a Cold Climate

> Of course I do not know any more than anybody else does, to what extent penguins manage to convey ideas to each other, but if you watch Mr and Mrs Penguin together it seems perfectly certain that they do somehow. At any rate, they do a great deal of love-making, becoming vastly sentimental in the process. A penguin's expression at these times is easily recognisable. The feathers round his throat seem to puff out and he lowers his head into them, so that his general attitude is rather in the shape of a question mark.
>
> – Cherry Kearton, *The Island of Penguins*, 1930

From the Antarctic Peninsula, the *Greg Mortimer* continued north-east to Elephant Island. Perennially enshrouded in cloud and guarded by super pods of fin whales, the island is most famous for its associations with Ernest Shackleton's *Endurance* calamities. It also has a healthy population of Chinstrap penguins.

While the man they called The Boss was off attempting his daring rescue, the sailors he left behind here ate both the eggs and flesh of this penguin population's forebears. 'Every effort was made to secure as large a stock of meat and blubber as possible, by the end of the month the supply was so low that only one hot meal a day could be served,' wrote Shackleton. 'Twice the usual number of penguin steaks were cooked at breakfast, and the ones intended for supper were kept hot in the pots by wrapping up in coats.'

Anchoring in front of a glacier just by Point Wild,* we bounced out in high swell to see these gothic little birds with their black tongues and inscrutable eyes. Like most penguins, Chinstraps are often very aggressive towards one another, and the telltale marking that runs under their heads can look as though it's attaching a helmet to a belligerent little soldier. On board the ill-fated *Belgica*, Emile Racoviță described these distinguishing markings as 'a thin black line that curls up its white cheek like a musketeer's moustache. This gives the penguin a pugnacious air, which corresponds well to its character.'

That night we sailed into open ocean towards South Georgia. With Chinstraps on my mind and my glass topped up with free wine, I decided to tell a table full of strangers my Antarctic engagement story. I had done this on prior Antarctic trips and realised I could make it funny or sad, depending on who was listening. In 2022, the audience was an Australian couple that liked to feud publicly, an American sales agent with curly brown hair and sapphires for eyes, and a Canadian kayak guide with a rubber face and perfect teeth. The story goes like this:

When we got engaged in December 2010, we weren't ready to tie the knot – we were in the middle of what would become almost 18 months of backpacking around the world, but the

---

* Point Wild is so named because it was temporarily governed by Shackleton's right-hand man, Frank Wild, though its perennial wildness could easily have earned it the same name.

chance to propose in Antarctica seemed too extraordinary to pass up, the bragging rights too tempting.

Even so, it was a late decision, and on the morning before boarding in the Argentinian town of Ushuaia, I pretended to need seasickness medication for the journey, then scrambled to the shops to buy a ring. It wasn't expensive and it wasn't showy, and I told myself that with six more months in unpredictable South America ahead of us, this was for the best.

For the next eight days, it stayed in my pocket. Occasionally I'd reach for it like Bilbo Baggins, my nervous fingers tracing its outline through my thick jacket to reassure myself that it was still secret, still safe. The ring stayed there as we took three days to cross a this-time spiteful Drake Passage; stayed there when we saw penguins for the first time, too. It almost made an appearance when we spotted our first humpback whales, but that experience was already so overwhelming, my hands so shaky, that I decided to wait once more. It would have come out that night when an amber sunset rolled into a blushing dawn, but I stood on the frozen deck alone, entranced by the sky as my would-be fiancée slept.

The eighth day was to be our final one in Antarctica, and I was almost out of time. Whatever was to come next, I had to ask her to marry me. I strode to the bridge – a man with a purpose – and explained my situation to Captain Ernesto Barria. The Chilean, a dashing specimen who caught the eye of every woman on board, nodded his approval and showed me the charts.

Our final stop was to be an island volcano. A millennia-old eruption had blasted open one of its sides, flooding it with seawater, creating a natural bay for 19th- and early 20th-century whalers to do their putrid work. Now it is a popular safe harbour

An Inconvenience of Penguins

for cruise ships to anchor.* Despite the violence of that volcanic event, the island retained some of its elemental energy and is still active. It's also home to one of the largest Chinstrap penguin colonies in the world, a lunatic collection of almost 200,000 noisy birds strewn across a rocky mountainside. It sounded ideal, dramatic, preposterous.

I looked closer at the chart to which Captain Barria pointed. 'We are here, the island is there,' he said. From this god's-eye position it looked like a sagging letter C. Then I saw the name. I double-checked with the captain, but he'd anticipated my question. 'Sorry, yes, the place we are going is called Deception Island.'†

Understandably, this would become pretty funny over the years, and depending on how we were getting on and who we were talking to, the story would either be that we got engaged on an active volcano in Antarctica or that I dithered so long I had to pop the question on a blackened island called Deception.

In any case, on that particular day, the sun had inarguably shone, she'd said yes, and we walked back to the dark shore where a small detachment of Chinstraps stood around like waiters at a poorly attended reception.

Back on board we were greeted as though we were lucky survivors from the Heroic Age of Antarctic Exploration. An obese Coloradan called Jim made a show of loudly buying us

---

* It's also a popular spot for the polar plunge, a supposedly innocuous bit of tourism where visitors are invited to run or jump into frigid Antarctic water from the shore or ship. On Deception Island, guides tell passengers that the volcano still warms the water and will make things easier as they run in. This is not, in a traditional sense, true.

† Regardless of my tone, that detail always gets a laugh.

champagne, then spent dinner flush-faced and slurring, implying that the ship's inevitable rocking would be the result of us consummating the engagement. I hated Jim, a porcine capitalist who said things like, 'I'll vote for any president so long as I can keep my guns,' but even he couldn't have ruined that day.

Penguins are often said to be monogamous, and much is made of their faithfulness, an aspirational human characteristic projected on to a bird at the far reaches of the world. It happens to be wishful thinking – though rarely promiscuous, penguins are not, as the popular myth holds, guaranteed to partner for life. Emperors, so celebrated and admired, only retain their partner between seasons around 15 per cent of the time, mostly because they are compelled to mate with anyone who has survived another deadly winter. Female Adélies, meanwhile, have been seen to mate with other males if their partner returns late to the nest, then have their cuckold incubate the interloper's egg.

Chinstrap penguins are among the more monogamous species, with over 80 per cent of their partners finding one another again at the start of the breeding season, despite the ludicrous distances and manifold complications they face in the interim. Reunited, they greet each other with grandiose courtship displays and ecstatic calls, flippers held back, heads thrown around as they cry in each other's faces. All being well, they then form a nest and begin a season-long pitched battle with their neighbours. The system has worked very well – Chinstraps are one of the most abundant of all penguin species, with around 8 million breeding pairs thought to exist in Antarctica and a handful of subantarctic islands around the continent.*

---

* Sadly the number is now likely to be much lower than this 2018 estimate.

An Inconvenience of Penguins

More than most penguins, they lend themselves to anthropomorphism, and few have made that easier than Roy and Silo, a pair of Chinstraps held at Central Park Zoo in the late 1990s.

That Roy and Silo were both male and had sex was one thing; that they were so comfortable as a couple that they tried to incubate a rock was another. Zoo staff, presumably equal parts heartbroken and curious, eventually gave them a surrogate egg, which the dads dutifully raised as well as any heterosexual penguin couple.

'Things went perfectly,' reported the *New York Times* in 2004. 'Roy and Silo sat on it for the typical 34 days until a chick, Tango, was born.* For the next two and a half months they raised Tango, keeping her warm and feeding her food from their beaks until she could go out into the world on her own.'

A year later, the same newspaper reported that Silo had perhaps just been going through a phase – poor Roy was dumped in favour of a female called Scrappy. Nonetheless, a children's book about their same-sex parenting, *And Tango Makes Three*, was released in 2005, immediately upsetting histrionic religious groups in the United States who declared it immoral. Since its release, this illustrated book aimed at three-to-eight-year-olds has been one of the most frequently banned titles in American schools.

Many more homosexual penguins have been recorded in captivity, though none received quite the same amount of media attention as the boys from Manhattan. In 2019 African penguins in Amersfoort in the Netherlands stole a heterosexual couple's egg then tried – and failed – to raise it as their own. In a Danish zoo, a gay couple kidnapped a chick as the mother

---

* Tango was also thought to enter into a same-sex partnership when she matured, raising a nature-nurture debate that I will not enter into here.

was swimming, while in London two females were said to have more benignly 'adopted' a chick at the Sea Life aquarium. There are dozens of similar examples of this behaviour. It seems inevitable that the pattern is repeated, if not readily observed, in the wild; in most penguin species male and female birds look so alike that it's impossible to tell their gender by sight alone. Even the act of copulation is not definitive – they are so alike that X-rays sometimes fail to tell them apart, with scientists only able to finally sex the birds with blood tests or if scans show eggs inside a female.

Nonetheless, spending even brief spells around colonies seeing couples mutually preening each other, or sharing their egg incubation,* then delicately caring for their offspring, it's easy to ignore the knowledge that they are animals driven by instinct, and instead make-believe that their tenderness is something akin to love.

I normally leave this bit out of the engagement-in-Antarctica story, mostly for fear of tipping the mood from amusing dinnertime anecdote to something less droll, but as you're here . . .

November 2015, a different Antarctic voyage, and my wife and I were trudging uphill through knee-deep snow, trying to get back to the rocky cliff known as The Window back on Deception Island. The trip had taken us to South Georgia, then down to the Peninsula, and was now making a final journey back north. The day had started at Baily Head, a notoriously difficult landing on a chaotic outer shore of Deception which has seen dozens of expedition staff and passengers dunked and

---

* For Chinstraps the incubation takes around five weeks, with the parents alternating in six-day stints.

An Inconvenience of Penguins

drenched over the years. The Chinstraps make light of such conditions – they seem to prefer to nest where there's rough surf – and Baily Head holds such appeal that they have colonised in extraordinary numbers. Leading from the cold water, across snow fallen on the volcano, the birds follow along a well-worn path, known as a penguin highway. The Baily Head commute is one of the most spectacular and heavily trafficked anywhere in penguindom.

We spent the morning watching the black-tongued birds marching around and bickering, then reboarded so the ship could take us back into the shelter of Whalers Bay. Five years had passed since our engagement, and though we were returning at a similar time of year, snow made navigation and hiking newly challenging. To our relief, no other passengers followed us on our little pilgrimage.

When we finally arrived – hot, bothered and on the brink of argument – to what we almost agreed was the spot, we paused for a quick kiss and a couple of photos. Some other passengers were already heading back to the ship. There was no time to hang around, so we had a final look, promised each other to come back again one day, and started our descent.

Neither of us had any idea that within 12 months, our marriage would be over.

Antarctica sometimes occupies a strangely elegiac corner of my heart, but for years as a journalist I embarked on the convoluted and unprofitable business of finding a way to return. If I have anything in common with the men of the Heroic Age, it is perhaps this compulsion.

In the early 1900s, their voyages would take years, with wives and sweethearts left at home. Correspondence was virtually

Love in a Cold Climate

impossible in the interim, the only hope being mail carried by whalers who took more direct routes from Europe to hunting waters off the coasts of places like subantarctic South Georgia.

When Robert Falcon Scott's fatal expedition to the South Pole turned to catastrophe in early 1912, his wife, Kathleen, sent dozens of letters out into the vastness of the ocean, with no idea that her husband was already long dead.* When his body was found that November, a missive to Kathleen written by Scott as he accepted his doom was found among his possessions. There is affection in that remarkable document, but a lot of the prose from his deathbed is almost instructional. 'I want you to take the whole thing sensibly, as I'm sure you will,' he wrote. 'The boy will give you comfort – I had looked forward to bringing him up with you, but it is a satisfaction to feel that he is safe with you.' This is followed by specific directions on how he would like his son, Peter, then just two, to be raised.

Later, as Scott's condition worsened and the man with the scythe waited outside the tent, panic and sincerity rose through some of his lines, but in the letter's near-1,000 words, love is only explicitly mentioned once: 'You know I have loved you, you know my thoughts have constantly dwelt on you . . .'

By comparison, letters between the Australian explorer Douglas Mawson and fiancée Paquita Delprat were much more open in their affection, making the long gaps in correspondence even more torturous. 'This everlasting silence is almost unbearable,' Paquita wrote at one point, unaware that in a frozen hut overlooking Commonwealth Bay, partner Douglas was midway through one of the continent's great survival tales.

---

* Many historians have alleged that while Robert was away, Kathleen Scott was considerably less monogamous than the average Chinstrap penguin.

An Inconvenience of Penguins

Mawson's story of Antarctic misadventure is less well known than his British counterparts', but it is just as unlikely and culminated in a lone, month-long trek across ice following the death of the rest of his party. On completing this epic solo trip, Mawson found that he had just missed a rescue ship home, but that five men had waited behind for him at Cape Denison. Together they endured another nine months stuck overwintering in Antarctica, a prison sentence that stretched their bodies and minds to breaking point.

As soon as he was well enough, Douglas began feverishly writing to Paquita. Though he knew the letters couldn't be sent until he was rescued, Mawson's prose was eager and romantic. Love it never lacked.*

'I have entered the subject of love with you as presiding deity and raced off goodness knows where – please forgive,' he wrote on a long night in the brutal winter of 1913. 'When we are together there won't be any side attractions – love will mean nothing but ever so near your heart, as near as you will allow.'

Fewer letters between Shackleton and his long-suffering wife Emily have been published, and while occasional quotes have become part of the Antarctic canon, the expedition leader wrote openly of preferring life at sea to life at home, too.† When he finally died on an expedition in 1922, his shipmates tried to repatriate him, via Montevideo, Uruguay, only to receive a telegram from Emily telling them that Ernest should

---

* Of the figures of the Heroic Age, Mawson was one of the few expedition leaders to live happily ever after, dying at the age of 76, still married to Paquita after 44 years.

† Among Shackleton's most repeated lines is the famous: 'I thought you'd rather have a live donkey than a dead lion.'

be buried back on South Georgia. She may well have mourned her husband, but she also knew what he loved the most.

Watching penguins interact, their version of love can feel just as cold. Violence is ever present, and for every moment of tender preening, there's a flash of objectionable or repugnant behaviour. When breeding season comes, they become creatures of pure, uncalculated instinct, with males entering bloody combat to win or defend their mate. They pound each other with flippers and bite, twisting their enemy's skin. I've seen penguins with gaping head wounds, their blood appearing especially crimson on their white feathers. I saw a Chinstrap on Elephant Island that had lost an eye, presumably to a rival.

It has ever been thus. As Dr Murray Levick wrote while observing a breeding colony over a century ago: 'Soon there were many cocks on the war-path. Little knots of them were to be seen about the rookery, the lust of battle in them, watching and fighting each other with desperate jealousy, and the later the season advanced the more berserk they became.'

The mating is no gentler. Males whack their would-be partners with their wings, trying to force their head down, hoping to make them prone and open to copulation. Sometimes the penguin underneath will fight back or run away. Other times they hold their wings up to deny the aggressor a platform. If the deed does take place, the male's claws dig in to try and keep balance while they attempt the dreadful docking of their cloaca. There is only a brief peace in the immediate seconds following insemination.

Between their seasons of sex and violence, Chinstraps spend months at sea, beyond our reckoning. Despite the chaos and danger of that life, when the southern oceans melt, they come back in their millions, improbably returning to the same beach to be with the same partner. Four out of five Chinstrap couples are able to do this, and while we may be tempted to think they do so out of a sense of honour, duty or even love, it's just as likely their fidelity is driven by the genetic knowledge that their old partner is fertile and reliable. Faithfulness also means avoiding the traumatic business of securing a new mate again.

Dr Levick sailed on Scott's final Antarctic expedition, and while he wasn't selected for the leader's hopeless march to the South Pole, he was assigned to be part of the calamitous Northern Party. He and five other sailors almost died while enduring a winter in an ice cave on Inexpressible Island, but prior to that suffering, Levick spent the summer at Cape Adare observing a gigantic Adélie colony, thought to be the world's largest. At such extreme latitudes, only Adélie and Emperor penguins survive – Chinstraps and all other species nest farther north, enjoying longer summers and less frantic breeding seasons. Levick discovered that the Adélies' drive to procreate had troubling results.

The doctor's detailed account of his time at Cape Adare over the summer of 1911–12 was published in 1914, but so scandalous were his notes on penguin breeding behaviour that it had to be heavily edited into something fit for public consumption.

Levick hid the most outrageous and upsetting elements by writing them in Greek and it took almost a century for a salacious pamphlet with these details to be translated. Even then the content was shocking, with stories of gang-rape of an injured penguin, the sexualised murder of chicks, and penguins so crazed with hormones that they mated with rocks that bore even a passing resemblance to a bird. Prior to its uncovering, a sanitised published report only hinted at what he'd seen:

Love in a Cold Climate

> Many of the colonies, especially those nearer the water, are plagued by little knots of 'hooligans' who hang about their outskirts, and should a chick go astray it stands a good chance of losing its life at their hands. The crimes which they commit are such as to find no place in this book, but it is interesting indeed to note that, when nature intends them to find employment, these birds, like men, degenerate in idleness.

When the pamphlet was finally published, the homosexuality was its least outrageous element.* Levick was likely the first person to record such behaviour but didn't feel he could write publicly about it at the time. Much like *And Tango Makes Three*, which was published seven years before the notorious pamphlet, there was a desire by some to censor and ban stories that didn't match their sensibilities. Perhaps the sex lives of penguins have always been too much for us.

In recent years, I have sent letters from expedition cruises that have occasionally tried to ape the tone of the great explorers, full of the kind of verbosity and pomp men like Levick employed liberally. Despite the insurmountable gaps in language, I continue to want to feel some kind of kinship with those authors. This is partly because each time I travel south and peer through a porthole, I see approximately what they did: a land of untrammelled beauty, little altered in a century, still implausibly full of penguins.

---

* 'I saw what I took to be a cock copulating with a hen. When he had finished, however, and got off, the apparent hen turned out to be a cock, and the act was again performed with their positions reversed, the original "hen" climbing on to the back of the original cock, whereupon the nature of their proceeding was disclosed.'

An Inconvenience of Penguins

I'd seen much of the world by the time I first visited Antarctica, but it immediately showed me something new. Whatever I thought the maximum emotional heft a destination could offer was forever trumped. The mountains, the whales . . . the penguins. Up became down, my heart moved from left to right, my arteries were rewired. There was a me who hadn't been down there and then there was someone else.

Each time I return to port now, I disembark certain I will spend the rest of my life attempting to make the journey once more, comfortable with the knowledge that my love for the place has long outlasted my marriage. There, and only there, I feel what Mawson described as 'a rapturous wonder – the rare thrill of unreality'.

I set out on the *Greg Mortimer* knowing what would come. After the hollow grey of the Drake Passage, the penguins – Chinstraps and more – were waiting, as were seals and so many whales their blows sprouted like a great forest from the surface of the cold ocean. Yet, equal to the fauna, I found Antarctica's ice to be the voyage's most mesmerising element, especially on the grey days when the bergs seemed to generate their own light, pumping out vivid blues like gas flames. On those mornings they appeared like huge paper lanterns, waiting to float into the heavens – or like pieces of heaven had floated into them.

The largest of these wandering titans, the tabular icebergs, are born from the face of glaciers and can roam the southern oceans for decades. As one of our Zodiacs got close to one, we felt the very atmosphere alter in its shadow: the air grew colder; the water was tranquillised; wind changed direction. Sound itself moved differently. Witnesses became humbled or frightened, but they were mostly silenced by its omnipotence. I don't believe in spirits, I follow no gods, but the scale and perfection felt unquestionably magical.

Perhaps it's a facile comparison but this glacial ice and love have a lot in common. At their best, their light is equally intoxicating, but they also grow and they shrink, advance and retreat, melt and sometimes reform. There are often cracks, which are usually resealed, but once in a while a vital piece breaks off, never to be returned.

4

Penguins in the Shit

> In vain we reproved them for this cruelty. Condemned to long obedience in the solitude of the seas, this class of men feel pleasure in exercising cruel tyranny over animals when the occasion offers. The ground was covered with wounded birds struggling in death. At our arrival a profound calm prevailed in this secluded spot; now everything seemed to say: Man has passed this way.
> – Alexander von Humboldt, *Personal Narrative of Travels to the Equinoctial Regions of America, During the Years 1799–1804 – Volume 3*

The penguin stood looking at the box and the box stood looking at the penguin. Neither was sure what to do next. 'It's a juvenile – pretty rare at the moment,' whispered naturalist Leo Doig Alba, standing next to me in our mobile hide. 'Those guys are usually a little bit more relaxed, but don't make any sudden movements.'

I hoped the innocent juvenile would be helpful for photographs – helpful for simple observation, even. In the wide world of penguin naivety, the adult Humboldt is a rare and committed cynic. They do not wander up to peck boots. They do not shelter under tripods.

They run. They are afraid.

Penguins in the Shit

Six months had passed since my last polar trip, and now in Peru for the fourth bird, penguin spotting had become a very different sport. To get a closer look at them, Leo had constructed the hide, approximately the size of a phone box, covered in a sandy-coloured canvas. We were joined by research assistant Lyanne Ampuero, and all three of us had awkwardly shuffled half a kilometre towards a huge colony of seabirds. Underfoot it was impossible to tell what was dust, sand or guano, the assorted droppings of cormorants, boobies and pelicans. Antarctic snow felt very far away.

As we approached a black barrier of guanay cormorants,[*] they calmly parted to allow our weird vehicle to pass. The large, webbed feet which make them such expert swimmers clacked on the white crust beneath us. 'For some reason they don't see anything weird when a big box walks around,' whispered Lyanne as we edged forward and I stifled a giggle.

Outside the hide, a foul wind blew and blew. 'Just don't breathe too deeply,' Leo said. 'The smell isn't too bad today though, right?'

I didn't agree with the handsome Peruvian. The stench of guano hanging over the Punta San Juan marine reserve on Peru's south-western coast was as strong as any I'd ever experienced, a dazzling reek so sharp that breathing quickly became unappealing. On the hazy horizon, 30 wind turbines hung above the nearby town of Marcona as though they were trying to clean the rancid air. When I stepped out of the hide, it was hard to shake the feeling I was breathing in atomised shit. That night, when I finally got back to my woeful hotel, my beard was starched with the stuff.

---

[*] Birds that are such prolific defecators they are named after their waste.

An Inconvenience of Penguins

And yet, the scene was tremendously vital, life abundant on a scale that actually did remind me of Antarctica. In a yawning bay, sea lions and fur seals played with kelp in the surf, while little waddles of Humboldt penguins left all their grace in the water and awkwardly made their way up the beach. Everywhere there were guanay cormorants, taking off and landing in great tornados, occasionally joined by Peruvian boobies and Peruvian pelicans. It was an entire ecosystem at work, as majestic as it was chaotic, all drawn here to feast on upwellings of sardines in the Humboldt Current offshore.

Despite and because of this menagerie's stench, the 150-acre Punta San Juan site has long needed protection. A conservation project has existed here in one form or another since 1940, partly to protect the 250,000 cormorants, 3,000 penguins and other species, but mostly to secure their valuable waste product, which has been used as a fertiliser for centuries. To guard the site, the peninsula has been walled off, effectively creating an island on which the birds can thrive.* Guano harvesting used to be a violent and indiscriminate process – the cause of the ancestral wariness in the Humboldt penguins – and the wall kept shit bandits and most other predators out.

The juvenile Humboldt penguin was more curious than any adult, so with permission from my guides I edged out of the hide and began taking photos. The bird had fledged and lost its down but hadn't really settled into its adult plumage yet, its blacks more of a charcoal grey, the whites appearing to have a golden tinge. Perhaps most strikingly, the species' signature

---

* The peninsula security is sensitive enough that it isn't open to the public. I'd sent numerous emails and had to be interviewed on Zoom by the project coordinators ahead of my visit.

Penguins in the Shit

pink face was only the colour of a baby's feet. Like the little Galapagos bird, the Humboldt is one of the banded penguins, though from a distance it's more similar in looks to the Magellanic and African species. Up close, though, the adults become distinct from their cousins thanks to upsettingly florid faces which call to mind those of scorched British holidaymakers.

Like the adults, this juvenile was dependent on the guano for a home – penguins of course create plenty of their own waste, but the huge plain over which we'd walked had predominantly been lacquered by the more abundant seabirds.

Just as in the Galapagos, the penguin craned its neck, looked at me out of one eye, then the other.* It turned and did the same again.

Then in the distance there was a short alarm, followed by the first explosion.

It's nowhere, really. Nowhere good at least. A place without colour or imagination, a mining town, almost invisible on the map. A place of dust. Marcona was built by and for industry, thrown up without thought beyond making profit for the corporation. Back then, in 1952, it was for an American firm named the Marcona Mining Company, but today it's for the Chinese-owned Shougang Mining Company. The latter does not have a reputation as South America's best employer. A 2010 *New York Times* report on their operations reads:

> Resentment also emerged when Shougang did not invest a promised $150 million in the mine and the town's infrastructure, opting instead to pay a $14 million fine for failing

---

* Virtually all penguin species do this because they are monocular – I was essentially being sized-up.

to do so, and left blocks of housing once occupied by workers vacant in a town with an acute housing shortage.

Shougang does not seem the sort of company that cares about conservation, and certainly not about penguins.* If anyone back in their Beijing headquarters knows anything about the mine's avian neighbours, it is perhaps only that they are a nuisance. The firm's blasting for iron ore happens frequently within earshot of tens of thousands of seabirds – during my visit warning alarms went off multiple times a day. Other times we just heard explosions.

The story of mining in South America is generally one of misery and avarice, whether in the form of the great guano thefts, Spanish colonials sending indigenous workers into Bolivia's notorious Cerro Rico de Potosí to chase silver, or Chile's 33 copper miners who spent 69 days trapped underground during the infamous 2010 Copiapó incident.†

Marcona has its own victims, including the 21-year-old Wilber Huamanñahui, who was shot dead while protesting conditions at Shougang in 2009. The company denied any involvement. His 18-year-old widow said: 'I know there will never be justice for his killing.'

Later, as Covid-19 landed with devastating force in Peru, 20 Shougang employees died. Their families sued for negligence, claiming the company failed to provide safe working conditions. 'There is a direct causal relationship between the neglect

---

* Though its website argues that it 'adheres to the development concept of "lucid waters and lush mountains are invaluable assets"', whatever that means.

† The 'rich mountain' of Potosí is also known as the Mountain That Eats Men.

Penguins in the Shit

of the company and the death of these people,' argued Marco Rios, a lawyer representing the bereaved.

Marcona's human population: 17,000. Feral dog population: a hundred or more. There was – and perhaps still is – also a rooster I wished the pack would hunt every morning. It woke at 4am, screeching and vengeful, and only shut up around 6am, by which time I was already doomed to consciousness.

I had arrived in the dark, the best way to approach a town like this. I'd have avoided it if I could, but the penguins of Punta San Juan were barely a 10-minute drive from its centre. The journey from home had taken 44.5 hours, a tedious, frequently painful trip from Glasgow to Edinburgh then London by train, then a flight to Madrid, then another 12 hours on the next flight to Lima before a long drive south. I had built this trip into a month of working on various travel writing assignments in Peru, Chile and Bolivia, none of which would involve penguins, but all of which would provide occasional pampering. There was no support for this initial leg, however, and it was brutal.*

There had been confusion and tension trying to hire a car at the airport, but after three hours I was finally able to start what I thought would be an eight-hour drive. In the end, with stops, traffic jams and roadworks, it took more like 11. Periodic texts would arrive from the conservationists of the Punta San Juan Program who had agreed to meet me in Marcona. I wanted to tell them that for every hour I drove south it felt I was being carried two north. Before the end, I was crushing a can of vile

---

* A fortnight later in a luxe Andean hotel, I told a guide about this journey, and she winced and nodded at the details, as though I was telling her of a family tragedy.

An Inconvenience of Penguins

energy drink in my twitching hands and periodically screaming in the car to keep myself awake.

The police stopped me only once, asking to see documents they hoped I wouldn't have. I've been detained by cops like this in many countries and know the body language and tone that precede a bribe.* Often there is theatre, occasionally there is a smile – though not in Russia, of course. In Peru, I adopted the first and often most successful tactic to avoid being separated from my cash, embodying a foppish, largely affable, Hugh Grant-type persona, smiling, offering the correct documents and uttering not a word of Spanish. The officer – perspiring and incommunicative – soon waved me on without my having to reach for any Peruvian sols. As I pulled away I thought: *There's none of this wretchedness in Antarctica.*

The road tolls fleeced me with far greater efficiency, though at least the Pan-American Highway was generally in good shape. There was a very notable exception when leaving the city of Ica, where a bridge had been demolished resulting in tailbacks so soporific I resorted to slapping myself and getting out of the car to stretch as though I were preparing for a bare-knuckle fight.

The interminable drive finally led to a desert, cold and intimidating, then, after a final climb, I took a long right to crest a hill. From there I could see the poorly wired lights of Marcona and the infinite black Pacific lying beyond. Dreadfully, I was still another hour from my hotel.

I bumped through the dark, following a marker on a downloaded Google map, hoping for the best as dust erupted from

---

* Bulgaria, India, Kazakhstan, Kyrgyzstan, Russia, Tanzania, Tajikistan, Uganda, Ukraine . . .

Penguins in the Shit

the unsealed roads and bloomed in my headlights. Having rocked the suspension of my car through this awful visibility all the way to the southern limit of the town, I pulled over to what I thought might be the accommodation.

A newish tower, four storeys high, there were no indications that this was the Hotel Malath Beach – no sign, no lights, no life. I texted the project coordinator, who reassured me that I was in the right place. A minute later, a security gate opened.

A cheery receptionist greeted me, a man so wide it looked as though his leather jacket had been ripped from a bull and directly wrapped around his huge, soft shoulders. He reassured me that everything was OK, that he had functioning Wi-Fi, and that I shouldn't drink the tap water. I was muted by fatigue, too tired to grumble about the lack of elevator. By the time I'd dragged my bags to the third floor, it was midnight, and I was extremely grateful to collapse into bed.

The following morning, I opened the window and saw a ramshackle collection of huts and half-finished buildings across the road. Again, from the *New York Times*: 'On the other side of Marcona from Playa Hermosa, some workers at the mine live in bleak company housing. Others rent squalid rooms in the town. A lower class of squatters subsists on Marcona's edge in a driftwood shantytown, Ruta del Sol.'

For the next three days, this was home.

Not enough people are familiar with Alexander von Humboldt today, but in the 1800s he was globally renowned as a genius polymath, the most celebrated scientist of his age. In 1869, on the 100th anniversary of his birth, 25,000 people gathered outside Central Park in New York just to see the unveiling of a bust of the German.* During Humboldt's lifetime, Charles Darwin, Thomas Jefferson and Henry David Thoreau lavished him with praise. Ralph Waldo Emerson compared him to Aristotle and Julius Caesar, a 'wonder of the world' who arrived 'as if to show us the possibilities of the human mind, the force and the range of the faculties – a universal man, not only possessed of great particular talents, but they were symmetrical, his parts were well put together.'

Humboldt had early theories about continental drift, as well as the spread of plants, currents and species around the world. He described human-driven climate change before such terms existed. Scientist after scientist, philosopher after philosopher would later say they owed their careers to him. He understood extinction and got to the edge of evolutionary theory. A master scientist, he saw interconnectivity, the lines through things. 'In this great chain of causes and effects,' he wrote, 'no single fact can be considered in isolation.'

He was also a fantastic traveller – durable, daring and whenever possible pumped full of coffee, which he referred to as 'concentrated sunshine'.† A man of enormous curiosity who was religiously tolerant and despised slavery, his fantastic voyages covered vast swathes of the world in the name of science, not empire.

His five-year quest around the Americas is widely recognised as his greatest expedition. Arriving in Venezuela in 1799, he discovered new species of birds, witnessed a meteor shower, then

---

* He still looks out of the western border of the park today, when hot dog vendors aren't blocking his view.

† His final words were: 'How grand these rays! They seem to beckon Earth to heaven.' It's not known if this was also a reference to coffee.

Penguins in the Shit

developed a theory about how deforestation was a scourge of nature. He spent four months in the jungle, where he was zapped by electric eels and met rarely contacted Amerindian tribes. Next, he sailed north through the Caribbean before looping back down to Colombia, where he travelled for nine months. Having crossed into Ecuador, he climbed peaks higher than any Westerner had previously managed and discovered that the magnetic equator was 500 miles south of the geographic version.

Finally in Lima, Peru, three and a half years after leaving Europe, he'd timed his arrival to witness a transit of Mercury across the sun on 2 November 1802. Of more earthly concern was the cold current hugging the western coast of South America from southern Chile to northern Peru. This nutrient-rich, bountiful water supplies the Galapagos Islands – and many other places besides – with its extraordinary biodiversity. Today, it is known as the Humboldt Current, though the man himself protested the name, saying all he had done was measure it – local fishermen had known of it long before him.

Similarly, Humboldt didn't discover the penguins that were found in huge numbers along this same coast. Until as recently as the 1970s these were still referred to as Peruvian penguins, but they too now bear his name.

As I read more about Humboldt's magnificent mind and looked out across the bleak cement of Marcona – explosions going off in the distance, seabirds disappearing from the shore – I wondered what he would make of man's impact on the world today. Then I wondered: how would he react if he knew he had inadvertently been a trigger for such enormous biological destruction that it nearly caused the extinction of his own penguin?

•

An Inconvenience of Penguins

Around the time of the transit of Mercury, the 33-year-old Humboldt found himself wandering the docks of Callao, which today has been subsumed by the sprawling Lima metropolitan area. Among the cargo being brought ashore was a yellowish white substance the locals referred to as *wanu*, which stank so powerfully of ammonia it made the European sneeze uncontrollably. Asking around for more information, he found that this was guano, the dried excreta of seabirds from the nearby Chincha Islands. It was being brought ashore because as far back as the Incan Empire, it was renowned as an excellent fertiliser.

Intrigued, Humboldt collected samples, which he dutifully held on to for two years before handing them over to French scientists for study. The results were so promising that within a few years, huge, greedy armadas of European and then American ships were sailing to the Peruvian coast to rip guano from the ground. At some places it was 50m deep, so old it was fossilised. The miners didn't care about its history, nor that it provided important nesting for penguins, boobies, pelicans and Inca terns. White gold had been struck and nothing could get in the way of turning a profit.

As a 2023 *New Yorker* article states: 'When Humboldt lugged his sack of bird shit to Europe, it seems safe to say, he had no idea what lay ahead – the wrecking of the guano islands, the Bou Craa conveyor belt, the war in Western Sahara, aquatic dead zones, and, potentially, phosphogeddon.'*

One way or another, this exploitation was always going to happen. Rapacious, bloody European expansion into South America was unstoppable, but there is a terrible irony that a

---

* An expansion of dead zones leading to an oceanwide oxygen crash.

Penguins in the Shit

man like Humboldt contributed to the death of hundreds of thousands, perhaps millions, of penguins named after him.

I was thinking about this as I prepared to take a forlorn walk down to Playa Los Pinguinos on my second morning in Marcona. I asked the cheery hotel manager if there was a chance of seeing penguins there and he laughed with a bit too much gusto. I showed him photos from Punta San Juan instead and garbled some Spanish about it being so beautiful just north of the city. He squinted at my phone: *'¡Que lindo! ¡Fantástico!'* he replied, flicking his hand.

Outside, the sky was an unhealthy shade of beige or grey, exsanguinated at all times and exacerbated by seasonal winds known as *paracas*.* I spent a few unhappy years living in the UAE under skies like these, unsure where the horizon might be, or if the firmament would ever look blue again. Environments like this are as un-Antarctic as a humid jungle, and yet for the Humboldt penguin they are also a happy home.

In the mid-19th century there may have been as many as a million of these birds globally, but the relentless guano mining meant that by 1982 there were just 21,000. Then the same apocalyptic El Niño that had devastated the Galapagos arrived in 1983, massively reducing the productivity of the Humboldt Current, eviscerating the population further to leave fewer than 6,000 survivors. Fifteen years after that, another El Niño resulted in a lost year of chicks in Punta San Juan and conservationists feared extinction within a couple of decades. Today, thanks in part to their efforts, the numbers have stabilised, with a total population estimate now sitting at around 40,000 penguins.

---

* This name is also given to a Peruvian culture that predated the Incans by about 2,000 years.

An Inconvenience of Penguins

Though they are also found in Chile, Peru has the largest number of remaining Humboldts, and of the 17 colonies along its long, dry coast, none is larger than Punta San Juan. The penguins have shown some degree of adaptability, and during times of food shortage they have been known to migrate; they do not just lie down and accept their doom, but beyond conservation work they aren't being given much chance to thrive.

Along with warming seas and competition from fisheries, a new problem for the penguins arose in 2022.* Artificial alternatives to guano had largely reduced the pressure on the reserves, allowing seabird populations to recover. Then Russia, one of the world's largest producers of fertiliser, invaded Ukraine, and Russian products became the subject of sanctions and boycotts. A global shortage quickly emerged. Before long, a near-forgotten enemy of Humboldt penguins returned: guano bandits. There were surely few clearer examples that the war in Ukraine was global than this – they may have been over 12,000km distant from the front line, but the penguins of Peru became casualties of the conflict.

I returned to Punta San Juan in the afternoon, driving out through the sandy northern reaches of Marcona. The centre of town is dominated by an obscene local government building, a gaudy piece of architecture complete with a folly of a bridge which goes nowhere and is used by no one. I bought some delicious empanadas from a stall nearby, where the woman serving me shook her head at the building, said some things in

---

* In the 1990s, over 1,000 birds were counted dead as bycatch when fishermen emptied their nets near Punta San Juan.

Penguins in the Shit

too-quick Spanish, and handed me a small plastic bag of mercilessly spicy hot sauce.

The proximity of Marcona and its iron mines to Punta San Juan and its guano reserves is coincidental. The rich peninsula had been walled off for a decade by the time the town was founded. Back then, Punta San Juan was not the teeming avian centre it is today – once the area was protected, it became so appealing that the birds literally flocked here. Authorities cared little about the welfare of the animals; they were only determined to protect their valuable resource. It was a selfish sort of conservation, but it worked.

When I returned for a second tour that afternoon, it felt like a particular privilege – the guanay cormorants were roosting in such numbers their bodies had turned the white world black. Humboldt penguins were somewhere in this impenetrable barrier, as were burly Peruvian pelicans, but both were difficult to spot amid the chaos of the diving birds. Once in a while, I also spotted Inca terns, another species dependent on both the Humboldt Current and the guano deposits. Smaller than the rest of the birds at Punta San Juan, they had the most outrageous markings: a red bill fringed with what looked like yellow lipstick and something like a white moustache flowing flamboyantly from their black heads.

As sunset came, we retreated, shuffling back in the hide until we were distant enough for the birds not to see us. Panic with this number of animals would inevitably result in fatalities. Mega-penguin colonies in the Antarctic region can be dangerous places for their inhabitants, but there's exponentially more risk of injury when all that biomass can take flight.

The Punta San Juan Program headquarters was a short drive from the gates of the reserve, a single-storey building

An Inconvenience of Penguins

in a newish neighbourhood that felt distant from downtown Marcona, despite its proximity.* Inside, various staff said hello and offered me tea while I waited for project director Susana Cárdenas-Alayza to sit down and talk shit.

Having spent almost 20 years at the site, Susana knew more about the region's politics, problems and poop than most people. She'd come initially to study sea lions and fur seals, but as her role grew so did her focus. The programme now existed to facilitate education, conservation and land management, protecting the guano and its inhabitants in equal measure.

'If you look up and down the coast, north and south of the wall, the habitat will look similar, but it's only here that you see the pinnipeds, the guano birds and the penguins all densely packing together,' she said, adding that the beaches in Marcona bearing animal names were now empty, not because of pollution or harassment from iron mines, but because the territory at Punta San Juan had become so much more appealing. The fauna had essentially migrated. I mentioned that it sounded like a honey trap, and she laughed, saying, 'No! It's more like they've been welcomed to this excellent resort.'

Susana spoke with little prompting for an hour, often with the sort of obstinance you'd want in a person defending wildlife against humankind. After a couple of days in her company, I had no idea if she liked me any more or less than at the start, but her candour and directness with matters of conservation were a delight. Local and national governments, international conservation bodies, fishermen, tourists and inevitably the Shougang Mining Company all took a tongue-lashing at one

---

* A Humboldt penguin statue on the roof let me know it was the right place.

Penguins in the Shit

point or another.* She had a smile that suggested cheekiness or menace, and I suppose your interpretation of it would depend on whether or not she was talking about you.

The director seemed surprisingly tolerant of the limited guano collection that still went on. We were speaking in September 2022, three years since the last legal harvest at Punta San Juan, and she seemed grudgingly accepting of the precautions taken before it began. After long consultations about breeding cycles, El Niños and the health of the colony, hundreds of workers would arrive for back-breaking graft Susana called 'artisanal'. They would be forced to work by hand, first building a temporary wall within the reserve so the birds couldn't see what they were up to. This no doubt had practical implications, but it was just as easy to imagine it was done to hide their shame.

A sustainable collection for organic farmers once every five years was one thing, but the effects of the invasion of Ukraine were quite another. Susana explained: 'Peru hasn't been able to get the fertiliser it's been buying from Russia, so farmers started putting pressure on the government, and eventually the president promised he'd try and find it in the form of guano.'

Some got a share legally. Others were more desperate. 'We haven't had it here because the environment is too dry for agriculture anyway, but in reserves and guano islands near valleys, we've heard about illegal extraction. All that has happened this year because of the war – Russia is impacting on our penguins, man.'

After we spoke, I retreated to town and to a very bad restaurant. The team had warned me not to go, but nowhere else

---

* So much so that I was later asked to leave some of the most barbed quotes out of my writing.

An Inconvenience of Penguins

seemed open so I climbed up some stairs slippery with dust and pulled up a plastic chair. Unkind eyes greeted me, men who'd come here straight from shifts at the mine. There wasn't a woman in sight. I thought: *I bet prostitution is rife in this town.*

If there was a menu, I wasn't offered it, but instead got some sad plantain, followed by room-temperature chicken served in a mystery sauce seasoned with the threat of dysentery. I had a powerful urge to drink, but the waiter said they had nothing. In the corner, a TV blared out a folk concert in Lima. The panning shots of the crowd seemed impossibly vivacious compared to the grim cadavers around me. I still had a lot of travel ahead, and on some level this trip had been a success, but I made a promise to myself never to return to Marcona.

The next morning, at the start of the 11-hour drive back to the capital, I stopped at the edge of town. On a gable end of one of the grey buildings, skilled artists had painted a mural depicting a girl in bell-bottom jeans, sitting down, hugging her knees. Above, penguins appeared to be flying, suggesting she was either on the ocean floor or perhaps dreaming. To the left, a Humboldt as large as the child seemed to have a wing around her shoulder, as though it was consoling her. As I got back in the car, I thought that, if anything, it should be the other way around.

5

Think of the Children

> Bleached remains of thousands of penguins were scattered all over the platform, mostly young birds that had succumbed to the severity of the climate. Thousands of years hence, if the species should become extinct, those remains, frozen and buried among the debris, will be available as proof of what once existed in these gelid regions now just habitable, then, perhaps, not at all.
>
> – Louis Bernacchi, landing at Cape Adare, 1899

I'd always fantasised that if a crevasse ever opened beneath me, I'd sense it, or somehow be able to react, heroically saving myself and likely the rest of my party. Perhaps this arrogance is a form of victim-blaming – to fall into a glacier is surely the act of a careless, slow person. I would be better. As someone with no mountaineering experience – I can't even ski – I have no idea where I got this idiotic notion.

While my legs dangled uselessly above the abyss, I took a moment to revisit this hubris, then focused on my breathing and tried to work out how I was going to extricate myself. Luck and my camera bag had stopped me from falling all the way in, but I was still in trouble.

My arms were splayed either side of a hole near the top of a hill at Prospect Point on the Antarctic Peninsula. Below, blue,

An Inconvenience of Penguins

granular ice crumbled further away any time I pawed at it with a boot. It was impossible to tell where my full body weight would take me – I only knew that I hadn't found bottom and didn't want to. My expedition teammates were 10 minutes or more down the hill. I was too scared to reach for my radio in case I lost my grip of the crevasse rim. My layers of polar clothing began to feel suffocating as my temperature soared.

I looked at the sky, breathing, breathing.

My weight was all on my arms and my bag, which had mercifully wedged in the snow. My camera was in my right hand, so I threw it away from the hole in order to better attempt an awkward half-climb out. As I made a little progress, part of the rim collapsed. I slipped and for a moment my breathing stopped altogether.

Next, I kicked my heels into the ice walls, trying to firm up a surface to get some purchase. This done, I pushed myself slowly up and out, side-rolling on to the snow. Lying on my back, I was so hot I thought I might melt through to the base rock.

After a couple of moments, I commando-crawled back to grab my camera, convinced until the last second that the whole island might disappear beneath me. It's a horrible thing to distrust the ground.

I looked down the hill and saw the first cruise ship passengers were heading towards me, their photography guide. Nine months after my last visit to Antarctica, I had returned, no longer as a travel writer but now part of the ship's expedition team, a newbie very obviously out of his depth. I stood and beat the snow from my staff jacket.

The passengers were making conveniently slow progress. Beyond them, three Adélie penguins stood on an ice floe. There was no chance to appreciate penguin number five as I only

Think of the Children

had a few minutes to compose myself, get ready for the guests and pretend like nothing had happened. I had pleaded for this guiding job. I had really wanted to be in Antarctica more – just perhaps not so literally.

'Aark!' said the Adélies beyond. 'Aark! Aark!'

Not that they'd know anything about it, but Adélie penguins have always been a major driver of Antarctic tourism. Being such committedly southern birds saw them recorded in many diaries of men obsessively pushing towards the South Pole during the Heroic Age of Antarctic Exploration. They charmed Scott, Cherry-Garrard and even old stone-faced Amundsen, who, when shooting some for food, described them as 'extraordinarily amusing, and as inquisitive as an animal can be'.

His contemporaries were more expansive. Scott lacked plenty as a leader, but he could write – even the moribund instructions to Kathleen were well composed – and his descriptions of Adélies are worth reading in full.

> The Adélie penguin on land is almost wholly ludicrous. Whether sleeping, quarrelling, or playing, whether curious, frightened, or angry, its interest is continuously humorous; but the Adélie penguin in the water is another thing: as it darts to and fro a fathom or two below the surface, as it leaps porpoise-like into the air or swims skimmingly over the rippling surface of a pool, it excites nothing but admiration. Its speed probably appears greater than it is, but the ability to twist and turn and the general control of movement is both beautiful and wonderful.

However, it was the diarist of Scott's expedition and the gatekeeper of the *Terra Nova*'s story who wrote the most quoted line about Adélies – perhaps about any penguin species. Apsley Cherry-Garrard had the benefit of a decade of rumination by the time he sat down to write *The Worst Journey in the World*,* and yet it's hard to imagine a more perfect description of these ridiculous little birds than that of the Englishman: 'They are extraordinarily like children, these little people of the Antarctic world, either like children, or like old men, full of their own importance and late for dinner, in their black tailcoats and white shirt-fronts – and rather portly withal.'

Part of their popularity comes from their singular markings. Though they are in the brushtailed genus, closely related to Gentoos and Chinstraps, they appear very distinct, with off-white, almost icy blue rings encircling their eyes. This gives them a permanently shocked look, as though they're trying to warn of some mortal danger; they have eyes that have seen traumatic things.

Much is made of the Emperors with their epic marches and astonishing ability to endure Antarctic winter, but the little Adélies nest just as far south and in larger numbers. Over the last 19 million years they have evolved the good sense to escape the apocalyptic polar night, but that doesn't mean they shouldn't be revered like their big cousins.

Their extreme latitudes also make them quite nutty, though – sexually schizophrenic and especially quick to violence. There is famous footage of one defending a crèche of Emperor chicks from a giant petrel – an adult Adélie, the smallest bird in the scene, heroically sticks up for an entirely separate species, apparently spoiling for a fight.

Long-time Penguin-botherer Batman would not be shocked by that video. The Penguin has appeared as a Gotham villain

---

* A decade of rumination and the guiding hand of George Bernard Shaw.

Think of the Children

in many guises since 1941, occasionally as a stylish mobster, at other times as a disgusting pervert. Having learned about the sexual proclivities of the Adélies, when I rewatched Danny DeVito's repugnant turn as The Penguin in *Batman Returns*, I couldn't help thinking that his drooling, handsy performance had been thoroughly researched. He even looks a little like an inverted Adélie, with black rings around eyes set in a ghostly white face.

The realism admittedly wobbles elsewhere in the film as a baby Oswald Cobblepot is dumped into a Gotham sewer for murdering a single cat.* Like a faecal baby Moses, he floats along the rancid water and is inexplicably met by what looks like King penguins in the depths of the system. There he becomes a sort of evil Mowgli figure, raised by the birds. Towards the end of the movie, he mobilises penguin stormtroopers to destroy the city; Gotham Plaza is to be blown up by dozens of real penguins wearing rockets and radio-controlled skullcaps. Fortunately, Alfred – the wily old butler – jams The Penguin's signal and sends the birds back into the sewer. Defeated, Cobblepot seems to choke to death on his own indignation. His coffin is later carried by Emperor and King pallbearers, an achievement considering their slender shoulders.†

•

---

* Would a cat get the same treatment for murdering a penguin? I think not.

† It makes no sense, of course, but that Penguin is a lot prouder of his moniker than Colin Farrell's reincarnation in the 2024 HBO Max series of the same name. The Irishman's Oz Cobb in *The Penguin* is a much more serious villain; the nickname relates to his unfortunate waddling limp and prodigious beak-like nose. Knowing that he is effectively being bullied each time he's called The Penguin, he lashes out – violence which at least mimics that of the birds.

An Inconvenience of Penguins

The first Antarctic penguin I ever saw was an Adélie in 2010 on my debut trip to the Peninsula.* I'd seen an African penguin a year earlier, but on floury sand closer to the Tropic of Capricorn than the Antarctic Circle it felt somehow inauthentic.

This lone Adélie was plainly different – a true polar bird on the storied continent, surrounded by snow and mountains wearing glaciers like feather boas. I knew so little about penguins that I didn't challenge an inaccurate story the expedition team told us about its name. They said that the bird was named by the French explorer Jules Dumont d'Urville in honour of his wife, Adéle. This seemed like a fine way to apologise for his extended absenteeism: 'Look, *ma chérie*, I have named a cute little penguin after you.' In fact, Jules had given 430,000km^2 of Antarctic territory his wife's name; the Adélie penguins were first recorded in this Adélie Land, and the name came from there, rather than directly from the often-abandoned Adéle.†

When we saw that first penguin, several of us fell on to the snow, encouraged by our expedition photographer to get as low as possible for the best shots.‡ The bird looked tall and proud, those shocked and shocking eyes peering right down the lens. Perhaps the vagrant was lost, perhaps it'd been shunned by its colony, but it was alone and no doubt a little confused by all the humans prostrating themselves as though in worship.

If we were reverent in that moment, things fell back into a more common nonsense when we watched them lining up to

---

* It didn't look like a pervert, but then do they ever?

† Two years later, as they lay dying together in the Versailles rail disaster of 1842, I wonder if any of these gestures were remembered by the Dumont d'Urvilles.

‡ This was in the good old days, before fear of seal attacks and avian flu led to reputable operators banning their guests from lying down in Antarctica.

Think of the Children

go into the water at Paulet Island. Standing on an ice ledge, 25 or more Adélies looked at the water as though it were a portal to another dimension, hesitant, unsure and yet irresistibly curious. The birds had to go in the water to feed – their lives and the lives of their chicks depended on it – but they queued bamboozled by the prospect, at once afraid and hypnotically drawn, before finally the penguin at the front was nudged by one behind. Once the first fell in, its flippers and feet scrabbling in thin air, others tumbled after it, and as momentum gathered, all the birds clumsily followed suit. Each time entering the water may as well be the first time for an Antarctic penguin.

I had travelled as a journalist but would have been counted among the 37,000 visitors to Antarctica that season. Twelve years later, I was contracted to make the journey multiple times a year, no longer as a passenger but as crew, one of hundreds of guides shepherding over 100,000 visitors around the continent during the austral summer. Now *I* was telling people how to behave around the Adélies.

When the time came, the decision to begin diluting my travel writing career was an easy one. It was clear that postpandemic the travel industry would come back, snarling, roaring and vengeful, but if writers were hesitant to promote places like Israel or Saudi Arabia before 2020, few could afford such morals afterwards. If you wanted a job, you had to write positively about wherever paid.

In that first year of the disease, advertising dried up, magazines folded and staff were made redundant. Many experienced people chose to leave the industry permanently. Unsurprisingly this led to a decline in quality and the demise of imagination. To pitch a story about somewhere unknown or unpredictable was to be met with silence, while churning out copy about an ad-buying resort was to guarantee employment. A pal pointed out that none of this was travel writing – at best we were covering tourism. I considered my options, thought back to the Universal Credit days of 2020, then began filing copy as shallow as a week-old puddle.

When I wasn't effectively writing ads, I pitched weird stories about rarely visited parts of the world and was largely ignored – people only seemed to want fairy tales about holidaymaking. An inevitable AI writers' apocalypse loomed on the horizon, but checking social media I'd see no shortage of peers promoting listicles on Abu Dhabi spas while their profile photo had them gazing to the horizon, their jaws set hard against the dying sun.

These sorts of unhelpful and probably unreasonable thoughts had been lurking somewhere in my mind for years, so when alternative employment came along, I found myself diving on it like a fumbled rugby ball. The fact that this option – photography guiding – happened to be in Antarctica only made me react more quickly.

As a travel writer I'm often asked where my favourite place is. I usually answer the Antarctic region then reference an obscure chess documentary.* In it a talking head called Frederic Friedel explains how superhuman Garry Kasparov was compared to his contemporaries at his peak. 'Grandmasters, there are many hundreds of them now,' says Friedel in *Game Over: Kasparov and the Machine*. 'And there are a few grandmasters who are so far superior to their colleagues that they should introduce something like a super-grandmaster. And one could argue that Kasparov needs his own category all to himself . . . he is beyond.'

---

* For ease other times I just say Argentina, India or Japan.

Think of the Children

That is Antarctica for me, a Kasparov – an incontestable, overwhelming phenomenon with which it is unfair to compare anywhere else. As soon as I got access to the internet after the 2010 trip, I looked up jobs with the British Antarctic Survey, only to find they wanted people with either a PhD or time served as a carpenter, chef or electrician. Sadly, neither high science nor a practical trade was on my CV, and they had no use for a soft-handed writer.

Still, I couldn't shake the idea of getting back to the penguins. After the first trip south, I backpacked for seven months in Latin America, then one in the US, then spent three months volunteering in post-earthquake Japan. It was all useful distraction, but when I got home there was no avoiding the uncomfortable knowledge that I was not in Antarctica and had no active plan to return. As the celebrated Australian expedition photographer Frank Hurley put it: 'After life in the vastness of a vacant continent, civilisation seemed disappointingly narrow, cramped, superficial, and empty.'

Having already been hosted by them for four sponsored media trips south, in late 2022 Aurora Expeditions gave in and offered me a guiding job.[*] I would have cleaned toilets to be on one of their ships – to be paid an honest wage and have colleagues immediately felt better than much of the lone work I'd been doing as a travel writer.[†] I also wouldn't have to haggle with miserly cynics in media accounts departments; I'd be paid on time.

---

[*] Another reason to accept was that this saved me from trying and failing to adequately write about the overwhelming experience of being in Antarctica.

[†] As a student, I spent two years working as a part-time cleaner in a psychiatric hospital, and so cleaning toilets actually is a skill on my CV.

An Inconvenience of Penguins

All of this, plus almost unrestricted access to penguins. Fewer than a third of the 18 species breed in Antarctica proper, yet it's impossible to think of the birds without the ice. Perhaps if I got to know one, I could better understand the other – or perhaps both would remain distant and alien. In any case, I had a chance to find out.

Long before stuffy colonial sailors travelled looking to plunder Antarctica, the ancient Greeks speculated that there must be a southern land to balance the icy expanses of the north: if there was an Arktos, there must be an Antarktos.* Centuries later, the first ships that travelled south were quickly rebuffed by the unassailable environment. Whatever was there seemed protected by an endless vortex of wind and waves spinning defensively, a buzzsaw around the world's last-explored place.

Its myths were partly dispelled when the first European ships pushed through in the 18th and 19th centuries; first Captain Cook, then Dumont d'Urville, then James Clark Ross embarked on voyages focused on discovery, cartography and empire. Many rocks were christened on behalf of distant monarchs and colonial flags flown until carried away by polar gales. Each of the expeditions met penguins along the way, and while the French were charmed by the Adélies, the Englishman Ross found himself in pitched battles as he tried to claim their land:

> Inconceivable myriads of penguins completely covered the whole surface of the island, along the ledges of the precipices, and even to the summits of the hills, attacking us

---

* One has penguins, the other has polar bears. An easy way to remember it is that there would be no skinny polar bears if they had access to penguins.

Think of the Children

vigorously as we waded through their ranks, and pecking at us with their sharp beaks, disputing possession.

It took until the last days of the 19th century for people to overwinter so far south, when de Gerlache and the penguin-eating crew of the *Belgica* were trapped in sea ice. The Heroic Age of Antarctic Exploration followed, with mankind's focus shifting from understanding to domination. Soon the word 'conquer' was being employed.

Whaling next brought people to the continent, and later a handful came south as paying passengers to witness this *terra australis incognita*. They were soon outnumbered by representatives of nations squabbling over increasingly petty territorial claims. Drunk on Second World War victory, the United States charged down in 1946. Parts of Japan still lay in irradiated rubble when Operation Highjump saw 70 ships carry 4,700 personnel to Antarctica. Just two months later, with four men dead and having failed in 'consolidating and extending the United States' sovereignty', they withdrew, chased away by worse-than-anticipated climactic conditions.

The Antarctic Treaty was signed in 1959 and went some way to calming things down. Initially a dozen nations agreed to keep Antarctica for peace and science.[*] As of 2025, there are 57 countries on the list.

Odd things still happened periodically, futile attempts to claim ownership of this ungovernable place. In late 1977, a heavily pregnant Silvia Morella de Palma was flown down to Esperanza Base on the Antarctic Peninsula by the same Argentinian dictatorship that would later invade the Falkland Islands.

---

[*] Argentina, Australia, Belgium, Chile, France, Japan, New Zealand, Norway, South Africa, United Kingdom, United States, USSR.

An Inconvenience of Penguins

When baby Emilio arrived a few weeks later, he became the first person to ever be born on the continent.* According to his LinkedIn profile, today he lives in Barcelona, works as a construction analyst and has exquisitely maintained veneers.

Much of this history is covered in lectures on board modern expedition cruise ships, but the presenters rarely get round to talking about Antarctic tourism itself. By the time of Palma's birth, guests had been paying to sail to this one-time fortress for over a decade, but it wasn't until the 1990s that something like today's industry emerged.

The Australian climber, geologist and expedition leader Greg Mortimer was there in the early days, founding a small travel company that would go on to be Aurora Expeditions. Today he is semi-retired, though he still leads the occasional expedition cruise on a ship which, to his great embarrassment, carries his name.† Despite a lifetime of high adventure, extraordinary guts and outrageous fortune, the Australian has a habit of trying to wave such acknowledgement and grand gestures away.

In the early days, a ship like the *Greg Mortimer* was a far-off fantasy, the nascent industry instead relying on fuel-inefficient Russian ships newly liberated by the demise of the Soviet Empire. Marketing was restricted to pre-internet brochures, a little word-of-mouth, and people's seemingly innate desire to be around penguins.

There was considerable risk in those early enterprises, though ample freedom to explore, too. Greg first took people

---

* An Adélie colony has long surrounded Esperanza and there is a reasonable chance some of the birds would have heard poor Silvia screaming in the grips of labour.

† Which leaves me pondering if it's too late to rechristen it the *Greg Mortified*.

Think of the Children

down in 1991 and immediately saw the effect Antarctica had on its rare visitors. 'We had an ice ship to play with and no one around – we could go where we liked, do what we wanted,' he told me. 'That attracted a certain type of person, a pretty rambunctious group of mavericks, and that made for a nice cocktail. I saw the impact it had on everyone, including ourselves.'

The delivery method has changed little in the intervening decades – refitted or purpose-built polar ships travel south with guests, far from any coastguard and with only a rough idea of where they are going. The organisers rely on Antarctica's many marvels doing much of the hard work while they instead focus on keeping everyone safe, and the environment safe from them. I experienced a version of this formula in 2010 when I saw my first Adélie, and not much had changed by the time its relatives were watching me fall into a crevasse as a guide.

Expedition cruising starts with a plan, which immediately goes out of the window and flutters away into irrelevance. Landings are often already booked or blown out by unwelcoming weather, meaning alternatives must be hastily found. As the number of tourists has tripled in a little over a decade, competition for spots can be fierce. In this world of chance, seeing penguins is one of the few guarantees.

'The enticement of seeing penguins is a prime motivator of the entire industry,' admitted Greg, a militant geologist who has a habit of telling his guests that the birds are boring and that they should instead focus on the guano-spattered rocks beneath them.* 'No matter how hard I try to shut it down, people come for them. We see it every voyage.'

---

* Though I've heard this several times, I've never truly known if he's joking.

An Inconvenience of Penguins

By the time passengers disembark for their first excursions, their clothes will have been searched for foreign objects, all Velcro and wool vacuumed to pick up potentially invasive seeds. They will not be allowed to eat ashore or leave anything behind. Since 2022, in a bid to reduce the spread of avian flu, they cannot even touch the ground with anything other than disinfected boots, walking poles and camera tripods. If they have picked a ship with 500 or more passengers, they will be among the 30,000 annual visitors who are not permitted to land at all.

For us working on smaller ships, a good voyage is signified by passengers being so tired or overstimulated that they can hardly take any more by the last day. A really successful one will see them standing on their final shore, weeping with the knowledge they might never see all this grandeur again. Later in that 2022 trip, I had the unenviable job of shepherding a family from Washington past Adélie penguins and back to the ship while tears filled their eyes. As they sobbed and waved towards the birds, I remembered the same sense of loss during my first visit.

Expedition cruising should always demand more of its passengers than the soft experiences on offer in the Caribbean or Mediterranean aboard floating all-inclusive hotels. For Greg Mortimer the best trips result in 'the whole ship, as a group, shifted in their view of how the Earth works – understanding the levers and forces driving everything, and having personal experience of them'.

Most passengers engage with the on-board education programmes, but others spend depressing amounts of their time on their phones and computers. As Antarctica shrinks, we move closer to it, understand it better, dispel its mystery. In the early days without Wi-Fi, I felt profoundly connected to the place. Those were trips free from distraction, filled with time

Think of the Children

to read books about the continent while in situ, attend lectures or simply stand outside and watch it all roll sensationally past.

In 2018 aboard a ship operated by the French expedition cruise company Ponant, a cheer went up when the captain announced that free Wi-Fi would be available for the duration of the voyage. I watched pensionable tourists nod to each other, fleeting glee passing across their faces – the grandkids would be able to read their Facebook updates after all.[*] As the hubbub dissipated, I wondered how many I could throttle before security carried me out.

Connectivity provides a weapon for the passengers, too, a tool to verify what they're being told, or to challenge decisions coming from the expedition leader or even the bridge. It is an astonishing thing to see an uninformed landlubber question a hardened polar captain's navigation based on information they're getting from their smartphone.[†]

As much as internet access has changed the dynamic on the ships, it has not changed the passengers themselves. Typically white, wealthy and curious, they are often reasonable folk who have reached a point in their lives where money is no longer a concern, but time left on Earth most certainly is. Some are nice, most are interesting, but on every cruise there are also passengers who fall into distinct categories, individuals charged with the same privilege and social cues to the degree that they become almost interchangeable. They reveal this uniformity

---

[*] One of these same pensioners later missed a whale breaching while they were sitting on their iPad, wasting time.

[†] On my first guiding contract, as we sailed towards the Antarctic Circle, a passenger called the bridge at 5am to double-check that we were in fact heading south because their 'iPhone said we're going north'. The heroic crew managed to hold back their laughter until they hung up.

An Inconvenience of Penguins

mostly during the nightly recaps and briefings, when questions are invited by the expedition team.

An incomplete list of these archetypes includes: the person who opens with 'Not a question but a comment . . .'; the snide asider who believes they're saying something never previously observed; the person making a long and sincere thank you that wasn't asked for or needed but gets a baffling amount of applause anyway;* the Google warrior who researched a gotcha question two months ago and can hardly get it out for the amount of drool forming around their mouth; those who complain they are being overfed while accepting two canapes from a passing waiter; the doubter, who may also be the snide asider, who thinks they are being lied to or conned by the trained professionals currently keeping them alive.†

There are almost always climate questions and it's hard to know what the motivation is behind them, or what the expected answers are. Perhaps people want unknown statistics to beat others with back home; perhaps they want a thin answer to help them believe things aren't as bad as they fear. Do they really want to be told that several penguin species are going extinct? That this is largely because the world is savagely overpopulated with people? That their dozen grandchildren will grow to become increasingly parasitic and inevitably make things just that little bit worse? Mercifully I am only employed to talk about photography.

---

* Let's face it, an American.

† All of these people are generously described as 'challenging' by the team, but the absolute worst passenger in the world is the comedian who isn't funny, doesn't know it and loudly insists on bantering people into a coma.

Think of the Children

To see the passengers mix is always interesting, though, especially when they are united in joy around the birds. The cancer survivor. Those travelling with their decrepit parents. The honeymooners. The widows. The sick and the maimed, side by side with the entitled and the terrible. Then, once in a rare while, there are kids, whose joy around penguins is so brilliant that all shadows disappear.

The youngsters are easily pleased, but demands from adults in Antarctica frequently amaze me. If they don't get to visit the British base turned post office at Port Lockroy, there will be dejection. Fail to step on the Antarctic mainland and full-grown adults will question why they've even bothered coming in the first place. Mentioning that the thousands of islands around the continent's edge of course count does nothing to placate them; I occasionally point out that surely visiting Manhattan would constitute visiting North America and I am told it is simply not the same. The polar plunge stirs up similarly unreasonable passions. On one trip, I had a man around retirement age stomp – literally stomp up and down with clenched fists – in front of me when he was told bad weather meant it wasn't happening. They can be extraordinarily like children, these people of the Antarctic world.

Penguins – especially Adélies – also cause people to lose their minds; our job is to keep this insanity within the realms of decency. There is a likely apocryphal industry story of a passenger somehow sneaking a penguin on to their ship in a backpack and keeping it in their shower, ordering copious amounts of fish from room service to keep it alive, before finally being uncovered and quickly banned from ever landing again. I have no idea if that story is true, but I believe it could be.

It's not easy for us to be stoical, either, to ignore the absurd

An Inconvenience of Penguins

behaviour of the penguins and avoid falling into anthropomorphism. Take, for example, the middle of the season when Adélie chicks – dark grey fluffballs which look as though they've just been pulled from an old hoover – are growing and ravenous. After a few weeks of dependency, they are now able to run and harass their poor parents for food. There are limitless joys in visiting Antarctica and yet it's hard to think of many more amusing moments than watching The Chase, the moment when an adult penguin, gorged on krill and other pungent delicacies, attempts to run away from its hungry chicks and is inevitably pursued through the colony. As these birds stumble-sprint over rocks and other fellow citizens, they frequently slam their chins against the ice, tripping and flailing as though they're in a cruel Japanese game show. No matter how many times I go to Antarctica, the pure idiocy of these scenes makes me laugh.[*]

Yet for all that, it's getting increasingly hard to ignore the creeping fear that simply being there is exacerbating the region's rapid warming. Part of the mission of expedition ships is to educate their passengers on how they can protect the environment – to show rich, influential and hopefully motivated people what they are losing through their elected officials and life choices. But how many minds are really changed and behaviours truly altered is unknowable. In an angsty 2024 piece for *Outside Magazine*,[†] the naturalist guide Kara Weller wrote:

---

[*] Grim, pragmatic scientists say that the reason for this pursuit is to check which of the chicks is stronger, which one wants it more, and is therefore more likely to survive. Apologies about those nerds – I'm just relaying their information.

[†] One of the titles whose rank approach to paying monies owed helped drive me from the travel writing business.

Think of the Children

Will they act as ambassadors for these regions? My fellow naturalists and I fervently hope so. We feel conflicted by our presence and the presence of the passengers we guide. We love ice, but we also know that our carbon footprint, which contributes to melting, is greater for flying across the world to reach the ships that burn fossil fuels as they steam towards these ends of the Earth. We do our best to educate our passengers about climate change and have them understand what they are witnessing. Sometimes it doesn't feel like enough.

Despite all the inspections, the precautions and the pleading, there's no doubt that tourism does influence life in Antarctica, especially on the Peninsula, where the majority of the season's 50-plus cruise ships visit between October and March. Animals become habituated. Soot from exhausts darkens snow and can lead to accelerated melting. If 70,000 visitors land on the continent every year, then 140,000 boots are tramping across its surface.*

It doesn't help that, with soaring strings and soothing narration laid over footage of penguins preening at dawn, every big-budget nature series acts as a commercial for the place. Their often heavy-handed scripts drive 'last chance' tourism, hurrying people to spend big fees on travelling to the poles while they're still frozen. Since records began, the pandemic-blighted seasons of 2020 and 2021 were the only ones that failed to show a growth in tourist numbers.

The carbon cost of these trips is undoubtedly huge, but Antarctica is not a country and has no police force beyond what

---

* Not including the battalions of guides.

is agreed in treaties and handshakes. Nonetheless, the efforts to mitigate the impact of visitation are, to me, impressive. Tourist ships are used to transport scientists to bases, aid with medical emergencies and conduct citizen science projects. The scouting and study of avian flu in the region has primarily been done by the same expedition vessels. Some money from tourism, meanwhile, goes to supporting conservation, most notably the huge rat-eradication programme on South Georgia, which helped save colonies of millions of seabirds. There really are converts, too – I met one passenger whose life was turned upside down when his daughter told him, post-Antarctica, that she wasn't going to have children for fear our doomed climate offered no future.

If the world's estimated 35.6 million annual cruise ship passengers were made to be as fastidiously clean, follow rules as closely and give as generously as the 100,000 that visit Antarctica, the world really could be a better place. A more obvious threat to Antarctica comes not from the thousands of people walking along the predetermined sections of the spindly Peninsula, but the billions further afield. When Antarctic tourism bloomed in the early 1990s, the world population was around 5.5 billion; today it's over 8 billion. Earth has unceasing mouths to feed, and buns do not go back in the oven. Antarctica may be visited by many people, but they are not the only ones warming seas, slashing forests and seeding microplastics around the globe.

There are estimated to be 10 million mature Adélies in Antarctica, and most respected studies show this number is growing. Their population will continue to rise until resources disappear and the environment changes around them. At that point, having taken an evolutionary gamble on living in a world

Think of the Children

that wouldn't get too hot, things will get desperate and, despite their abundance, extinction will become a possibility. Ultimately their problems are our problems: as the planet warms, polar ice diminishes and the ocean acidifies, we may find out just how extraordinarily like these little people of the Antarctic world we really are.

6

'And then we heard the Emperors calling'

> When all the sick & wounded have been tended, when all their impoverished & broken-hearted homes have been restored, when every hospital is gorged with money, & every charitable subscription is closed, then & not till then would I concern myself with those penguins.
> – Winston Churchill, writing to his wife from a Flanders trench, 1916

There was chaos up on the Antarctic Peninsula. The first full tourist season since the start of the Covid-19 pandemic saw more ships than ever crammed into the region's limited landing sites; over 50 vessels sailed across the Drake Passage, a record fleet that brought saturation. Then a series of summer storms arrived, and everything got worse.

For one thing, there were no alternative spots to visit when popular locations and supposedly safe harbours got blown out; for another, already hectic flights that were supposed to bring more tourists to the continent simply could not fly. This left outgoing passengers unable to depart and forced inbound trips to be cancelled altogether. At one stage ships were queued by

'And then we heard the Emperors calling'

the icy airstrip at King George Island, waiting for passengers who would never arrive.[*]

I was hundreds of nautical miles to the south aboard Ponant's *Le Commandant Charcot*. My inaugural guiding season had ended without major incident and, after a few weeks home over New Year, I had come back south once more as a travel writer. I felt passingly guilty when expedition colleagues texted to say that the sea was churning and rancour growing up north, especially as I was having a run of clement weather and tranquil water that bordered on miraculous.

The French ship's main aim was to complete a rare Antarctic semi-circumnavigation, 12,150km from Argentina to New Zealand.[†] My main aim was to spend time with Emperors, the largest, most iconic and most regal of all penguins. After that, with the right planning, I could stay on in New Zealand and see another two or possibly three extra species. There were many reasons to make this long voyage aboard one of the world's newest and most durable icebreakers, but failing to see the big birds would be disastrous for me, especially as the cruise took 28 days to swap South America for Antarctica, then Antarctica for Oceania.

Despite their global fame, the Emperors' extreme breeding cycle gives them a mythic quality: the biggest extant penguin is the only one that incubates an egg through the impossible horrors of the Antarctic winter nights. The Emperor does this exclusively on sea ice, meaning it may spend its entire life

---

[*] An expensive way to learn that it's better not to cheat by flying and just take your medicine in the Drake Passage instead.

[†] Or 6,561 nautical miles, the equivalent of Glasgow to New York and back again.

An Inconvenience of Penguins

without ever setting foot on land. No other bird can make such a claim – not even the little Adélies which nest at similar latitudes, nor the wandering albatrosses which spend the majority of their lives on the wing. Penguins are birds designed for hardship, but the Emperor operates in a realm of masochism beyond compare. As the great Peter Matthiessen writes in *End of the Earth: Voyages to Antarctica*:

> Like all of its tribe, the Emperor is hard-eyed, hard-feathered, and hard-boiled, being no less instinct driven and pitiless than any other animal, not excluding such sentimental favourites as lovebirds, pandas, whales, ducklings, and kittens. It is only in its hardihood, its breeding cycle, and domestic accommodations that *A. forsteri* is aberrant and extraordinary.

Ponant's itinerary didn't guarantee seeing the Emperors. By the time we set sail in mid-January 2023, their rookeries would largely be empty, their obscenely cute chicks grown, or fledging, and the adults mostly at sea chasing a much-needed feast after months of starvation on ice. Chances to see my sixth penguin species would be opportunistic; as it turned out, they would also be plentiful.

Even with the enticing itinerary, the French company had sold fewer than half the berths on their expensive ship. Like several point-to-point voyages I'd been on, it seemed passengers simply didn't like flying into one place and out of another.* The

---

* Notably a later trip via Tristan da Cunha to see the Northern Rockhopper penguins, but also several Arctic trips as a guide, none of which are ever sold out.

'And then we heard the Emperors calling'

fact that this particular cruise came with a price tag of almost £40,000 per person probably didn't help. This was Antarctica for people with deep pockets, lots of time and hopefully an interest in exploration.

But not quite as much interest as they had in champagne. From the moment we stepped on the ship it was everywhere. A welcome drink, a drink to celebrate crossing the Antarctic Circle, a toast to anything at all. Champagne was served before every recap in the ship's wonderful lecture theatre, where the cup holders were perfectly designed for champagne flutes.[*] It was there during breakfast, lunch and dinner, and throughout the chintzy show the cruise manager stubbornly put on every night for crowds of two or three. The enormous price tag meant that most drinks were included, but the bubbles were poured like fizzy water, and some of the French guests drank it in exactly that manner.

The ship is named after the handsome, uncommonly successful French explorer Jean-Baptiste Charcot. Liberally muscled and moustachioed, prior to sailing south, he won two silver sailing medals in the 1900 Summer Olympic Games and married into the aristocratic Hugo family. He could have probably afforded a spot on the ship now carrying his name, but in 1904 and again in 1908 he used some of the family fortune to fund two trips to Antarctica. His wife, Jeanne Hugo, granddaughter of Victor, was evidently unimpressed by her husband's growing Antarctic obsession and divorced him on the grounds of desertion a year into the first of these voyages.

Like all the best men of the era, Charcot travelled for science and discovery, not conquest and dominion, charting hundreds

---

[*] But not mugs, pint glasses or any other drinking vessel.

An Inconvenience of Penguins

of kilometres of coastline, collecting samples of everything from fish to fossils. He also oversaw an early penguin tagging operation and was able to prove that survivors returned to the same rookery each spring. Unsurprisingly he also fell in love with the birds, often looking on them as companions:

> Penguins, destitute of all fear, come up to me and chatter away. I ask the penguins where their rookery is, but the rascals pretend not to understand, and it is no use my hunting for it, I cannot discover it. But we part nonetheless good friends.

Having to kill them for food always weighed heavy on the expedition leader:

> The poor penguins will be the first to suffer for this, since we must sacrifice some hundreds of them. I detest these massacres, however indispensable they are in our position, and they grieve me all the more because the birds here are so gentle and inoffensive.

In 1936, the 69-year-old Charcot, took his excellently named ship the *Pourquoi Pas?* to Iceland. His desire to explore was undulled by age, but on that trip it was finally extinguished by a cyclone which wrecked his ship, killing everyone on board save the master steersman.* Charcot died as he had lived – a national hero of France and science.

Like Douglas Mawson and Otto Nordenskjöld, Charcot's focus on science over personal glory has meant that history – particularly Anglocentric history – has forgotten much about

---

*   Brutally answering the ship's titular question of Why Not?

'And then we heard the Emperors calling'

him.* Sitting on board *Le Commandant Charcot*, I wondered what the Frenchman would have made of being drowned out by his contemporaries, daft Shackleton† and incompetent Scott. And what of this ship? He'd surely have appreciated that it sails under the French tricolour, albeit a version that counts as a flag of convenience.‡ The ambitious route would have likely got his approval, too. Even the champagne would have been endorsed – Charcot's expeditions were famous for including it in their stores.

Despite the £330 million icebreaker reintroducing his name to many around the world, there's no shaking the fact that Charcot's achievements, if not his whole life, have been overshadowed by the noisy flailing of his British counterparts.

For me, the most perplexing of these figures is Captain Robert Falcon Scott, who led two missions to reach the South Pole in 1901 and 1910. The second of these ventures – aboard the ship *Terra Nova* – is one of the most studied, heralded and latterly condemned expeditions in Antarctic history. Despite this, before getting on for my 28-day cruise halfway around the continent, I knew about it only in outline. This was largely because all my previous Antarctic experience had been on and around the Peninsula, most of which unavoidably focused on the dangerous machinations of Ernest Shackleton. To redress

---

* Nordenskjöld was an intrepid Swedish scientist who Charcot once volunteered to rescue when his Antarctic expedition turned to calamity in 1903.

† Or, to quote Winston Churchill, 'ridiculous Shackleton'.

‡ The euphemistic term for sailing under the flag of a foreign nation, primarily to avoid stricter regulations and dodge higher taxes. Favourite countries for this include Panama, The Bahamas and Malta. Ponant's proud French flag actually represents them being registered in the overseas territory of Wallis and Futuna.

An Inconvenience of Penguins

this imbalance, I decided to use my time aboard the *Charcot* to finally read Apsley Cherry-Garrard's seminal appraisal of Scott's final expedition, *The Worst Journey in the World*.

This was my 10th trip to Antarctica in 13 years. It was frankly embarrassing that I hadn't read what is often described as the best adventure travel book ever written. The ship's route would take me to several crucial locations of that catastrophic mission; it seemed like the perfect time to finally tackle its 700 pages.

Of course, our Antarctic expedition would be largely unrecognisable by comparison, but travelling between continents through the Bellingshausen, Amundsen and Ross Seas, it was still epic by modern tourism standards. While most cruises stick to the northern tip of the Antarctic Peninsula and now come with the guarantee of seeing other ships touring well-established routes, we were striking out for something different.

In 1910, the 24-year-old Cherry-Garrard sailed because of his own pioneering spirit, plus his willingness to train as an assistant zoologist – and because he made a £1,000 donation to Scott's expedition. By the time it ended, five men including Scott were dead, and Cherry-Garrard was fated to live the rest of his life as a traumatised witness and ultimate analyst of this infamous polar misadventure.

The *Terra Nova* carried expedition members 'whose specialist knowledge was in whales, porpoises, dolphins, fish, birds, parasites, plankton'. Like all expedition cruise ships, the *Charcot* too carried experts, many of whom gave lectures. Unlike most of its rivals, Ponant also took working scientists who had their own dedicated lab on board for fresh research.

On my trip a team from Laval University in Quebec were searching for nanoplastics, while a professor from the University

'And then we heard the Emperors calling'

of Southampton was verifying a theory about phytoplankton in the Southern Ocean. These scientists, all distractingly good-looking and keen to find out the limits of the free bar when not working,* found themselves in the same awkward halfway house as me. Not paying guests, nor expedition team; not there on holiday, but not exactly flat-out with honest graft, either. Consequently we spent long evenings together, no doubt the subject of gossip among the expedition team and passengers alike. I drank most nights with one or all the science team after dinner, but during meals I often drifted towards unappealing tables at the edges of the restaurants to read my book, holding it up like a shield lest anyone attempt to sit next to me.

After reaching the trunk of the Peninsula we turned into the Bellingshausen Sea, pushing west every day. At one point, the ship broke through an ice barrier that allowed us to hug Thurston Island. No other vessel had done this in a decade – and even then, it was the *Nathaniel B. Palmer*, the US government's icebreaker.† This was lonely water now.

West, west and west again, time zones dropping away every couple of days, the confusion of the dateline yet to come. By the time we reached the Amundsen Sea, we were one of the most remote ships on the planet, and yet the unyielding sun shone at all hours, suggesting nothing was really at risk. Occasionally we'd see Emperor penguins on the pack ice and my

---

* We were normally served by a young barman with a silly moustache who liked us well enough but had decided he hated almost all the French passengers.

† Ponant's ship exceeds the icebreaking capabilities of the *Palmer* – the only vessels with a higher ice rating are nuclear-powered Russian vessels, creaking relics from the Cold War.

heart would leap or break when they felt they had to flee as we thundered past them, shattering the sea.

Spotting them from the outer decks was fine, but I wanted to be on the regents' level, to look into their black marble eyes and see if I could identify something singular. The chance came near Siple Island when Captain Stanislas Devorsine wedged our ship into some fast ice and, happy that both it and the *Charcot* were secure, lowered gangways directly on to the snow.

Some passengers used this opportunity to recreate the most famous photo from Charcot's Antarctic expeditions. Taken during his 1904 voyage, it shows geologist and glaciologist Ernest Gourdon and photographer Paul Pleneau on ice, their ship also held fast behind them.* The men are apparently celebrating Bastille Day, sitting cross-legged on wicker chairs, a table between them. On it there is a box of cigars, a bottle of champagne and two glasses. Gourdon is pretending to read what must have been a very out-of-date newspaper, while Pleneau is wearing a beret, smoking a pipe and angrily looking down the lens like he wants to punch the photographer.†

I couldn't pretend to be interested in this bit of fancy dress, and besides, one of the mountaineering guides was going to lead a small penguin excursion across the ice. From the bridge, the expedition team had spotted what they thought might be a group of Emperors, though at such range it was hard to be certain – it was also a bit odd that so many adult birds were spending time together at this time of year, so far outside of the

---

* What's now called Pleneau Island on the Antarctic Peninsula is home to a healthy summer population of Gentoo penguins.

† Which is all the funnier as he *was* the photographer and had staged the whole thing.

'And then we heard the Emperors calling'

breeding season. When we were asked if anyone would like to take a closer look, my hand was the first in the air.

The walk across the ice took 20 minutes and from a distance, the towering birds contrasted starkly against the white expanse. Had I not known better, I might have thought they were people. As we edged closer, it was soon clear that many were moulting, some with more grace than others. Penguins spend so long in the abrasive sea that each year they need to replace all their feathers. Rather than do this in stages like many other birds, they instead undergo what is known as a catastrophic moult, an exhausting process whereby they lose their waterproofing and must starve on land until their tuxedo has been renewed.

Consequently, these birds rarely moved, but when they did, their sheer mass was impressive, almost intimidating. Each step seemed like a significant event, huge, horrible feet thudding into the ice with every stride. I'd heard about scientists trying to tag these birds, the target flinching and running away, a desperate researcher then grabbing the penguin's ankles, only to be dragged across the ice. I wasn't sure if that story was true until I saw the monstrous birds up close.

Standing up to 1.3m tall and weighing 45kg before their arduous breeding cycle begins, the Emperor is the world's largest penguin by a distance. They are 30 times the weight of Little penguins, their smallest extant cousin. That may be an unfair comparison, but at their biggest they are also more than double the weight of the next largest penguin, the King. Those birds are undoubtedly more handsome, but the Emperors carry themselves with the heft and confidence of heavyweight prize-fighters.

This mass is important for managing heat and enduring the brutality of Antarctic winter. No matter the temperature,

An Inconvenience of Penguins

during their famous huddles, the males generate extraordinary warmth – the centre of these groups can reach over 35°C, forcing penguins out to cool down before rotating back in again. So efficient is the insulation of the Emperor that the move to the cold exterior is not an act of benevolence to accommodate their fellow penguins, but to avoid overheating.

In summer, their powerful flippers carry them to record depths unmatched by any other bird. Down there, over 500m in the cold dark they chase fish and squid, flying as though in outer space. When foraging for their chicks, they can travel up to 500km away, then swim and walk all the way back to regurgitate meals for their greedy young. The female loses 20 per cent of her bodyweight when laying an egg; the male loses half of his while caring for it. Their instinct to parent is so strong that bereaved adults occasionally kidnap the young of other penguins, so all-consuming that scientists have observed rival foster parents pulling stray chicks apart while squabbling over who can look after them best. In every way, these birds live in extremis. As Gavin Francis puts it in his book *Empire Antarctica*:

> Emperor penguins live in a triptych world of sea, ice, and sky, devoid of bearing and recognisable landmarks. Patterns in the ice coastline change every year. Their internal landscape must be mapped with constellations, solar angulations, and magnetic contours that give Antarctica a depth and texture invisible to us.

No creature can endure alongside them – their lives are too hard on land, too dynamic at sea. All humans can do is observe them in summer, and so for this moment only could I be with them, reverent and awed in the company of powerful royalty. The endless sunshine twinkled on their white and gold feathers,

'And then we heard the Emperors calling'

glinted off the black. I laid out the rain sheet from my backpack, took out my camera and knelt before the Emperors.

The sea days continued with the seemingly infinite Ross Ice Shelf and the man his shipmates called Cherry as my companions. By this point, we had sailed to over 77 degrees south, where ice was so thick that landings had grown impossible, and our ship had to carefully pass through mazes of tabular icebergs the size of aircraft hangars and shopping malls.

When we sailed past Cape Crozier, my reading of *The Worst Journey* neatly synced with our location. Here on the foothills of Mount Terror, Cherry-Garrard, Henry 'Birdie' Bowers and Bill Wilson returned from a near-fatal foraging trip for Emperor eggs in the depths of winter,* only to find their tent blown away. All that remained was their sleeping bags and a half-igloo left for shelter.

It was the lowest point the author reached in his whole wretched time in Antarctica. This mission for Emperor eggs, not Scott's death march to the South Pole, was the worst journey in the world. 'Thus impiously I set out to die,' Cherry wrote, 'making up my mind that I was not going to try and keep warm, that it might not take too long, and thinking I would try and get some morphia from the medical case if it got very bad.' He then seemed to reach across the century and whisper directly in my ear, 'Yes! Comfortable, warm reader. Men do not fear death, they fear the pain of dying.' At that same

---

* Eggs which they hoped would contain embryos that could prove the Emperor a missing link between reptiles and birds, which of course they are not. Two of these eggs are still held in London's Natural History Museum today.

An Inconvenience of Penguins

moment, the daily schedule aboard the *Charcot* was offering a brioche-baking class.

Early in the trip I had decided to take a day to say yes to everything Ponant offered on board. It was to be called my Lovely Oui Day, but it never quite happened. By the time we turned away from Antarctica, my innards felt like melted cheese that had reformed and hardened – I simply couldn't face more excess. Antarctic explorers used to worry about scurvy in this part of the world, but if I was concerned about an antique ailment on the French cruise, it was gout.

The ship had a lot of those sorts of offerings – gluttonous cruisy things – but I kept being distracted from the itinerary by Cherry-Garrard's endless suffering and the wide magnificence of Antarctica. Still, the gap between my universe and the author's widened, no matter how much I wanted to believe we were sharing something. I was experiencing the sort of life he, Bowers and Wilson would have dreamed about as they lay freezing to death near the Emperor rookery.[*]

In half protest, I didn't attend the cooking classes for Arctic char, far Breton or pumpkin risotto with hazelnut and truffle. ('This journey had beggared our language: no words could express its horror.') I ignored the morning yoga, the stretching with Sarvan and the aquagym. ('Any man who undertakes big polar journeys must face the possibility of having to commit suicide to save his companions.') I eschewed the classes variously teaching cha-cha, salsa and tango. ('I could not have wept if I tried.') I was absent for the pre-dinner tastings of duck breast, newly shaved Ibérico ham and Kaviari caviar. ('All my

---

[*] Months later this was the fate that awaited Bowers and Wilson, who were found frozen solid alongside Scott in the austral spring of 1912.

'And then we heard the Emperors calling'

teeth, the nerves of which had been killed, split into pieces.') And I completely neglected the outdoor pool, the indoor pool and the cigar lounge.* ('Only the long shivering... in our dreadful sleeping-bags, hour after hour and night after night.') I didn't even use my voucher for a free massage in the spa.

But Alain Ducasse's fine-dining restaurant on deck five? That I did take advantage of, almost every night, always with a gluttonous eye locked on the *chariot de fromages*.† Thus impiously I set out to dine.

The least I could do was take Cherry's book along. There its multitudes stretched in front of me: an account of adventure and penguins certainly, but also one of the disintegration of bodies and minds, of what his generation would later call shell shock and we now call PTSD, and – perhaps more than anything – a story of a man plagued by survivors' guilt. It is a book of pain.

Eventually, we turned around the western tip of Ross Island and nudged into the McMurdo Sound, Mount Erebus looming above us, unimpeded by cloud. More ice lay ahead but by this point, I had grown to enjoy watching it yield under the ship, an odd kind of hypnotism cast by colour and sound. Whites, blues and diatom yellows in turning bergs were accompanied by a soundtrack of groans, frazzles and guttural rumbles – then, just as Cherry-Garrard experienced, 'A tiny crack, no bigger than a vein, would run shivering from our bows, which widened and widened until the whole ship passed through without difficulty.'

---

* The sole inhabitant of this smoky time machine was a neckless Corsican who spoke in croaks and looked so profoundly unhealthy I became convinced he would die and ruin the trip for everyone.

† On the expert advice of the sommelier, I discovered a combination of walnut-washed cheese and white port that I still dream of now.

An Inconvenience of Penguins

We were not, however, invincible. As we continued to Cape Evans, a conspiracy of wind and ice gathered behind us. Despite his ship's exceptional efficiency in polar water, Captain Devorsine – who had a decade of captaining icebreakers before joining Ponant – saw the danger clearly. 'You must always be careful with pressure,' he told me. 'When the ice is forced into the land, it can be dangerous – even for this ship.' Plans to go ashore at Scott's hut were delayed, time we filled by pushing south to look at the polar carbuncle that is McMurdo Station, a US base that can accommodate 1,000 members of staff in summer. Even in the sunshine there was no softening the ugliness of seeing industry in Antarctica.

When we finally reached the hut the following morning, it looked in incredibly good shape. Dedicated work by the New Zealand-based Antarctic Heritage Trust has restored and renovated this tragic command post, keeping it somewhere between a museum and a mausoleum. Inside, I found the stillness and the intimacy almost too much to bear. I saw old cans of pemmican made by J.D. Beauvais of Denmark, and remembered that it was Cherry-Garrard's favourite. Nearby, the writer had slept in the bunk below his dear friend Birdie Bowers. At the side of the Scotsman's bed, I found a five of hearts playing card wedged by the mattress and wondered if the wee man from Greenock had been cheating in some long-forgotten game.*

It was the huge table in the centre of the room that felt most haunted. Here the men partied, planned and plotted; later, the survivors gathered to mourn the senseless loss of Scott, Bowers, Wilson, Oates and Evans, none of whom made it back from

---

* Though this would have gone against Cherry's judgement that Bowers 'was transparently simple, straightforward, and unselfish'.

'And then we heard the Emperors calling'

the South Pole. Amundsen had beaten them by 34 days and already announced his victory to the world while the last men of the fatal British mission lay dying in the snow. Fortunately for his readers, Cherry-Garrard hadn't been selected to go with them.

The Ponant team generously gave me a few moments in the hut alone to take more photographs, but my heart wasn't really in it. The place felt uncanny, almost eerie. I stood by the table, listening closely, hoping to hear something, or perhaps say something meaningful – the silence was too terrible. Instead, I turned to leave, then paused to look around the hut once more, and wished the men of the *Terra Nova* had been able to return here as one.

I spent the rest of the day thinking about the historic British approach to Antarctic exploration, about how they ignored advice and how, unlike Amundsen, they arrogantly dismissed Inuit practices for polar travel. The Norwegian had taken dogs and he had won comfortably. Scott, like Shackleton, tried to use ponies, all of which died before or during the journey.* He also tried to use a rudimentary snowmobile, which proved even more useless. The Brits somehow saw nobility in man-hauling, the most arduous and masochistic of all transport methods, each crewmember dragging stores and camping equipment with them, often in a chain. It took exhausting weeks and months to travel in this fashion and was always liable to complications with crevasses and pressure ridges.

---

* In one striking episode, ponies were snatched from an ice floe by orca with what Bowers called 'huge black and yellow heads with sickening pig eyes'.

An Inconvenience of Penguins

I started to see something of the Emperor penguin in these men: like the birds they chose the most torturous way to live. Stubbornness had killed many of their peers. Despite the avoidable awfulness, people around the world still looked at them – the penguins and the explorers – as noble, brave souls worthy of worship. For his part, Cherry thought the penguins suffered even more than his comrades: 'Take it all in all, I do not believe anybody on Earth has a worse time than the Emperor penguin.'

Rémi Bigonneau had a more balanced view – at least of the Emperors. One of several marine biologists on board the *Charcot*, he studied penguins but sounded more like a philosopher when we spoke on the long crossing from Antarctica to New Zealand. 'It's strange that there's so much attention given for an animal that is so enigmatic,' he said during his detailed lecture on the birds. Over that hour he'd repeatedly demonstrated how globally adored they are, even in places with little or no connection to Antarctica. He showed us that the Emperor has appeared on stamps made in Mongolia, Romania, Vietnam, even the emirate of Umm Al Quwain. People occasionally printed Kings when they meant to have the larger penguins, and I was gladdened to hear this annoyed him as much as it did me.

I asked why he thought the Emperor had become so iconic. Was it simply the size? Their starring roles in *Happy Feet* and *March of the Penguins*? The Frenchman looked at it with much more despondence. 'Well, there's not much hope when you know that they are dependent on sea ice and we know that it is going to disappear,' he said, his heavily lined face drooping. 'The Emperor gets more attention because we know we won't have it for eternity.'

'And then we heard the Emperors calling'

But, I pointed out, their numbers were stable. In fact, the week we'd travelled a new paper had shown that an entirely new colony had been found via satellite imaging – even if their numbers weren't growing in a true sense, the extent of their global population was still being discovered.

Rémi listened to me patiently, then talked me through the breeding cycle. Emperors are thought to have spent the last 3 million years nesting in their very particular way, wholly on sea ice. Penguins are one of the most slowly evolving birds in the world, and in some ways one of the least adaptable. After so many million years on ice, they will not quickly come up with a plan B. 'For sure they are doomed,' he said. 'And if somehow they started to nest on land, it would be an evolution – they wouldn't be Emperors anymore.'

Seeing I was still sceptical, the naturalist described to me the passenger pigeon, a North American bird once so abundant its numbers were thought to be upwards of 3 billion – when they passed overhead the air grew cold 'as though standing under an eclipse'. But then people started to persecute them and eliminate their forest habitat. Farming began to industrialise, and from its position as the most numerous bird in the world, the passenger pigeon collapsed. By 1900, it was extinct in the wild. By 1914, not even a captive bird survived. True extinction had been reached.

'Emperor penguins have many abilities, evolved over many millions of years, that mean they are perfectly adapted to their environment. They can survive where no other birds – no other land animal – can. But as this environment is going to change, they will be in big trouble,' said Rémi, the lines of his face more furrowed than ever. 'They have survived so much – the rise of cetaceans and pinnipeds, shifting continents, the planet getting

An Inconvenience of Penguins

warmer and colder, but those things happened over thousands and thousands of years. The warming now, the changes – they are happening too quickly. For the Emperor, the collapse could happen quickly. You cannot mistake abundance for species security.'

7

Requiem for a Penguin

> At times in the past there evidently were many more species of penguins, both in general and in particular regions, than there are now. Most of them have become extinct. The word 'extinct' is confusingly used in two different senses. We call some species extinct even though they have living descendants . . . On the other hand, innumerable species, many more than have survived in any form, have become extinct in the fullest sense. They have been annihilated; they have died off without progeny.
> – George Gaylord Simpson, *Penguins: Past and Present, Here and There*, 1976

Having emerged from three years in frozen hell, the survivors on the *Terra Nova* arrived in Lyttelton Harbour, New Zealand, in 1913. They sailed into a world of colour and confusion. 'Always we looked for trees, people and houses,' wrote Cherry-Garrard. 'How different it was from the day we left and yet how much the same: as though we had dreamed some horrible nightmare and could scarcely believe we were not dreaming still.' The men were welcomed ashore and began to tell the incredible, terrible tale of Scott's fate.

One hundred and ten years later, not all ships were being greeted in the old harbour with such warmth. Standing on the outer decks of the *Charcot*, I felt a little sheepish when noticing some amateurish, plain-spoken graffiti just outside the port authority's boundary:

CRUISE SHIPS NO
NO GOOD

There were a few reasons for the local anger, one being a sudden drop in water quality since cruise ships the size of Imperial Star Destroyers began returning post-pandemic. Ours was a just a 200-passenger tiddler, but it would still need to resupply before heading all the way back around Antarctica. This would exacerbate another problem – a long-standing egg shortage caused by new animal welfare regulations. As one local told me later, 'We're lucky if we can buy six eggs at a time and the ships come in wanting tens of thousands.'

Literally a little town a mountain away from Christchurch, Lyttelton is a curious place where chain stores do not thrive, independence is championed and residents are likely to have facial piercings. These hipsters have had a tight grip on the town for years, but part of their particular brand of gentrification has seen the weekend farmers' market thrive and the excellence of the coffee soar.

It has an outrageously beautiful setting too, screwed into the bay like a knot in mahogany, with views over the harbour to the volcanic Banks Peninsula. I'd been at sea for a month, and this felt like ideal terra nova for me, a place to absorb the colour green and inhale the perfumes of late-summer flowers. I enjoyed a couple of decompression days before getting ready to head off in search of the Yellow-Eyed penguin.

I say 'in search of' these particular birds because unlike virtually all other species, they came with no guarantees. Indeed

Requiem for a Penguin

they'd evaded me once before on a miserably rainy day in 2014, when I'd pulled over a rented motorhome to sit in a hide and wait for the Yellow-Eyed troops to return to shore.

To my continuing indignation, they never showed, and after just an hour of waiting in the cold, damp hide, I gave up. Failing to see them again would be awful, and likely result in an undignified tantrum and the deletion of this entire book.

'Ah no, could you take a photo of the beach for me?' asked Ben Goldsworthy, a ranger from the Yellow-Eyed Penguin Trust (YEPT), a few days later as we made our way into a secluded cove on New Zealand's Otago Peninsula. Below, the sand was the off-white colour of a polar bear. Relentless summer sun ricocheted from it, dazzling my eyes – I asked what I was supposed to take a photo of.

'There, down by the water,' pointed Ben. Through the lens I saw a dark aberration on the beautiful beach. It was a dead penguin, lying in a foetal position, its black back turned to the sea, its white belly facing the otherwise pristine sand. This was the second Yellow-Eyed penguin I'd seen that day. The first one had been dead, too. I had never known penguin-spotting like this before.

We made our way gracelessly down a bank towards the carcass. Introduced marram grass covered the dunes to provide a bit of useful stability in the sand. It was helpful unless pointing downhill, in which case it acted like a chute. Ben had been coming here for years and made swift progress to the shore, while I slipped, stumbled and nervously clutched my camera. When I got to sea level, we walked silently up the beach in an odd sort of funerary procession.

In Latin it's *Megadyptes antipodes*, the Antipodean big diver.

An Inconvenience of Penguins

In English, it is the Yellow-Eyed penguin, but before either of those names, the Māori named it Hoiho – the noise shouter. All of those descriptions are accurate, though they do nothing to convey the incredibly precarious conservation status of these endangered penguins. As well as impatience, the reason I'd failed to see one in 2014 was the simple lack of living birds.

So scarce are the Hoiho these days that to see them in the wild, I had to throw myself on the mercy of the YEPT. Even then, prior to leaving for Otago, the organisation wanted to screen me face to face in a Christchurch public park. It felt like I was at a meeting between an informant and an FBI agent, and I wasn't sure which part I was playing.

Having evidently passed the exam, I was invited to the YEPT office in Dunedin to meet Ben Goldsworthy. It was there I saw the first Yellow-Eyed penguin, a taxidermied bird looking out across the desks, reminding Trust employees who they were working for. From there, we drove an hour east out to the peninsula in the hope of seeing these extinction-adjacent animals alive.

Now on the beach we walked under a high, loose sky, the temperature a seductive 23°C, the kind of day you wish could last forever, or even just a week in Scotland. On the North Island, an unprecedented second cyclone in a month was tearing up the countryside, ripping out forests and flooding vineyards, all the while serving as a warning of the implacable storms to come. But in Otago things were resolutely idyllic – or at least they had been until we spotted the dead penguin.

The victim had already lost its eyes, but it had barely decomposed otherwise. Ben photographed it in situ then to my surprise produced a plastic body bag and lifted the cadaver. The ranger had become an undertaker. I asked if I could hold it, and with a slightly raised eyebrow, he handed me the bag.

Through the thick plastic, I could see its neck twisted upwards, its eye sockets mercifully forced shut by the unnatural angle. Ben wiped his hand on his shorts and told me that an adult Yellow-Eyed penguin weighs around 6kg. This felt a lot heavier.

The ranger explained that most of the survivors on the South Island have been chipped, like domestic animals. The scanner needed to retrieve the info had been borrowed by another team, so he would take the dead penguin up the hill, where he'd get some phone reception, contact the guys, scan the bird, then come back for me. I was welcome to come if I liked, but I opted to sit at the back of the beach and keep an eye out for live Hoiho.

As the young ranger strode off across the beach, the bag swinging at his side, I looked at the little penguin-shaped depression left behind in the sand and wondered for a second if I might cry.

Just two weeks earlier, on a Zodiac off Cape Adare in Antarctica, I had celebrated the murder of an Adélie penguin, a fledgling which had made the irreversibly poor decision to swim in the ocean while a leopard seal was around. As the sea monster had thrashed the bird's flesh from its hide, turning it inside out, my heart had pumped with excitement and my nervous fingers desperately tried to capture the deadly moment on camera. In over a decade of visits to Antarctica, it was my first time witnessing this hunting behaviour. I tell you this so you perhaps understand why I cheered the violence as though in a Roman amphitheatre. Know too that hundreds of thousands of Adélies covered the shore, and that individual's death felt like acceptable collateral.

An Inconvenience of Penguins

Anyway, to visit a healthy Antarctic penguin colony is to walk through a necropolis. If the population is upwards of 50,000, the dead and the dying will be everywhere, and once the skuas and giant petrels have had their fill, the remains take a long time to disappear in the cold. I've tiptoed through rookeries where it's been hard to find a footing that didn't involve stepping on a penguin corpse. Yet the abundance of life is a great emotional anaesthetic to such horrors, and within a couple of landings, even first-time Antarctic visitors become inured to the body count.

Now I was alone on a silent beach: there was no excitement, no thrill, just a hollow where a futureless penguin had drawn its last breath. In the Galapagos I'd been told their species was in trouble, and later I'd get the same news in South Africa, but this was extinction at the sharp end, no longer theory but awful reality. There are thought to be as few as 170 breeding pairs of Hoiho left on New Zealand's South Island – the death of even one felt like it would be a meaningful blow to the community, something that deserved solemnity. As I sat on the sea grass looking down at the shallow sand grave, steady waves began to wash in, filling then flattening the space where the penguin had been.

Last night, on that warm, dark shore, how did the end come? Did it drown at sea? Did it fall on land? Did other penguins see it? Did it know it was dying? Was it afraid? And then, I suppose the question living things always want to know of the dead: did it hurt?

The Yellow-Eyed penguin is the only member of its genus. When it goes extinct the entire *Megadyptes* branch of the Spheniscidae family will be lost forever. Functional extinction – where the birds cease to have a meaningful impact on the

Requiem for a Penguin

ecosystem they once shaped – had already been reached for this population; total extinction is forecast for 2050. It was hard to look at this contraction as anything other than a tragedy, a failure to protect something beautiful and vulnerable.

And yet, this is often nature's way. There are 18 extant species of penguin; there are known to be at least 50 extinct species, too.* The majority of the lost penguins disappeared long before people evolved, though two subspecies of other Yellow-Eyed penguins were annihilated by early Polynesian settlers.

One of these now-extinct species had also lived here on the South Island but was eaten out of existence. Māori tradition does not record the name of this penguin, but it has been assigned the Latin name *Megadyptes waitaha*. Until bones of the Waitaha penguin were discovered in ancient Māori middens, Yellow-Eyed penguins were thought to only have existed on the southerly subantarctic islands of Auckland and Campbell.† Somehow sensing the demise of their Waitaha cousins on the South Island in the early 16th century, the Hoiho moved north, attempting to fill a niche and colonise the newly vacant land.

By 2023, it seemed clear this 500-year-old emigration experiment was failing. Penguins have been on Earth for 60 million years, meaning they only narrowly missed the dinosaurs. How many times did this sort of expansion happen? How many times did it fail? How many times could the failure have been prevented? And would it have been natural to intervene in any case?

---

* Fossils of more than half of these extinct species have been found around New Zealand and its outlying islands.

† Small, poorly studied populations of Hoiho continue to live on these two islands today.

An Inconvenience of Penguins

Today the Yellow-Eyed penguin is celebrated nationally and proudly printed on the five-dollar note, an honour it shares with Sir Edmund Hillary. Yet, for all the brand recognition, the donations and the work of conservation bodies across New Zealand, it is dying out. As many as 80 per cent of all new chicks do not return to nest from their first season at sea. What happens to them out in the wild ocean is unclear – only their absence is verifiable.

On the shore, a Pacific gull played chicken with the surf, running out to the wet sand to see what the retreating water had left behind. Further along the beach, a half-sleeping fur seal was caught by surprise when one particularly powerful wave slid up the beach and slapped it in the face. I was mourning the dead penguin, but the natural world was quickly moving on.

A little more than an hour after he'd left, Ben returned with the news that the victim had been a 19-year-old male. The data from the ID chip suggested he had bred at least twice, fulfilling his penguin duties over a life that would have been reaching its natural end anyway. The ranger couldn't say for sure what had been the cause of death, but he suspected avian malaria. 'For this one to make it back to land and die on the tideline makes me think it was some kind of disease issue, rather than old age,' he said. From the beach, the bird would be taken away, chilled in Dunedin, then couriered by plane to Massey University on the North Island, a flight as unnatural in death as it would have been in life. Once at the university, it would undergo an autopsy.*

---

* Three weeks later, Ben emailed to confirm avian malaria as the cause of death.

Requiem for a Penguin

'In learning that it was an old male, that it had bred and passed on its genes, it's not as bad as it could be,' said Ben, scoring marks in the sand with a twig. 'You never want to lose birds, but I'd take losing an old male over a young female as there aren't as many of those. This isn't how I thought our trip was going to go, sorry. I'm pretty gutted.'

It was 5pm and no living penguins had shown up yet. I asked Ben more about avian malaria (a long-standing problem worsening with wetter weather), diphtheria (bad but now curable in the local animal hospital) and the looming shadow of avian flu, which had almost miraculously not yet reached Oceania ('It's a fear – it could potentially stop us working with the penguins at all.').*

There was some comfort in knowing that if avian flu did reach the islands, it would not likely be too devastating for the Yellow-Eyes anyway. Not only were penguins globally showing remarkable resistance to the latest strain, but the Hoiho were natural social distancers, only colonising in the loosest sense. Clandestine and antisocial, they live very differently to their cold-weather cousins; they enter and return from sea in ones and twos, and only really mix to breed. They do not, like so many other penguins, leave land for weeks and months at a time, but prefer a sedentary life at the same beach all year round. They are not especially monogamous, nor loyal to individual nesting sites.

They are, however, fussy homeowners – their ideal nest is in a bush with three sides and a roof, plus a single front door which they can fastidiously monitor as the only access point.

---

* When I asked if humans could get avian malaria, Ben replied, 'Thankfully not – I'd definitely have it by now.'

An Inconvenience of Penguins

The Hoiho had once been a forest-dwelling bird, but so much of New Zealand's greenery has been razed for pasture that now they must make do with this sort of ersatz cover.

Looking across the cove, the penguins would only be visible when waddling to and from the sea – if they showed up at all. Their paranoia suggests heavy predation at some point in their evolution, though no one knows what would have hunted them. A large, flying raptor seems likely – the Hoiho have not shared the world with people, or any mammals, long enough to justify such habits otherwise.

The afternoon dragged on. Hope had dwindled and my bum had grown numb when Ben pointed towards the surf. A penguin clumsily made its way back on to land, then crept into thick cover. We approached quietly and the bird looked at us through dense bushes like a nosy neighbour through curtains. At this proximity I could finally appreciate its singularly narcotic looks.

The Hoiho appears like a Gentoo that's had a neon glowstick cracked over its head, or like its signature yellows have burst from its incredible eyes, breaking through a valley towards the top of its skull, staining everything in the vicinity. The titular eye itself of course looks jaundiced, but it's more intense than that, almost pulsing as though the penguin has some kind of unnatural power source inside. When I sat staring into those eyes, knowing how few pairs remained, it was hard to meet the bird's gaze. The waxy colour of a harvest moon, its eyes hosted a glare as sharp as it was unforgiving.

The YEPT was doing everything it could for the birds, nursing chicks to healthy weights, looking after orphans, building artificial nests, replanting native flora, targeting introduced

Requiem for a Penguin

fauna. I had no idea if any of it would work long term, but for now success for Ben and the team was seeing chicks they had hand-reared and saved from certain death come back to this beach to breed. 'So long as we keep getting funded, we'll keep trying. We need one good year when nothing goes wrong,' he said optimistically, though his hope made me want to avoid his gaze, too. 'On land we're doing everything we can, to the point that almost all are surviving here. But the numbers aren't decreasing on land – it's happening out there at sea. We can't help them when they're out there.'

In the water, their problems are legion. Sea lions and sharks savage them; occasionally barracuda do, too. Unknown numbers are being caught in fishing nets and most of those deaths are unrecorded – several conservationists believe this to be the largest reason for the population crash. On shore, poorly controlled dogs and introduced rats are known to kill adults and chicks alike. Do locals help? 'No one is against the conservation – they can see that the Hoiho need help so there's no active opposition, just some obstruction.'

I asked how this manifested and the ranger explained that some landowners choose not to let scientists on their land to study the penguins nearby. Protecting their stock and privacy are frequent excuses for this unhelpfulness. The land we were currently on was part of a farm but essentially managed by the Trust, one of five such sites around the region.* Ahead of the visit, I agreed not to name it specifically, so as not to tempt

---

* One hadn't had Yellow-Eyed penguins since the 1990s, but it was being planted with indigenous flora in the hopes of encouraging them to come back. In the meantime, dozens of Little penguins had moved into the prefab nests.

people to visit the Hoiho – unsupervised tourists tramping around would improve nothing.

The penguins don't help themselves much, either. Unlike the lookalike Gentoos, the Hoiho do not replace a lost egg. They don't, in Ben's parlance, 'triple clutch'. A lost egg or chick means no more attempts until the following season. When I asked what he would change about them, he quickly mentioned this low reproduction rate.

'I think people would be shocked if we finally got to the point of extinction,' he told me before we began to head back to the truck. 'Our media do tend to publish a lot of stuff though, so the public should know they're in dire straits. It would be a loss for sure. I like to think we'll find some kind of silver bullet that will fix everything and bring the numbers up real fast. I like to stay hopeful.'

Disappearance from the South Island wouldn't necessarily mean total species collapse, though. The small populations down on Auckland and Campbell Islands offer chances of survival, but they don't get anything like the amount of care or study of this northern detachment. It's an obvious concern that if an entire genus is reduced to just a few hundred birds on those outposts, the chance of true extinction would increase exponentially.

It was time to leave the cove. Despite the patient heroism of the YEPT, I saw little hope for the last of the Yellow-Eyed penguins on the South Island. Perhaps it was a natural failure, perhaps it was entirely man-made. There was a chance the disappearance of this species could allow another to thrive. That had happened before – the Hoiho themselves had capitalised on the extinction of a fellow penguin after all.

Requiem for a Penguin

I wanted to tell myself that it could happen again, but for now the tide continued to rise, the shallow grave had been erased, and all trace of the Yellow-Eyed penguin had vanished.

8

Out of Reach

> The penguins – ludicrous birds – in hundreds, drawn up in rank and file, stood to oppose us on our march, and it required not a little vigorous kicking to force our way through them.
>
> – Henry Armstrong, visiting Snares Islands aboard the *Amherst* in 1868

By the eighth week on the road, my energy began to desert me. At less than two months, the trip was hardly epic, but I was tired and could feel my 40th birthday approaching like a brick wall in the middle of a motorway.

In order to see the Yellow-Eyeds, and now possibly another two New Zealand penguins – the Fiordland and Snares – I had pulled every PR lever available, securing travel writing commissions to cover stories in different parts of the country. Careful planning and a lot of begging meant that I'd managed to extend my trip after the Ponant cruise while remaining more or less solvent. Even so, there was no shaking the fatigue of the road.

The cheese chariot and bottomless champagne of *Le Commandant Charcot* were distant memories. Instead, I ate as I do at home: prowling local supermarkets for items with discount labels, preferably things which didn't need cooking and hadn't quite turned green. Each bargain was a boon, but I didn't feel the usual ecstasy when buying semi-putrid sandwiches. I began to

Out of Reach

wonder if the demise of the Hoiho was still affecting me. Those birds were doomed, and now on the eve of another expedition cruise, I wondered what new miseries I would uncover on this next penguin voyage.

The plan was to join a short cruise on Heritage Expeditions' *Adventurer*, starting in the tourist-gorged city of Queenstown on the South Island. From there the ship's passengers would be bussed down to Invercargill and the port of Bluff, where we'd board for an eight-day trip. We'd visit Stewart and Ulva Islands, then the magnificent Fiordland National Park. Though it was out of season I might see the Fiordland penguins there, but either way we'd finish by heading south to the subantarctic islands known as the Snares. We'd only get a single morning around that tiny archipelago, but it has its own penguin species, a true endemic that I'd find nowhere else. So, with heavy arms I repacked, headed to the airport and got ready to return to sea.

Queenstown was over-touristed when I first visited in 2014, and nine years later everything was worse, except the scenery. It still looked majestic, idyllic in a way that hardly seemed plausible – pine trees dipped their roots in the waters of Lake Wakatipu and the entire place was fringed with snow-capped mountains, completing a flawless alpine aspect. This helped distract from the artificiality of the city itself. It felt like nothing existed downtown that wasn't a boutique, an overpriced outdoor shop or a tourist trap. There were a couple of pricey bars where there was no hope of meeting locals, and these were joined by savagely expensive restaurants.[*]

---

[*] And the notorious Fergburger, an indescribably overrated burger joint where you must queue for the best part of an hour for fine-I-suppose meat pucks.

An Inconvenience of Penguins

The following morning, I was on Heritage's bus, staring silently out of the window. Outside, the mountains formed a huge corona, but the vast basin it contained was mostly filled with uninteresting pastoral land. After three weeks in New Zealand the ruination of the countryside for agriculture had become loathsome. Ahead of me on the coach, 10 passenger heads gently bobbled with the rhythm of the road: eight grey, one bald and one unwisely dyed an overly insistent black.

There's such a thing as too much travelling, and as the bus rumbled on, I knew I'd reached that point again. It was familiar from my backpacking days, a feeling of weariness coupled with creeping disinterest. I was quite broke; I was very tired. I was also a bit lonely, but not enough to introduce myself to anyone. The sense of repetition was especially grinding when I had to talk. I'd introduced myself so many times in the preceding weeks that I was no longer sure what I'd said to whom. Conversations felt like echoes. I needed to break the cycle, probably by going home and sitting in silence. Hashtag wanderlust. Hashtag NeverStopExploring.

I hoped some penguins might snap me out of it. Until then I indulged a familiar fantasy: when I got on the ship, I'd keep myself to myself, stay out of the bar, replace the table wine with exercise, study, learn, absorb. It wouldn't happen, of course, but in the moment, I swore a blood oath to myself.*

The road south pressed on, passing through the flat town of Invercargill, finally reaching Bluff three hours after leaving Queenstown. It was as though the old gods had run out of mountains by the time they got down here and forgot to finish the job they'd done so wonderfully elsewhere. A flat expanse

---

* It's barely even going to last six paragraphs, don't worry.

Out of Reach

slid impotently into the ocean, and there, waiting for us in what might be the ugliest part of all New Zealand, was the *Heritage Adventurer*. It was to be my latest penguin vessel, but not so long ago this 32-year-old polar ship was behaving like a dangerous privateer's criminal sloop.

Almost exactly three years before I got on – and long before the Kiwi-owned Heritage Expeditions took charge – this Finnish-built, ice-strengthened ship was on the run. Back then, under the stewardship of the now defunct and widely despised One Ocean Expeditions, it was known as the *Resolute*. As the cruise company spiralled towards bankruptcy – avoiding paying its crew and expedition teams while still taking money from unsuspecting passengers – the ship was arrested twice in the Arctic before making a break south to attempt some kind of Antarctic season. When that fell apart, it was arrested again in Argentina and only released after four months. Following that final liberation, it sped back north, may or may not have strayed into protected Venezuelan waters, was pursued by their coastguard, then ended up ramming and sinking a patrol vessel.* Mercifully no one died, One Ocean's crooked owner was pursued in court, and eventually most people got most of the money they were owed.

But that was all then. Now, with a new paint job, a new name and a respectable company in charge, the *Adventurer* was ready for an easy cruise around the southern tip of New Zealand.

The same could not be said for me. As I sat through my fifth safety drill in two months, I realised I would be better

---

* Note to all coastguards: if you're going to obstruct a cruise ship, perhaps make sure its hull isn't reinforced for Antarctic ice.

retreating to my cabin rather than run the risk of screaming at a pensioner when they fumbled with their lifejacket buckles in front of me.

The battle to save the Yellow-Eyed penguin may have been on the brink of defeat, but New Zealand's wider conservation war continued apace. Even if victories are fleeting, all possums must be killed, every rodent annihilated, each mustelid destroyed. If they come back, do it all again. Four days after boarding, trapper and conservationist Darren Peters was in the ship's bar, making a case to me for the persecution of every land mammal introduced to his country.* If he had to choose just one to instantly obliterate, what would it be?

'Oh, brother,' the big, bald man said, before pausing for so long I could only read his silence as genuine contemplation. I sipped a gin and tonic as he rubbed his huge, leathery hands together. While I waited, I wondered how many animals had seen those big mitts right before the lights went out.

'I reckon if we left them long enough it'd be rats or mice,' he said eventually. 'Those nibbling bastards are the worst, but it's a difficult one. Maybe stoats, too, but they at least leave some things alive. It'd be one of those three bastards in any case.'

Peters was sailing with Heritage as part of an impressive line-up of conservationists on board to explain and interpret New Zealand's unique ecosystem for guests. Their programme of talks and lectures was amazingly detailed, so thorough that I wished more passengers had been on to experience them.

---

* Which is to say everything aside from three endemic bats – one of which is already extinct – and, I assume, human beings.

Out of Reach

Having travelled around the world helping efforts to control introduced predators, the trapper told me stories of sniping deer from helicopters, the mass murder of rodents, and – I was only so sure he didn't mean this literally – the 'nuking' of rabbits. He swore and laughed loudly and often, and not being offended by profanity or the demise of vermin, I found he almost single-handedly turned my mood around.*

'Look, all of us started loving animals – I don't want to kill the fucking things,' he said after a few drinks. 'But I will, because if we can't correct the bullshit we've done to our planet – no matter what level you're operating at – well, my philosophy is that *we'll* be fucked.'

At the start of the voyage we'd heard of the conservation challenges on Stewart Island, many of which relate to the 300 or so permanent residents of the pretty little town of Oban, the only settlement.† Even in seemingly wild places like this, protecting local fauna is tremendously complicated, in part because many of the residents have pet cats and dogs, some of which go feral, and some of which attack native animals and still come home for dinner.

On Stewart we saw people living right up against the wilderness, but after the ship sailed north, our guides told us with no small amount of theatre that we had arrived in the Fiordland National Park, a 'place where nature has won'.

The park dominates the south-west of the South Island, spreading across 12,600km² of largely uninhabitable land that

---

* The G&Ts were another possible factor.

† Stewart Island is also a home of the Hoiho, though their numbers are impossibly low, and we went nowhere near their residences.

has been protected by various government bodies since 1904. Over a couple of days sailing up and down the semi-mythic waters of the Doubtful and Dusky Sounds, we were told stories of Māori legends and European misadventure. Much of the geography was named in English by Captain James Cook during his three visits to the region in the 1770s. For all his talent as a navigator, the Englishman didn't have much skill when it came to christenings – while the Māori have names such as Rakiura ('Land of Glowing Skies'), Cook thought it fit to name an archipelago the Many Islands.

His diaries offered more insight: 'No country upon Earth can appear with a more rugged and barren aspect than this doth,' wrote the explorer in 1770. 'From the sea for as far inland as the eye can reach nothing is to be seen but the summits of these rocky mountains, which seem to lay so near one another as not to admit any valleys between them.'

Two hundred and fifty years later, fjord walls still rose sheer from the water, veined with innumerable waterfalls. Wildlife was everywhere – resident pods of bottlenose dolphins accompanied the ship in the Doubtful Sound, their blows disintegrating as spectra in the afternoon sun.

Yet dolphins weren't what I wanted to see. The park is also home to a penguin, the forest-dwelling Fiordland. Nine years earlier I'd seen one or two swimming in these waters, but that was at a different time of year, before they had gone to sea. This time, during a Zodiac cruise, we heard the unappealing call of one nearby but it disappeared before anyone could so much as take a photograph. I wish I had more to tell you about that encounter, but it was so brief as to seem imagined. Instead, over 18 months later, I would have to make an entirely separate

Out of Reach

penguin voyage, all the way back across the world to try and see this elusive crested bird properly.*

While people – European and Māori – failed to settle the Fiordland region, the pests they left behind proliferated. Mammals from deer to mice still lurk in the forests. At each of the landing sites in the national park we saw traps for possums and stoats, though many of us wished it was the plague of sandflies, known locally as *namu*, that were being targeted instead.

Polynesian settlers brought the first dogs and rats to New Zealand, but British colonisers made everything exponentially more dire, purposely introducing pests for all kinds of idiotic reasons. Having almost exterminated fur seals from outlying islands, it's possible to see a logic in their introducing possums and rabbits to generate a replacement fur trade. But they ran out of control, so they introduced mustelids (stoats, primarily) to chase them down. Naturally, these greedy killers did murder quite a few bunnies, but the hitherto untroubled birdlife had never met an enemy like this. They used to look to the air for threats, but now Death was running up branches towards them; stoats continue to slaughter unsuspecting birds today. This nascent attempt at conservation calls to mind the 'old lady who swallowed a fly', with British commanders sending increasingly alien animals to eliminate their mistakes, not realising they were only exacerbating the situation.

I can just about forgive that dipshittery, but their reasons for introducing British birds into the world's ultimate avian kingdom are unforgivable. One night on the ship I chanced upon a book containing a collection of articles from the *Otago Witness*

---

* Which was, of course, deeply annoying. I still hold this elusiveness against the Fiordland penguin today.

published between 1860 and 1910. They were mostly colourful fluff with titles like 'A Few Practical Notes For Holiday-Seekers' and 'Two Interesting Letters From Mr So-And-So', but others offered an insight into why protected parks and conservation are now so important in New Zealand.

One detailed the voyage of the *Warrior Queen*, which sailed from London on 28 November 1870, bringing with it an Ark-like collection of British birds, 'all of them in capital health and condition'. The avian cargo included 150 partridges, 150 hedge sparrows, 96 blackbirds, 70 chaffinches, 61 goldfinches, 60 skylarks, 50 twites, 50 redpolls, 50 yellowhammers, a dozen thrushes, 10 quails, 10 woodlarks, 'eight brace' of grouse, 'four reed sparrows and the same number of scarlet buntings', three bramble finches, 'several fancy ducks' and a single, condemned nightingale, which if it survived the voyage would have died as the loneliest bird in the world.

Twenty-two people were denied passage to the New World in order to accommodate these foreign birds. Why? 'It is to be hoped [we] will be rewarded by often listening to their songs in the beautiful island home to which we wish them a quick and pleasant passage.'

All of this idiocy has meant that modern New Zealanders have developed a particular set of skills when it comes to extermination. From the Galapagos to South Georgia to here in the motherland, they have pioneered initiatives designed to eliminate introduced species, always with the goal of allowing endemic fauna to thrive. On the Galapagos, they developed the brilliantly devious Judas Goat programme, through which a feral goat was captured and secured with a GPS collar. The naturally social animal would then be released and eventually seek out its kin, unwittingly betraying their location, at which

Out of Reach

point the New Zealanders would jump in helicopters and shoot them from the air. Meanwhile, on South Georgia, it was Kiwis who perfected the calculations that led to the eradication of rats and the salvation of millions of seabirds. They had lost so much to pests, and now their killer knowledge was being dispensed, alongside bullets and poison, globally.

'Most of New Zealand was cleared with an axe or a match,' said Lou Sanson on one of our landings in Dusky Sound. 'But not here.' Sanson spent decades in environmental work, most recently as director-general of New Zealand's Department of Conservation, or as everyone constantly referred to it, DOC.* Like Darren Peters, he had been brought on board by Heritage as a guest lecturer.

Sanson's tone oscillated between pride (he had overseen record increases in government spending on conservation) and concern (climate change was forcing many animals to adapt faster than was possible), but he was open about how things lay. For all his nation's successes with eradication abroad, many domestic projects failed. The mammals are many, the landscape sometimes impossible, and the logistics close to unimaginable. 'It's pretty shattering when it doesn't work,' said Sanson. Peters called every reinfestation 'a real kick in the guts'.

A 20-hour sail south gave the lecturers plenty of time to talk more about what we would see at our final destination, the Snares Islands, a place untouched by humans. On Stewart we'd seen people living with nature; in the Fiordland National Park we'd seen what happens when humans left an area to thrive.

---

* The great pity was that he'd retired from that role, meaning I couldn't legitimately ask: 'What's up, DOC?'

An Inconvenience of Penguins

The Snares was a truly wild place, so distant no pest could reach it, so inhospitable no person could live there. A pristine place.*

Actually, it's not quite right to say that no one has ever lived on the Snares. Discovered and named in 1791, these subantarctic islands were never seriously considered for settlement, but there is an incredible story from the early 1800s of four men being marooned there, having been kicked off their sealing ship in order to save rations. 'The Captain submitted to their choice whether they would go on shore, or starve afloat, stating it to be impossible for the provisions to hold out for the whole of the crew,' reads the report of another captain who rescued three survivors, a no doubt gruelling seven years later.

The stranded men lived on seabirds, seals and a few potatoes which they planted and, against astronomical odds, propagated on the main island.† No detailed record of their time on the Snares exists and much of their lives is unknown, but as I saw the archipelago emerge through a chilling fog, the impossibility of their fate was laid bare.

From a distance the islands looked like a jaw full of broken teeth, topped with stubborn trees. A biting wind, its enamel hardened down in Antarctica, charged around the sea cliffs. Having spent several days of the late Kiwi summer wearing shorts and soaking up the sun, this return to the cold caught me unprepared.

As we drew closer, I realised that thoughts of home had long disappeared. A new penguin was just a couple of nautical

---

* Though in an apparent bid to help castaways and shipwreck survivors, some animals were released, including, in 1890, several pairs of possums, kiwis and goats. Thankfully none survived long.

† We were told a possibly apocryphal story that researchers with permission to go ashore continue to find potatoes thriving today.

Out of Reach

miles away, and with shivering hands, I tried to note down what we were seeing. This included great masses of flying birds – Buller's albatrosses, cape petrels and red-billed gulls, all of which were dwarfed in number by massive fleets of the estimated 2 million sooty shearwaters living on this lonely outpost. The expedition team told us that almost half of the visits here are too tumultuous to get people off the ship, but the swell for us was insignificant – we'd at least be able to cruise the cliffs in front of us.

Right enough, the lee of the island provided enough stability for the crew to launch Zodiacs and I waved with new enthusiasm when I saw the drivers waiting patiently on their tillers. I almost floated to my cabin to get ready for this final excursion, but then a nauseating thing happened – the doors on the *Adventurer* developed a hydraulics issue and would not open. In the year or so I spent on ships researching this book, I'm not sure I ever felt more seasick than in that moment. I leaned over the gunwales and wondered very seriously what the consequences would be of jumping over the side and swimming to shore.

Half an hour later, the heroic, largely Filipino crew had fixed the problem, and we were skipping out into the boats. As we headed out through a cloud of sooty shearwaters, it quickly became clear that the protection afforded by the island was only a temporary reprieve. Turning around a headland towards the major Snares penguin colony, the swell changed from long, smooth rollers to chaotic, inconsistent waves which sloshed into our dinghy as though trying to escape the ocean.

I looked around at my shipmates for signs of weakness, offering a spare hat and gloves to anyone feeling the cold, but more generally trying to project an impression that everything

An Inconvenience of Penguins

was *fine* and that warm showers would be waiting for us just as soon as we'd seen the penguins.

Writing down thoughts soon became impossible, seawater making the ink bleed upsettingly across the page. Remembering that notes on the Emperors and the Hoiho were in the same book, I soon put it away altogether. The saltwater also made me nervous about my camera gear, and it wasn't until we'd entered a sheltered channel on the other side of the island that I felt I could start shooting again.

We were drenched, chilled, electrified – and the Snares penguins were waiting for us in abundance.

Today there are six species of penguin found in New Zealand territory, four of which are endemic.* Of those, the Snares are, in some ways, the least remarkable. A crested penguin, it is so similar to other species that accurate identification requires big lenses and a bird nerd on hand to be certain of what you're seeing.

Appearing almost identical to the Fiordland penguins, the Snares' only real physical point of difference is a subtle light-coloured highlight at the back of their beak, near its hinge. Otherwise, they have yellow crests and red, hungover eyes like the rest of their family. They likewise seem to prefer entering and exiting the ocean at its most hectic access points.

They are only their own species by the narrowest of margins. One of their clearest tells, however, is their location – they nest exclusively here, and though once in a while a vagrant will drift north, the entire 30,000-strong population is otherwise found at this point 48 degrees south. Why they have not

---

* Erect-Crested, Fiordland, Snares, Yellow-Eyed.

GALAPAGOS

GENTOO

CHINSTRAP

HUMBOLDT

ADÉLIE

EMPEROR

YELLOW-EYED/HOIHO

SNARES

AFRICAN

SOUTHERN ROCKHOPPER

MACARONI

MAGELLANIC

KING

NORTHERN ROCKHOPPER

LITTLE

FIORDLAND/TAWAKI

ROYAL

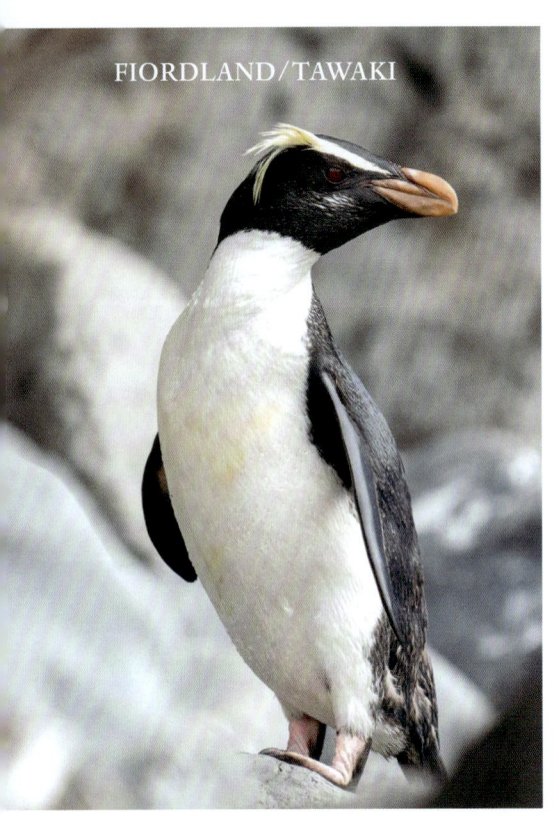

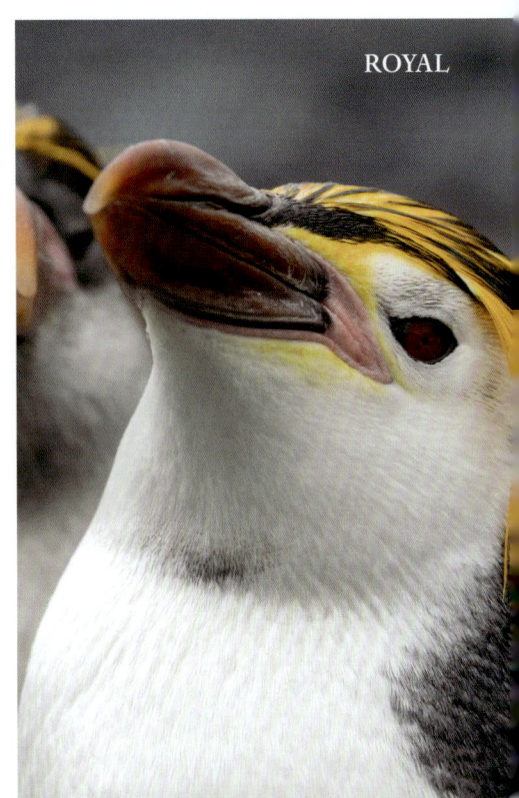

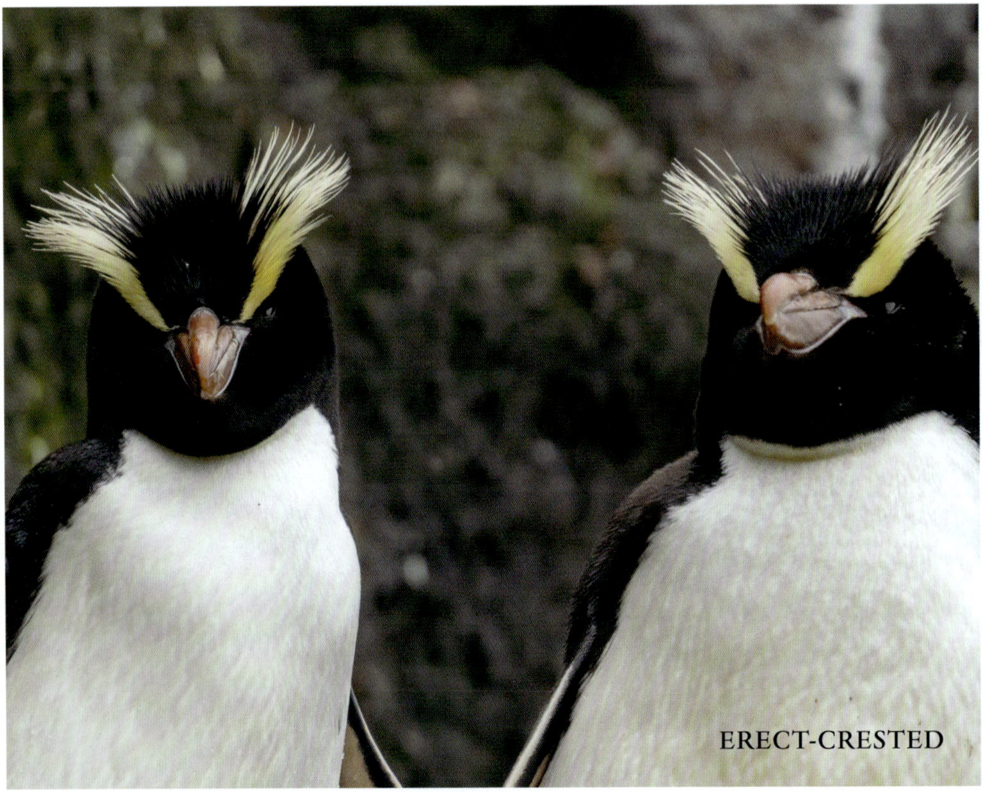
ERECT-CRESTED

Out of Reach

expanded their territory to any of the other subantarctic islands is unknown.

Being able to remain rodent-free makes the Snares a rarity among New Zealand's subantarctic islands – perhaps that alone has made them feel comfortable enough never to migrate. The lack of pests is also the reason the skies and shores are full of life. So determined is DOC to keep it this way that no landings are possible, save for a few licensed researchers for limited periods of the year.* All my observation, then, would be from the Zodiac, but thankfully the penguins' abundance meant this still counted as good access.

Birders in the boat kept eyes peeled for other endemics – including the Snares tomtit, which looks like a black snowball with legs – but my focus was exclusively on the penguins. Our Zodiac driver, an excitable Canadian, told us that some Snares penguins had been observed roosting in the subantarctic tree daisies which covered the island, some making it as high as 3m. This struck me as incredibly profound, some ancient muscle memory from deep within their genes telling the birds: reach higher, your relatives love it up here.

When we got into more placid channels, I looked for this behaviour but couldn't see it from the water. Instead, I watched hundreds of penguins stomping around on land, busy with some important business or other but never too rushed to miss the chance for a fight with a passer-by. Like other crested penguins, the Snares have a habit of walking around with their flippers held in front of them, as though carrying an invisible box. This added to their impression of mysterious industriousness.

---

* Also a huge amount of the ground is honeycombed with shearwater burrows, making it difficult to navigate.

An Inconvenience of Penguins

They may have been massively outnumbered by flying birds, but the penguin population seemed very healthy here. Seeing them in boisterous groups and photographing their little periscope heads as they popped out of the water was a relief after the bleak experience with the Hoiho. Here was a Snares penguin stumbling down a hill; there was another belly-flopping out of the water and on to bare rock; yet another was shitting on its neighbour.* All was right in this penguin world, and all was funny.

My camera was full and the people around me were very ready to return to the warm, dry ship by the time we turned away. I had no idea how long Heritage had had us out in the Zodiac, only that I was grateful they had pushed it as much as they did. Darren Peters happened to be in the same boat and had noted the time. Ever the trapper, he said, 'That was the bait that got me here – just those three fucking hours.'

That night we sailed all the way back to Bluff, where the following morning we were quickly transferred on to buses for the drive back to overdeveloped Queenstown. Passengers spent their time dozing and sorting photos. I used it to talk to Lou Sanson again, all the while trying to ignore how uncannily he looked like the feverish British comic Harry Hill. We talked about DOC's controversial use of poison, about the environment and the future. We also discussed the Yellow-Eyed penguins, and he said that while he admired the work of all conservation groups, 'You can't hand-rear an entire species. That just doesn't work.'

Still, the trapping, the replanting, the reintroductions – they were working, often imperfectly but offering measurable progress. Knowing how pathetically far behind we were in the

---

* Literally, of course.

Out of Reach

UK – how comparatively disinterested we are in virtually any type of conservation – I couldn't help but admire all the Kiwi effort, all that money being spent to right man-made wrongs.

There were reasons to be optimistic about the future of New Zealand, but as we nudged north, I spotted a fable playing out in real time. A stoat and a rabbit danced around each other in a fallow field, a public duel in a dusty arena: two foreign animals fighting a battle where there could be no winner.

9

Extinction Events

> But that hardly mattered because we had the pleasures and distractions of such a panoramic tableau: we watched ships trawling, stately oil tankers moving slowly across the horizon; we saw gulls spearing fish from the sea and seals cavorting on the waves; we laughed at the colony of penguins, which resembled a brigade of clumsy, flat-footed soldiers.
>
> – Nelson Mandela, *Long Walk to Freedom*, 1994

When the shouting started, part of me prepared for conflict. From the top of a gentle hill came an ungentle accent – a woman with a strong Afrikaner inflection was roaring at me as I approached my car. I was staying at an Airbnb in Simon's Town, half an hour or so south of Cape Town, and assumed I'd parked in the wrong place. I'd apologise then ramp things up only if necessary. It sounded like the South African was way ahead of me.

That accent is pre-tuned for belligerence – during two dull years working in an office in Dubai, I spent long, frightened hours listening to an all-Afrikaner sales team essentially intimidate clients into buying ads. It was a remarkably successful tactic and hearing that same mean-sounding brogue again gave me the chills, right up until we were face to face and I realised

Extinction Events

this lady was being a good citizen. Her chief concern was the welfare of penguins.

'You must always check under your car here, hey,' she said. 'The penguins get everywhere, and I saw one near here. Get down and check – that's the way when you're in Simon's Town.'

I humoured her and got on my hands and knees like I was looking for an old football, and sure enough, between the front tyres there was an African penguin, caught halfway between bewilderment and embarrassment. It felt like I'd uncovered a prankster mid-deed. I stood up and thanked the woman, then reassured her I'd check from now on. Over the next three days, I found penguins half the time I approached the car.

For Europeans, the African penguin is likely the most quickly accessible wild penguin in the world.[*] The withered remnants of the Namibian population may be a little nearer, and it'd be a close thing with the Northern Rockhoppers on Tristan da Cunha, but as I was to find out, reaching them is much more complicated. For speed of travel, nothing requires less effort than the colonies in South Africa.

This is especially true over the austral winter, when the majority of penguin species are at sea or in regions inaccessible to ordinary ships. Most birds use this time to forage far and wide before slowly returning to shore in spring to lay eggs and breed again. With far more favourable conditions, the African penguin is more relaxed, instead raising its chicks through winter. This made it one of the few species I could visit in September, when most destinations further south were essentially closed

---

[*] It's sometimes referred to as the Cape penguin, and it was also formerly called the Jackass or Black-Footed.

An Inconvenience of Penguins

by inclement weather. Six restful months had passed since New Zealand, and I was no longer jaded – almost halfway through the list, it was again time to head south.

After a flight to Cape Town International and a 45-minute drive to Simon's Town, the most famous colony awaited at Boulders Beach. The ease of access has long made this small population among the most visited penguins in the world and, despite the species' numbers crashing, shows like Netflix's cloyingly cutesy *Penguin Town* have driven more and more traffic to them. It's now thought that over a million people visit every year. Dozens of street stalls, shops and penguin-branded cafés have sprung up to meet the thunderous footfall. With just over a week to spend on assignment for the *Financial Times* in South Africa, I'd see the penguins in several locations, wild and in captivity, dead and in recovery, but the rampagingly popular Simon's Town was the most hectic.

The penguins here were the first I ever saw, back in 2009, crossed off a list I didn't know I was going to keep. I'd last seen them on a trip in 2017, when access to the beach was still unfettered and tourists were very likely to interfere with the birds. On that occasion a girl of about six chased a penguin around the beach while her potbellied father watched on, recording the harassment on his phone. I very nearly *said something*, but he too was armed with the Afrikaner accent, so I just looked on sternly and tutted like a disapproving octogenarian.

It was gladdening, then, to see that in the intervening years Simon's Town had installed boardwalks and fences to keep visitors away from the birds – or at least far enough that physical contact was impossible. This protects the penguins and allows the Southern African Foundation for the Conservation of Coastal Birds (SANCCOB*) to collect passive income from tourists.

These are not the prettiest of penguins. Like all four of the banded penguin species, African penguins are predominantly black and white, the only exception being a salmon-pink arc that stretches out from their eye like an inverted comma. They are most similar in appearance to the Magellanics of South America, though with just one black band, rather than two, across its chest. Like all of the *Spheniscus* genus, it sounds like a donkey when it brays and its beak is lined and layered, like blackened tree bark. It predominantly nests underground and, unless part of this colony at Boulders Beach, is likely to be quite skittish when out in the open.

There are somewhere between 2,000 and 3,000 penguins at this site, but they only arrived here in 1982, after a short migration from Dyer Island. Just two penguins were spotted initially, then dozens, then hundreds, now thousands. If human visitors have a negative impact on these birds, it was hard to see how it was manifesting here.

Inside the crowd I was quickly relieved that man and beast had been separated. Sometimes in Antarctica and subantarctic territories visitors experience cosmic revelations about the planet, wildlife and occasionally themselves. South Africa, by contrast, offered a mass tourism experience. With so many visitors every year, the penguins were undoubtedly habituated to the noise and stupidity of humankind – they seemed wholly unbothered by the firing squad of lenses pointing at them as they emerged from fynbos vegetation, charged down sandy

---

* The imprecision of this acronym really grates, but I suppose it'd be difficult to say SAFCCB aloud.

slopes and continued under the boardwalk and out to sea. Some people walked into each other while reviewing seconds-old footage of this transit on their smartphones, while some penguins walked into each other because they were penguins.

It was a warm and windy Sunday in 2023, the crowd was international, and the penguins' appeal universal. Everyone quickly became children together: some laughed, some cried and some had tantrums when they couldn't see as well as their playmates. Daft things were said in all kinds of languages. Most contemptible were guides making up stories about orca attacks and the threat of leopard seals in these waters, both a virtual impossibility. My own guiding work wasn't due to restart for three months, but my lip trembled with a desire to correct the inaccuracies.

Other tourists couldn't help themselves with selfies or roaring things like, 'Let's go, buddy!' at the bemused birds. Another standout was a Canadian lady who menaced one penguin with, 'I'll take you to Ottawa,' before adding in a baby voice, 'We have so much snow there.'

The African penguin is a warm-weather creature, and this one was unlikely to have ever known freezing temperatures in its short life. It was a mercy that it didn't understand this threat of death by exposure, but with the volume of people coming here every day, the bird was likely to have heard worse. Few animals have such ability to disrupt higher brain functions and infantilise their observers as the penguin.

Despite the weight of the tourists, it was hard to be too damning of the boardwalks. They provided broadly the same service as a zoo without any need for imprisonment, and like other penguin colonies I'd seen in Antarctica and South

Extinction Events

America, the ability to coexist with people was to these penguins' benefit. Humans had either persecuted or scared off predators; humans had also provided artificial burrows in the bushes to encourage the birds not to stray too far into town – and under cars.

Of course, we hadn't made it all better for them. There were still occasional stories of lithe caracals taking birds, especially chicks. Further round the coast, much more muscular leopards had raided the colony at Betty's Bay. Over the years, the local press also carried stories about pets attacking penguins, including one nauseating incident in 2022 in which two huskies slaughtered 19 birds before they were brought under control.

Perhaps it's the Arctic and Antarctic regions colliding, but something about penguins stirs up irrepressible avicide in huskies. Robert Falcon Scott knew about it a century ago, though the violence seemed not to trouble him much:

> The great problem with [the huskies] has been due to the fatuous conduct of the penguins . . . They waddle forward, poking their heads to and fro in their usually absurd way, in spite of a string of howling dogs straining to get them. 'Hulloa!' they seem to say, 'here's a game – what do all you ridiculous things want?' And they come a few steps nearer. The dogs make a rush as far as their leashes or harness allow. The penguins are not daunted in the least, but their ruffs go up and they squawk with semblance of anger, for all the world as though they were rebuking a rude stranger – their attitude might be imagined to convey, 'Oh, that's the sort of animal you are; well, you've come to the wrong place – we aren't going to be bluffed and bounced by you,' and then the final fatal steps forward are taken and they

come within reach. There is a spring, a squawk, a horrid red patch on the snow, and the incident is closed. Nothing can stop these silly birds. Members of our party rush to head them off, only to be met with evasions – the penguins squawk and duck as much as to say, 'What's it to do with you, you silly ass? Let us alone.'

Once in a while, though, weird things happen, things that are much harder to explain than a diluted wolf savaging a flightless bird. In 2021 on Boulders Beach, locals awoke to the upsetting scene of 63 seemingly healthy adult penguins dead. They called SANCCOB, who came and collected the cadavers.

An hour's drive north at the main SANCCOB facility, I spoke to David Roberts, the vet who was handed the case as though it were a murder investigation. 'Normally when there are a lot of dead penguins in one place it's because of disease outbreak or predation, but there were no signs of wounds, and if it was disease, they shouldn't all die in one spot,' said the vet. Fresh-faced and long-haired, he exuded such bespectacled kindness I briefly worried that I'd have bullied him at school.

'Over 60 boxes came in, so we started doing post-mortems. By the end of the day, we found they had lots of internal bleeding and inflammation in their kidneys. The day before we'd received a penguin from the same area that had a lot of blood in its urine. We kept it in ICU but it died overnight. The whole thing left us scratching our heads. We wondered about toxins, perhaps water polluted with heavy metals. Someone found an onion lying in the sand and we even wondered: could penguins be hyperallergic to onions?'

Eventually, the team went back to Boulders Beach and after a prolonged search found the culprits: dozens of dead bees, all of which had been furious enough to commit suicide in their attack on the penguins. No one knew what had set them off, only that nothing like this had ever been recorded before.

The vet and I were speaking just outside an enclosure in which a couple of dozen penguins were milling around, preening and pratfalling. Some had bright bandages on their flippers, while others were fledging or in the middle of their catastrophic moults. Overall, they appeared as most penguins do, which is to say incompetent, disbelieving in personal hygiene, and in need of a babysitter. Roberts said that while they were surprisingly vulnerable to the bee stings, they had shown remarkable resilience towards the highly pathogenic strain of avian flu that had been rampaging around the world for the last couple of years. Local terns and cormorants hadn't been so lucky, but for reasons unknown, penguins – here and globally – appeared to be resistant.

The bee incident was an anomaly, a freak occurrence that may never happen again on that scale, but other systemic problems were far more threatening to the birds. The African penguin, this coastal icon, was disappearing while simultaneously delighting people into buying thousands of t-shirts in Simon's Town. In front of so many witnesses, this most charismatic megafauna was facing functional extinction within the next five to ten years.

A little over a century ago there were thought to be as many as 2 million of the birds, while today's freefalling population is estimated to be around just 30,000. As I'd heard in New Zealand with the Hoiho, Roberts told me that birds were heading out to sea to forage and simply not coming back. Chicks were then starving. SANCCOB's hospital hadn't had this many

An Inconvenience of Penguins

underweight penguins since the catastrophic MV *Treasure* oil spill of 2000.*

All this wretched damage and loss wasn't happening to a population out on some uninhabited island at the edge of the map – it was happening to the world's most accessible penguins.

I asked Roberts what he thought of the species' prospects.

'I think they're poor. Without drastic action the number will continue to decline,' he replied as volunteer nurses brought a newly admitted penguin past us and into the clinic. 'Drastic action is needed with fish stocks and the environment they're in, and that requires members of the general public to put pressure on politicians. Without that, all the stuff we do here isn't going to be a long-term solution.'

The volunteers held the African penguin like it was a rugby ball. Some wore foam guards on their arms to protect against its vicious wing slaps, while others wore goggles or arced their heads out of pecking range. What was thought to be a bite from a fur seal still seeped fresh blood. As the examiners pulled the bird's foot down to see the wound, a fresh red pulse surged up – even from my mammalian perspective it looked painful. The penguin fought and fought, with no idea that these people, at least, were trying to help it.

Days passed along the coastline of the Western Cape, sunshine and wind as insistent as each other. I'd facilitated the trip by writing an article about the so-called Marine Big Five, a marketing term for a fairly arbitrary list of creatures – including African penguins – easily found along this vast coast. The

---

* This on the back of other major spills which directly affected penguins in 1971 and 1994.

original safari Big Five was compiled to note how dangerous the buffalo, elephant, leopard, lion and rhino were to hunters. Unless you identify as a sardine, it's hard to look at the African penguin in a similar light. The same goes for the dolphins and southern right whales, which also find themselves on the list. There is more obvious menace posed by cape fur seals, and certainly by great white sharks, but the Marine Big Five seemed to have been chosen more or less at random.

Still, the research to see them was no hardship. There are few cities with a more beautiful setting than Cape Town, one of those places where if you removed every hint of human settlement, you'd be left with a landscape so gorgeous it'd still get visitors. Rio de Janeiro has similar beauty, as do Hong Kong and Edinburgh.*

Table Mountain casts its considerable shadow across parts of the city, sitting fat and plump in its own peninsula like an almighty yolk. Towns and villages – including Simon's Town – must make do along the border, though no one begrudges this sentinel overlooking the city.

There are other populations of African penguins within a couple of hours of the colossal landmark. Betty's Bay, to the east, is home to the largest population, while due north Robben Island still has a few hangers-on, too. That particular colony has undergone rapid decline in the last few decades and won't be anywhere near as impressive as it was when Nelson Mandela occasionally admired it, when Apartheid-era prison guards let him outside during his long imprisonment on the island.

Instead of pursuing those birds, I drove east to Gansbaai, a fishing town on the eastern bracket of Walker Bay. In 2017, I'd

---

* Though as a Glaswegian it pains me to say so.

An Inconvenience of Penguins

made the same journey with a friend, a teacher who'd used a chunk of his summer holiday to come on my work trip. We'd spent most of our time driving a motorhome around South Africa, Lesotho and Swaziland before flying to Cape Town for a few days of hiking and eating.* As part of that leg, we decided to head to Gansbaai, the self-styled shark cage diving capital of the world. The villains we'd booked with let us make the three-hour drive before telling us that they had a problem: there were no great white sharks left.

Marine biologist Alison Towner couldn't help but smile when I told her this story over lunch, in a restaurant just outside of Gansbaai: 'I had the same thing, these new theories, all this new tech ready to try out, and then the orcas turned up.'

The story of quite what happened to the sharks is strange, so strange that even though I'd already read about it, hearing it from someone who'd made it the subject of their PhD was still shocking. In 2015, dead bodies of large sevengill and great white sharks started washing up on shore. Their livers had been so exactly removed it looked like the work of a surgeon, artist or deviant.

At the start of *Jaws 2* there's a scene very much like this: a 7.5m-long orca has washed up, its face half bitten off, its spilled entrails being attended by a squabble of gulls. Chief Brody arrives and posits that a massive great white has taken megalodon-sized chunks out of the cetacean. The killer has been killed, or as Brody helpfully puts it, 'Well, it's obvious that a big fish took a bite out of this big fish.'

When the reverse started in real life and part-eaten sharks

---

* The *Guardian* held my feature about that road trip for so long that by the time it ran, Swaziland had been renamed to Eswatini.

Extinction Events

began washing up, Towner told me the mystery was solved a little more quickly. 'The question was on everyone's mind: could it be these two orcas that have just arrived? No one knows them or knows where they came from. They're both males. They're highly distinctive with flopped-over dorsal fins, which are really not common with wild orcas.'

These noticeably flaccid fins are only present in 4 per cent of non-captive killer whales, and it's thought to indicate illness or an immune system issue. Because their dorsals leaned to opposing sides, the orcas were christened Port and Starboard.* The pair was soon witnessed eviscerating sharks, removing their livers with precision that couldn't have been matched by a human at sea.

There are several problems with the orcas behaving this way. It devastated the multimillion-rand business of shark cage diving around Gansbaai for one thing. For another, it scared large sharks off down the coast, to beaches they rarely used to visit. Surfers and swimmers were now being maimed and killed in places they once thought safe.† Between the loss of business and the increased risk to human life, there had been dark talk of culling these two – and it was just two – hooligans, though Towner doubted that would ultimately happen.

'It's also caused problems for your friends, the penguins,' she added. 'African penguins are now really endangered and can't tolerate any more pressure on their numbers. If you remove white sharks from the Dyer Island system, immediately cape fur seal behaviour shifts. Their stress hormones have all

---

* Which is fine and everything, but given their kink for eating liver, I'd have gone with Hannibal and Lecter.

† Towner preferred the term 'fatal bite incidents'.

dropped. One day we heard of them killing seven penguins in a row, not to eat them but to steal their stomach contents – just because they can.'

The sharks used to patrol Dyer Island in such numbers that one channel off its southern tip was christened Shark Alley. Penguins live on Dyer, too, but they're being steadily pushed out by the soaring numbers of cape fur seals, the preferred prey of the great whites.

Since the arrival of Port and Starboard, people had adapted, too. To bring back some kind of shark diving experience, the industry had pivoted to dropping people in with bronze whaler sharks,* but while the fish can grow to 3m and school unlike the individualist great whites, they sounded like inferior substitutes. What is bronze if not the medal of compensation?

Still, later that day, I gave it a go, sailing out from Gansbaai to jump in and watch these killer fish emerge from cataract water, baited all the way to the bars of the cage. The lack of visibility came in part from heavy chumming, which had the simultaneous effect of attracting sharks, sending gulls into a frenzy and making one woman in my group vomit when she accidentally swallowed some of the rancid sea.

On a second outing that day, we spun around the island on a whale-watching boat, colossal southern right whales never out of sight.† The abundance of pinnipeds was much harder to ignore. Fur seal recovery around here has shot far beyond mere stabilisation, bouncing back with such force that they now put pressure on other species. From the boat, I watched the noisy mammals crowd beaches and hang from shipwrecks like rag-

---

*   Also known as copper sharks.

†   Colossal and honestly quite boring.

gedy protestors, their case already won, barking now in what might have been triumph.

Not far from this pungent colony, the boat captain surprised passengers by bringing out two large cardboard boxes. Inside were four penguins which had been rehabilitated by SANCCOB and were now deemed well enough to get back out into the pitiless ocean. The boxes were turned upside down, and the penguins unceremoniously dumped in the water, little flakes of dried guano spinning out behind them.

The greatest African penguin colony ever known to exist was on Dassen Island. Around 55km from Cape Town, it is today reached by a long and featureless drive north from the city, followed by a 45-minute boat ride from the port town of Yzerfontein. After some gentle negotiation with conservationists working on the island, I was allowed to head out to visit this legendary colony.

In 1930, the naturalist and photographer Cherry Kearton published *The Island of Penguins*, an account of spending 'many months' living on Dassen with 'five million penguins'. That number was impossibly high, but the birds undoubtedly swarmed the island at the time:

> Penguins are found in many parts of the southern seas. But nowhere are they to be seen in such profusion as on this island – the principal breeding ground of the Blackfooted Penguins who, because of the unpleasant noise of braying which they make, are known as Jackass Penguins. Here they are so numerous that in places one can barely walk between their nesting-burrows, and it is no uncommon thing for two pairs of nesting penguins to find themselves

so crowded for space that their burrows run into each other. In the four-square miles of the island there are six principal colonies – and each of them contains, at a rough estimate, three-quarters of a million penguins.

Along with brother Richard, Cherry Kearton was one of the earliest naturalists to work with film. Queen Victoria was still on the throne when the brothers began photographing the natural world, starting with bird nests in their native England and progressing to shooting safari animals from hollowed-out model buffalos in Africa.

As a child, David Attenborough saw Cherry Kearton's film from Dassen Island, *Dassen: An Adventure in Search of Laughter, Featuring Nature's Greatest Little Comedians*. Decades later, Attenborough explained he was 'at the age of eight taken to see a film lecture presented by Cherry Kearton. [It] captured my childish imagination and made me dream of travelling to far-off places to film wild animals.'

Kearton's book from that expedition is often verbose and funny, and his conduct around the penguins predictably unrefined. He purposely blocks penguin highways; he bodily moves birds from one place to another. His naturalist leanings rarely stretch beyond colourful observation, while scientifically unhelpful anthropomorphism is present in almost every sentence. And yet, reading *The Island of Penguins*, I found it impossible not to feel joy – both my own and Kearton's.

> I trust I have done him no injustice, for though like everyone else I laugh at him, I also like him . . . I hope this book is worthy of the penguins, I must also hope that if perchance my visit to the island has added a chapter to the unwritten nature lore of the island's inhabitants, they

Extinction Events

– though doubtless they laughed at me – found as much that was likeable in me as I found in them.

There were never 5 million penguins on Dassen, or anywhere, and unbeknown to Kearton their numbers were already in sharp decline when he visited. Still, he would have experienced vitality alien to any visitor today.

When I parked at the dock at Yzerfontein, a boat called *Pikkewyn* was being unloaded from a trailer.* Two young seamen greeted me curtly, mentioning that I must be 'one of those guys who actually turns up when he says he's going to'. I asked what that meant, but they didn't answer.

Before long any need for awkward conversation was lost to the bouncing waves and roaring engine. Some common dolphins tried to keep pace with us, but the ocean was reasonable, and the boat skipped like a stone.

From a distance, Dassen's profile was unremarkable: low-slung and beige, its only notable feature seemed to be an antique lighthouse. Today the island is officially closed to outsiders, with just a handful of researchers coming and going, keeping eyes on numbers of penguins, pelicans, terns and several other seabird species, as well as an improbably dense population of angulate tortoises. When he visited Dassen seven decades after watching Cherry Kearton's film, it was these tortoises, not African penguins, that David Attenborough came to film.

As we got closer, only a faint smell of guano reached out to the ship. It was already clear that there would be no wall of penguins. I would not, as Kearton had done, 'compare my arrival on the island with that of Gulliver at Lilliput'. From hundreds

---

* *Pikkewyn* is penguin in Afrikaans.

An Inconvenience of Penguins

of thousands, perhaps even a million penguins, the estimated population had fallen below 2,000 breeding pairs in 2023.

The island was littered with crumbling buildings and signs of old, salt-gnawed industry. In one room, dozens of empty penguin eggs sat in old paint buckets. Above, a small exhibition – unseen by anyone aside from rangers, conservationists and the odd volunteer – detailed the fatal combinations of guano extraction and egg collecting that saw the penguin population drop by 95 per cent in the first 60 years of the last century. Walls were built to concentrate areas where the penguins would lay so the clutches could be stolen with greater efficiency. The eggs were mostly eaten or sold to the mainland, but they were thought to be so eternally abundant that workers would crack them open and use the albumen as soap.

Today, instead of a great sea of penguins, the scrubland is dominated by tortoises and introduced rabbits which don't even have the decency to have fabled races against one another. While the Boulders Beach penguin population has learned to trust and essentially ignore people, the surviving birds on Dassen are understandably fearful. When I finally did find a few dozen penguins here, I saw them reacting to me from a distance, looking over their shoulders and shuffling away as though they'd seen me unsheathe a blade.

By the time conservationist Johan Visagie arrived on Dassen in the early 2000s, the great colony was in long decline. Wild-haired, with eyes heavily guarded by wraparound shades, he lit a cigarette that burned without being smoked as he talked in a heavy Afrikaner accent.

'Just from Dassen we've lost 75,000 individual penguins, everything has been declining,' he said, rolling vowels around his mouth like marbles. 'They haven't rocked up somewhere

Extinction Events

else. Boats would have reported something if they'd seen lots of dead birds at sea. No shark can eat that many penguins. It can't be seals. They haven't washed up dead. It's a mystery, a conspiracy theorist's dream, but even for their long-term survival and study there aren't any bodies to look at. Things are bleak at the moment. There's too much in-fighting between conservation and fisheries sectors, each one criticising the other's sciences and stats. Until they reach some kind of agreement, who knows?'

If the African penguin was to disappear, what would it mean for conservation?[*] I asked this question to Visagie and to penguin experts around the world. Some were so despondent they thought it almost irrelevant, but the South African was still angry enough to see it as something dire, harrowing and ultimately embarrassing.

'They're indicator species of marine health. Something like penguins that can't fly, that need high-energy expenditure to reach its food – if they start struggling, then it's a very early indication of an unhealthy system. I've seen them decrease so seriously now and we're not even finding out why. What do you do about that?'

I of course had no answer. Orcas and bees weren't to blame for the demise of an entire species. At every turn, from the insatiable theft of their eggs to the oiling of the water to the industrial removal of their food sources, humans had plainly pushed the African penguin to the brink of extinction.

'Apart from the loss of an iconic species, it would be a failure on our side. We have the opportunity . . .' Visagie paused for

---

[*] Before I'd finished writing this book, the African penguin's conservation status was downgraded to critically endangered.

a moment to order his thoughts and look at his cigarette. 'We're supposed to have the skill sets to stop this. It's either a lack of drive or will from someone higher up. Everyone on the ground is doing what they can. Something is absolutely lacking.'

Before we left Dassen Island, I was handed a small package to take back to the boat. It had been wrapped tightly in a bin bag and crudely sealed with packaging tape. It was the size of a loaf of bread that had failed to rise. I knew what it was before volunteer Yandisa told me. The African penguin inside had been found that morning and had likely died of starvation, another chick whose parent never returned one day. According to the label, its decomposition level was 'Fresh'.

10

Fear and Loathing in Las Malvinas

> Regretting – in a flare-up of the old spirit of pure science – that we could not photograph these anomalous creatures, we shortly left them to their squawking and pushed on toward the abyss whose openness was now so positively proved to us, and whose exact direction occasional penguin tracks made clear.
>
> – H. P. Lovecraft, *At the Mountains of Madness*, 1936

The peculiarities began at the reception desk at RAF Brize Norton, Oxfordshire. I was checking in for a semi-militarised flight to the Falklands, via Ascension Island, when the shift manager looked at my passport and said he recognised me. When I tried to tell him this was unlikely, he only got louder, ignoring the growing queue.

How long had I lived on the islands? I told him that I'd only visited for a day here and there over the years. That couldn't be true, he blared – did I drink in the Victory Bar? It annoyed him when I said I didn't. Still, he insisted he knew me and would soon work out how. It sounded like a threat.

I nervously moved into the base to board an AirTanker bound for the Falklands. It was November 2023 – there was still enough time to see Southern Rockhoppers and Macaronis here,

An Inconvenience of Penguins

then Magellanics in Argentina before my second guiding season in Antarctica. The journey should really have been quite simple, but the plane was already 24 hours late because of cyclonic weather spinning around the South Atlantic. I had no idea that longer, less explicable delays were yet to come.

Welsh Guards comprised around half of the passengers, and despite repeated warnings about drunkenness coming over the public address system, several looked and certainly smelled as though they'd partied until the moment they'd had to talk to a superior officer. Much later, when things had gone wrong, I heard one of them refer to his unhappy sobriety as 'dry hour nine'.

Still, we all boarded the AirTanker together – civilians and squaddies alike – filling just about half the seats, giving us all room to snooze for the eight-hour night flight.[*]

They call it The Cage and not without reason. The holding area at Ascension Island's military airport has the look and feel of a prison exercise yard, without room to actually exercise. Ordinarily it would be used for a couple of hours while the plane refuelled, but as news broke that ours had developed a mechanical problem, we tried to settle in for a longer wait.

The troops stood out in the sun, smoking and regretting their hangovers. Very young and very red-eyed, most of them sported unerringly straight moustaches that seemed a bit too well-developed for the first days of Movember. After a bit of sunburn, many moved inside to watch the news. There was

---

[*] Just in case I was in any doubt over my status, each boarding pass had a space for rank and mine upsettingly said 'Mister'.

Fear and Loathing in Las Malvinas

some interest in King Charles's first address to parliament, but there was more in the updates on Israel's ongoing invasion of Palestine – when that came on, muscled arms got folded and those preposterous moustaches drooped slightly. They knew better than I ever could what regional escalation might mean. Rather than dwell for too long, someone changed the channel to *Loose Women*.

Water was handed out. It helped a little, then, after a few hours of boredom, a flawlessly bald man delivered the news that our plane's hydraulics issue was worse than first thought. Either parts or a replacement plane would need to be flown from the UK. Until then, we would be staying on Ascension. The military would provide us with food and shelter, and we would be transferred from this cage to a much larger one at the RAF Travellers Hill barracks.

I'd visited the Falklands several times before, but always with strict time constrictions to get back to one ship or another. This time the local tourist board was hosting me, an arrangement that would maximise my time on the islands if only the military arrangements weren't so untidy.*

Like the Falklands, South Georgia and Tristan da Cunha, Ascension is a British Overseas Territory; unlike those cousins, it has no penguins. Outside, the land was all emaciated shrubs and sizzling rocks, the sort of post-apocalyptic landscape only likely to be tolerated by goats, rattlesnakes and flies.

---

* The local government presumably receives a significant subsidy to use this route, rather than the circuitous but more reliable commercial alternative via Chile. Such is the ongoing bitterness over the 1982 conflict in the Falklands that travelling more directly via Argentina is almost impossible.

An Inconvenience of Penguins

We passed a security checkpoint and were shown to spartan accommodations. I was assigned a bed that looked as though it had been designed for a ricket-ridden Victorian, one of four squeezed into an ungenerous dorm. The mattress felt as though it had been stuffed with lumps of lava rock. An update arrived: as we hadn't officially crossed the border, we weren't allowed to leave the compound. Through no fault of our own we were now in something like a borstal.

Nonetheless, there weren't too many complaints. Perhaps it was the military surroundings, perhaps it was just fear, but we followed our instructions, even when the mosquitos started biting, even when great ladles of mystery meal were being splatted on to our plates in the mess, and even later when my roommates erupted into Beethovian symphonies of snoring and flatulence.

The closest I heard to actual disgruntlement came when they announced alcohol would not be served while they showed Champions League football in the bar. The Welsh Guards stared at the locked-up booze with greedy, hostile eyes but the rules were clear: we were in transit, and we weren't allowed to drink. One of them left in disgust from my table, leaving a packet of cigarettes behind. I glanced inside and saw there were two left. Despite not being a smoker, I pocketed them. The Falklands always has an element of time-travel about it, so it was probably still OK to smoke indoors – they might be a useful gift for an interviewee.*

The following morning, after a breakfast of rubber eggs and grey coffee, we were told a replacement plane was inbound. To

---

* Actually smoking indoors *is* banned on the islands, though the legislation came four years after mainland UK.

Fear and Loathing in Las Malvinas

kill time until this next escape attempt, I took a walk around the compound. Myna birds noisily hopped between the azaleas and a melancholic sheep staggered down the dusty road. The place had the feel of a gated compound in Saudi Arabia.*

That afternoon, back in The Cage, I spoke to an elderly Falklander who said she just wanted to go home and was wearied by the whole experience. We were now expected to land at 1am local time, more than 50 hours late. Nearby a young Gurkha with a kind face sat staring out across the runway at our useless plane. He was heading back to the Falklands after two weeks of R&R in the UK. I asked how familiar he was with making this journey. 'This is my first time,' he said. 'First and last.'

I spent the following day in and around Stanley, capital of the Falklands. By now I was too late to fly to half the places the tourist board had planned to send me to during what was supposed to have been a penguin-packed six-day stay. Largely because it was on my mind since the odd conversation in Brize Norton, I decided to head to the Victory Bar.†

The islanders have not forgotten, and many have not forgiven, what happened in 1982 when their extremely rural and formerly sleepy lives were turned upside down by invading Argentinian forces. As the name suggests, the Victory Bar is a hub for that unhealthy vein of nostalgia, a place where around Armistice Day, talk of remembrance can comingle with vengeance under rows of Union Jack bunting.

---

* It is similarly difficult to become a permanent citizen – immigration law for the island states that no one has the right to permanently live here.

† Also, because there's not a great deal else to do in Stanley.

An Inconvenience of Penguins

Around me, islanders drank pints of Iron Lady IPA, named in honour of their heroic prime minister, Margaret Thatcher.* I instead ordered a pint of Rockhopper, named in honour of the penguins I had come to see. Nearby two men discussed their inability to ever trust Argentinians again. 'When they smile atcha, it's like a clown doing it,' said a moist man with a black fringe smeared across his forehead. 'It's like it's painted on. Makes me shiver, it does.'

I couldn't quite hear what his drinking partner said in reply as a group of women nearby were collectively swiping through Tinder profiles on a single phone. When the account holder paused on one, a friend loudly stepped in: 'Not him! He's the sleaziest cunt on the islands!' Next was a serviceman. 'Well, if you're just after a shag . . .' I kept my eyes down and concentrated on the warm beer.

Walking back to the hotel I decided it might be a fine time to try one of the cigs I'd picked up on Ascension for myself. I've never been able to smoke, not really – every time it reaches the top of my lungs I cough as though suffering a gas attack on a battlefield in Ypres.† For a while I thought I might take it up as a Covid lockdown hobby but was so broke I couldn't afford it. The price had at least been right on this scavenged Marlboro, but despite my best efforts to resist, it still hit the back of my throat like a wasp and it took everything I had not to vomit over a wall into a nearby garden.

•

---

* Despite being a widely despised figure in Scotland, this beer has been given an orange and blue label that exactly matches the colour of Irn Bru, Scotland's national drink. It's shameless stuff, it really is.

† This actually happened to my great-grandfather in the First World War and is probably an insensitive simile, but he was a nasty man so it's staying in.

Fear and Loathing in Las Malvinas

Over 700 mostly uninhabited islands make up the Falklands. Bridges are a rarity and newish roads only so useful when looking to get out to the fringes of the archipelago. Most of the distant transport instead depends on the Falkland Islands Government Aviation Service (FIGAS), which uses a fleet of just-post-war propeller planes to move around.

My route was from Stanley to Sea Lion Island to Bleaker Island but may as well have been advertised as a 40-minute scenic flight. We took off from tarmac and landed on grass, flying over the low, treeless landscapes of dozens of islands and islets. From the air, kelp forests appeared like brushed hair, while on the ocean's surface, white horses galloped into each other in messy confusion. Most of the land was golden – a little too dry for late spring – and if there were sheep farms, they were difficult to spot.

As we approached Sea Lion, the pilots pointed out a pod of orcas ominously making their way along the smashed coast. I was still looking for them as we made our final approach, and so was surprised by a rookery of Gentoos just a few yards from the grass runway.

Bleaker was 15 minutes from here and the pattern was repeated: a large, seemingly barren island awaited, as did a grass runway attended by plane-spotting penguins.* A second before we touched down, an upland goose shot across our nose. As I laughed nervously the pilot shrugged it off. 'We bump into them occasionally, but it's not usually a big deal.'

While there are hundreds of Gentoos and a few thousand Magellanic penguins on the island, my reason for coming was

---

* Bleaker is not named because of its bleakness but is rather a corruption of Breaker Island, so named because of waves endlessly breaking across it.

An Inconvenience of Penguins

the healthy population of Southern Rockhoppers, the pugnacious crested penguins which live on the Falklands in greater numbers than anywhere else. As both writer and guide, I'd had some of my most transcendent and ethereal moments in the company of these birds at West Point and Saunders Islands in the north-west of the archipelago. There, large colonies tumbled down hillsides, interspersed with thousands of black-browed albatrosses, huge noble birds that projected such grace and calm that they seemed to pacify the raucous penguins. I'd wanted more of that sort of thing, but without being told by an expedition leader to hurry back to a ship.

I was met by Nick Rendell, custodian of the island. His family tend to cattle and sheep, manage the only accommodation, and moreover keep a close eye on the extraordinary wildlife that was here long before any of the stock. Nick first gave me a quick tour of the centre of the island, including a visit down to a sea lion colony. Their numbers have not rebounded since the bloody days of exploitation and he wondered if perhaps they were being out-competed for food by birdlife. 'Plus, they're really rubbish breeders,' he said. 'At least ours are. You see so many dead pups every year.'

Despite apparently struggling, their beach had the continuous rancour of any pinniped stronghold, with blustering males charging one another, stampeding over the females they were trying to impress or at least control. From high in the tussock, not for the first time I thought it looked like an awful lot of hassle to be a seal, at least the ones that form colonies like this. The biting, the confusion, the violent stupidity, all worsened by surging hormones – it reminded me of adolescent nights out, without even the hope of a kebab.

Here, though, there was also fear, a generational hangover

from the days when sailors would harvest hides that would later be turned into gloves and boots in Europe. So likely were the sea lions to flee at the sight of a human now that Nick told me to stay hidden in the grass when observing them.

After an hour or so above the colony, I checked in to the little cottage at the heart of the island. I'd be one of five guests, awkwardly joining middle-aged couples from Italy and China. *No matter*, I thought, *I won't have much to do with them.* And besides, with all the time I'd lost on simply getting to the Falklands, I wanted to make the most of my dwindling days with my 10th penguin species.

It took about 20 minutes to walk to the penguins. The last 50m or so were through tussock grass higher than my head, meaning before I saw the birds, I heard them calling, their almost squelchy voices sounding as distinct from Gentoos' honking as Italian does from Mandarin. Of the five clifftop penguin neighbourhoods, two seemed very exposed and, to my wimpy thinking, too close to the edge. Perhaps coincidentally, the largest rookery instead nuzzled further back in a bay of tussock, providing at least an idea of shelter from gales whiplashing around the headland.

It was hard to stand in these gusts, especially wearing my camera bag, which acted like a cumbersome sail. By Falklands' standards these conditions were not particularly outrageous – hurricane-strength wind is not uncommon, and in Stanley islanders like to brag about full shipping containers being moved when things get really lively. How true that is I don't know, but the relentlessness of the wind suggested trees had made a wise decision in not rooting here.

Even the native Rockhoppers found it tricky at times. When

An Inconvenience of Penguins

one tried to balance on a foot to scratch behind its golden locks, a gust almost blew it over, the bird only just correcting its balance before embarrassing itself in front of its peers. Mostly the wind made little weathervanes of their crests, rendering the yellow strands stiff this way or that, often giving the impression that their ridiculous fringes could do with a trim – or at the very least a little hairband.

In the middle of the huddle, a couple of Falkland imperial cormorants hung around, presumably confused about why everyone else looked so small and tubby these days. 'The shags all moved inland,' Nick Rendell had told me earlier.* 'I dunno why. They used to all nest together, them and the Rockies, but now they're in the middle of a big field by the house. It's good for us because they turn the soil, and their guano is full of nitrogen.' Before I had a chance to ask anything he'd added, 'And I guess the separation will be good if bird flu really gets here.'

Like many crested penguin species, Southern Rockhoppers are strangers to decorum. Short and sturdily built, they are not the most cantankerous penguins but carry themselves with the assuredness of diminutive bouncers.† While the Gentoos on Bleaker could seem aloof and the Magellanics were always on the brink of disappearing into their burrows, the Rockhoppers invited confrontation. I couldn't help wondering if the absence of beatific albatrosses in this colony allowed the penguins to indulge their most base instincts.

It was nesting season, so the Southern Rockhoppers were more primed for violence than any other time of the year. A marauding neighbour is very capable of breaking an egg as it

---

* Shag being an alternative and obviously superior name for a cormorant.

† Most scientists I spoke to said the cranky title would go to the Macaroni.

bounds through the colony, so parents snapped and snarled at all who came close. In those moments, tone and stance changed: a lunge forward, a slash of the beak, wings splayed and posture held, much like the flourish of a superhero or villain. I spent hours out there watching this, totally alone, the recreational violence and ecstatic calls a source of unending entertainment.

Before heading back to the cottage, I went out to the cliff edge to watch the birds returning from the sea, the part of the day when they must hop across the greatest number of rocks. The jump comes in stages – legs, wings and beak all working in approximate unison – and, though impressive, it never looks entirely natural. Imagine a tiny pantomime horse, but with two rabbits inside a penguin outfit, and you're more or less there. Like so much in the world of penguins, it seemed miraculous that it worked for even one individual, let alone multitudes.

I left early after breakfast the next morning, collecting a packed lunch and heading back to the rookery as soon as seemed polite. The walk took me past the thousands-strong colony of cormorants, and almost right into a few brown skuas which were so well camouflaged against the heather they may as well have been invisible. A couple of these punished my trespass with screeching attacks, dive-bombing as I fled, squealing.

After being swooped by the skuas, I thought perhaps I'd smoke the last cig I'd picked up on Ascension. My grandfather used to tell me that his first cigarette came after he'd descended from a crow's nest on board a Second World War destroyer in the High Arctic.* When he got back to the deck, unable to tell

---

* This was the son of the nasty man I mentioned earlier, and a comparative hero.

whether his shivering was caused by cold or terror, his commanding officer handed him a smoke. It calmed him down, so he spent the next 60 years rolling his own.

I tapped the packet, and as the last tube slid out, so did a little square of paper. I quickly pinned it down and examined it. Its edges were no more than 5mm long but in the centre there was an illustration of Saturn, complete with tiny rings.

It had been a long time since I'd taken LSD, and even then it had been passed to me in a festival crowd and I'd stuck it in my mouth without looking. In the morning sun on Bleaker Island, I had time to study the innocuous tab, such a harmless and inconsequential thing. A couple of times I had to stop it being carried away in the wind – it could easily be scavenged, and if skuas got into acid, who knew when the chaos would end?

I weighed the situation for myself, but rather than think too much, I took a bite at the paper, attempting to split it rather than gobble the whole dose. But the target was small and my nibble inaccurate, and almost three-quarters immediately disappeared. Deciding it was nonsensical to leave the tiny remnant on its own, I stuck it under my tongue, too. I waited a couple of minutes and then . . .

. . . nothing.

For a long time, nothing at all happened. I sat back down and waited for some interstellar experience, but it was determined not to arrive.

Sheltering in the tussock, I became invisible to the penguins, which soon began hopping over to the grass around me, tearing it out with impressive force, then going back to their would-be nests and releasing it, only for the clifftop wind to blow it all away. Having achieved nothing, they came for more.

Things continued as shambolically as they always do before

Fear and Loathing in Las Malvinas

a hideous fight broke out, with two penguins savaging a prone and seemingly lame individual for longer than I have ever seen. The victim seemed so listless that for a time I wondered if it could perhaps have avian flu. The disease hadn't yet reached the Falklands, but this behaviour – especially the lack of will to fight back – was so unusual that I had no other explanation.[*] It would be a hell of a coincidence if I'd discovered the first case having just eaten a powerful hallucinogenic, but what if?

The pecking and the beating with wings became too much to witness. I decided to relocate to a more peaceful neighbourhood, but when I stood up, I felt about three inches taller. I looked at the penguins and they seemed smaller. At my back the tussock danced and danced. One of the Southern Rockhoppers stretched to its full height and shook itself, its feathers suddenly seeming iridescent as they settled back on its little chest.[†] It was time to get away from the cliff edge.

The Rockhoppers are one of Bleaker's main attractions, and though there were just four other visitors on the island, I thought it best to move on as the acid took hold. To maintain isolation, I'd head north towards a huge white-sand beach and its widespread population of Gentoos, which would hopefully get no human traffic.

Stumbling back through the high grass towards the open fields, I began to giggle at my situation, and feeling quite camouflaged decided to hide out for a couple of moments to compose myself. I passed this time by having a snack while my

---

[*] I later heard a theory that the prone penguin could have been on top of an egg and was simply refusing to move. When I returned on the final morning, there was no sign of it, dead or alive.

[†] To my mind its full height was only 6–7cm at this point.

An Inconvenience of Penguins

brain spun up and out of my ears. I reached into the picnic bag I'd been given at the cottage and pulled out a chocolate biscuit. When I saw it was a Penguin, a part of my mind calved off and splashed down in ungovernable laughter.

I'm not sure how long I spent on the ground, but when I righted myself, I knew I had to get back to the Rockhoppers to ask if they thought the biscuit was inappropriate. A moment later that seemed impossibly ugly. Was I perpetuating an outdated image of penguins? Was this biscuit their version of the racist Robertson's marmalade branding? Would the Rockhoppers even take offence given the bird on the wrapper was approximately a King?[*] I wanted to ask all these things and more, but a light paranoia had worked its way into my skull and so I dusted myself down and stumbled away to seek out the company of the Gentoos.

Much of the next few hours was a mysterious jumble, but certain images endure.

— Out in the open fields, the wind was unchallenged, at one point so strong that it lifted dried cowpats whole and sent them spinning like wheels bouncing away from a cartoon car crash.
— Until I touched it, for quite some time I was convinced that a tundra of daisies was really snow.
— I became afraid that in one field I was going to drop through a crevasse into a penguin netherworld, dug out and ruled by burrowing Magellanics.

---

[*] It's actually a tricky bird to ID. The burnished oranges on its neck suggest a King penguin, but it also has orange feet, which are particular to Gentoos. In any case, I doubt it's an Emperor – unlike the birds on the biscuit wrappers, those joyless giants never smile.

Fear and Loathing in Las Malvinas

— I sat down on a fence post and listened to the wind and sea and for a few perfect moments couldn't tell where they ended and I began. When I came to, I was crying.

Days later I arrived at the beach. The Gentoos were at the far end, but by now my vision had grown so untrustworthy, I knew I'd have to get closer to be sure. Walking over the sand my legs became heavy and shorter again. No matter how long I walked, the beach remained stubbornly gigantic. Ahead penguins seamlessly moved hither and yon, their spatula feet coping much better on the surface than my leaden boots.

Finally, I found a rock not spattered with guano and sank against it. After a few moments in this little windbreak I felt utterly relaxed, listening to the sound of the ocean and the distant calls of the penguins, almost able to completely ignore the half-buried spinal column of a long-retired bird between my feet. I lay back and watched the clouds do extraordinary things, then slowly drifted up to meet them.

I wasn't sure how much time had passed, but when I awoke, I was shivering and a penguin was picking at my boots. The orange of its mouth was incredible, the rainbow hues of its chest feathers wondrous. Equally powerful was my sense of guilt when I startled it by sitting up. The Gentoo half hopped away, looking over its shoulder at me, the betrayer. 'I'm sorry,' I half shouted as it kept moving. 'I'm not sure things are going to be OK!'

The shivering worsened – the sun that had been so dazzling all morning was long gone. I wasn't sure how far I'd walked, nor how long it would take to get back, but with so few people on the island, if I didn't make it back for dinner, there would be concern. They might even come looking for me.

An Inconvenience of Penguins

The return journey was more arduous than psychedelic, but every time I was sure I was free from the drug, it would snatch me back and I'd be talking to Arctic terns or overthinking how many skuas it would take to devour a cow. On and on the path went, the world flitting between cold sobriety and warm madness.

Unsure of the direction back to the cottage, I let birds guide me. The cormorants' relocation to just outside the accommodation was handy, especially now at the close of day as they arrowed through the sky, pointing me home. The penguins, for their part, were useless.

Eventually I could see Bleaker's tiny settlement, but instead of relief, I felt dread. The LSD had not quite finished with me, but a meal in company awaited. I couldn't feign a lack of hunger, I couldn't ask for room service, and I certainly couldn't go elsewhere.

Sneaking into my room, I looked in the mirror. A barely recognisable face greeted me, an embarrassing combination of wind and sunburn giving me the appearance of a committed Brexiteer. My pupils danced like sea anemone, one large then suddenly small, but never the same size as its neighbour. I showered, washed my face, and prayed it would all go away.

It didn't.

Xin felt a little confused, even ambushed by my question. Was it true that the Chinese symbols for penguin can also be read as 'business goose'?

I'd managed to keep my gibbering to a minimum over dinner, but after watching my potatoes swim around the plate for a little too long, I decided I had to give my mind something else to do.

Fear and Loathing in Las Malvinas

Xin looked at me and I looked at her and hoped that the anemone had settled down.

'I heard that penguin in Chinese translates as business goose,' I repeated, glancing away in case I looked mental. 'I heard that last year but you're the first Mandarin speaker I've been able to ask directly.'

Gazing at me like a weary parent, she slowly explained that there were many ways to read the symbols, but that business goose was not necessarily accurate.

'Something like enterprise goose would be better,' she said to my enormous disappointment. 'I think someone has told you a joke.'

I wanted to tell her that it had been an internet meme for months and that people around the world had celebrated the inarguable logic of calling a bird in a suit a business goose, but there seemed to be no room for negotiation. I soon began to fret that I'd caused offence by assuming any knowledge of Mandarin. I looked at the Italian couple who had sat in silence, flummoxed by the weirdness of the conversation. I had no allies, so I instead chased down a potato, thanked everyone for their company and fled to my room.

Lying on the bed my brain raced and raced, no longer fun and silly but incessant and mad. Hours passed like this. When I finally fell asleep, insane dreams of Rockhoppers awaited me. In one, the birds flew at my face with snapping beaks while I tried to assure them I didn't have avian flu.

11

War and Penguin

> It sometimes happens, though, that he shows fight, and then it is wiser to keep out of range of his flippers; for in these he has a very powerful weapon, which might easily break a man's arm. If you wish to attack him, it is better to do so from behind; both flippers must be seized firmly at the same time and bent backwards along his back; then the fight is over.
> – Roald Amundsen, *The South Pole*, 1912

When I was a child, if the weather was warm and we weren't in school and there'd been planning by people more influential than me, my council block would mobilise and fall into open conflict with the one next to it. All the kids from our building and all from our hated neighbours' would get tooled up with guns and grenades, then rush downstairs to watery war. In artillery we had an advantage: one of the boys two doors along had been given a stolen Super Soaker for a birthday or Christmas. For some reason, my mother often kept an arsenal of water balloons, too. We felt ready.

Yet we were always at a tactical disadvantage because although we had a parent or two who would occasionally tip out a pan of icy water as though over a castle rampart, the other block had Mick, who was in his mid-30s for one thing, and a Falklands War veteran for another.

War and Penguin

Water fights with Mick were always fun, but guaranteed our block would lose. I remember trying to sneak round corners, not hearing anything and then bang: two in the face and two in the crotch to make it look as though we'd pissed ourselves. The soldier would then vanish in search of new targets, his straight back sliding along the wall. Other times, when we thought it was all done and time to go home, he'd lob water balloons from upper verandas as though they were mortars. He rarely missed.

Mick never spoke about his time in the Falklands, and if he was carrying trauma, unlike his battle training, he kept it hidden. I knew nothing of his experience, but then I knew nothing of the war – Argentina had invaded almost exactly a year before I was born.

Like Piper Alpha, Lockerbie and later Dunblane, the word Falklands cast a long shadow across my childhood, becoming a place where I knew bad things had happened, suffering only adults should really know about, if anyone had to know at all. No one ever spoke about that British Overseas Territory or the conflict with affection. I didn't really know where in the world it was, nor anything about its people or its wildlife. I just knew that for some its name meant death, and that a stain like that is almost impossible to remove.

Something I didn't tell you about Ascension Island earlier: while we were waiting for our replacement plane, I met another veteran. Short, with ever-so-slightly bowed legs and too-big glasses, he asked if he could sit next to me in the packed mess in RAF Travellers Hill. He was carrying a heaped tray of fried breakfast items and wearing a polo shirt which commemorated the 30-year anniversary of the Falklands War. His name was Oz, he said, and he'd been a young sailor in the Navy when the fighting

An Inconvenience of Penguins

began, part of the enormous, hastily assembled task force that was sent across the Atlantic to push back the invaders.

Argentina simultaneously began their attempted conquest on South Georgia, a sneak-attack during which they'd have presumably had to step over penguins to get to the few British personnel stationed on that more-distant outpost. The conflict on the Falklands was much larger. On 2 April as the main assault began, it was quickly clear that Britain was woefully underprepared to defend the farming communities living there. As the Argentinian junta sought to rally national support for their failing government, Britain scrambled its armed forces for the 12,500km dash south. Margaret Thatcher's own floundering government finally had a cause around which most of the nation could gather – like General Galtieri, her office would be cemented or crushed depending on what happened in the Falklands.

For men and boys like Oz, things were simpler – they only had to do what they were told. I didn't really have to ask any questions while the man of war spoke. His candour about his PTSD, his alcoholism, the sexual abuse he'd suffered as a kid and again in the forces, the images of the dead and dying he'd seen, his subsequent breakdown . . . it all came tumbling out of him like potatoes from a burst sack. Salvation for Oz had finally come with counselling and therapeutic painting. Now his brain was more at ease, he felt able to return to the Falklands for Remembrance Sunday – perhaps not for final closure, but another step towards feeling better.

When I felt the conversation lighten, I asked if by any chance he'd remembered seeing penguins during the conflict. I didn't want to be rude or flippant, I said, but I'd wondered how many young Brits sent down to that hostile environment saw

War and Penguin

penguins for the first time while bullets were flying. I'd wondered if they'd been a distraction, or even a comfort.

'Actually, I do – some of the lads were taking shots at them,' said Oz, nudging his big glasses up his nose with one hand and fiddling with an unlit cigarette in the other. He'd managed to get control of his drinking but still smoked with rare enthusiasm for someone in 2023. 'They weren't doing it for fun, but 'cause they didn't know what they were. We were putting scare charges in the water every six minutes because we were afraid of Argie frogmen attaching limpet mines to our ships. The guys didn't know if they were something to do with that, so they'd shoot.' This tallied with other accounts I'd read of military men mistaking swimming penguins for torpedoes. 'Anyway,' added Oz, 'being Navy, they'd have missed.'

The conflict still colours everything in the Falklands, even all these years later. Write the name into Google and the next suggested word will be 'War'. Before travelling to the islands, I watched a series of documentaries about the events of 1982, but the more I learned and tried to understand, the more harrowing it became. Not just because of the medieval hand-to-hand conflict in Goose Green, or the brutal conquering of Mount Tumbledown, but because of how avoidable it all was. Argentina never stood a chance of winning that war, nor holding the islands, but they sent teenage conscripts to be butchered by the SAS and Gurkha regiments so elusive and deadly the young Argentinians began to fear the islands were full of phantoms.

Worse: in the years prior to the invasion Britain was seriously considering leasing the islands to Argentina anyway. Had Galtieri really wanted the Falklands as something more than a trophy to stoke dwindling nationalism, he could have just

An Inconvenience of Penguins

waited.* Instead, almost a thousand people died, and more than double were officially injured.† The average age of British soldiers serving was 23. The average age of the Argentinian conscripts is not known.

Today it's very hard to convince anyone – friends, editors and no doubt readers – that the Falkland Islands are worth visiting. If you are sceptical, I would tell you that it is home to more penguin species than Antarctica. It of course doesn't have the biomass of that ultimate continent, but it does have the edge when it comes to diversity, offering several endemic creatures as well as many of Antarctica's whale, seal and bird species. If you're afraid of the Drake Passage or simply cannot afford a visit south, the Falkland Islands are a worthwhile alternative.

For my purposes, I was keen to see some Macaronis up close. They nest in far greater numbers on South Georgia, but here they and the Southern Rockhoppers have a very unusual relationship.

Another thing I didn't tell you earlier: when I was up on that cliff on Bleaker Island, before my brain became unreliable, I saw a single Macaroni penguin. Single but not alone, it was surrounded by Southern Rockhoppers which looked like they had become the visitor's hosts and perhaps friends. There was one bird with which the Macaroni had evidently created an especially close bond – the interloper had found itself a sweetheart.

---

* Even then, the islanders were deeply opposed to the idea.

† British losses: 225 killed, 775 injured, 107 captured. Argentinian losses: 649 killed, 1,657 injured, 11,313 captured. Total number traumatised by conflict: unknown.

War and Penguin

There is only a smattering of Macaronis on the Falklands, with fewer than 50 birds making the archipelago their home. When considering it is the most abundant penguin species in the world, with an estimated 18 million individuals around the Antarctic region, this tiny detachment seems insignificant, except for one fact: here and only here are they known to hybridise with another penguin.

Cross-species breeding is not totally unheard of – just off Chiloé in Chile, Humboldt and Magellanic penguins cohabit burrows and occasionally produce chicks.* However, those birds have near-identical markings and to novice eyes can seem indistinguishable. The Macaroni and the Southern Rockhopper are far more distinct, with differences something like those between a rottweiler and a Labrador. One is larger, more muscular and aggressive, the other a calmer and perhaps dumber second-cousin.

On the cliff on Bleaker, I saw the lone Macaroni gently preen its smaller Rockhopper partner, which was sitting on their egg. The former had a deeper, darker beak, and a much more flamboyant crest, a rich golden colour forming a proper mane, rather than the paler eyebrow crest of its partner. Its baby, when it hatched, would eventually show traits of both these penguins.

'I can usually tell the hybrid chicks straight away,' said local birding guide Andy Pollard when I interviewed him later. 'Although you can't see it when they're really small, only when they come back as adults the following year. I don't know how long it's been going on, but we can say at least 20 years.'

Unlike, say, mules, are these penguins fertile? Andy said they were, though they usually bred again with Southern

---

* Would they be called Humbellanics or Mageboldts? I'd consider either.

Rockhoppers, largely diluting the Macaroni traits back out again. 'We just don't really have enough Macaronis here,' he said. 'I mean, of all the birds to breed with again when they come back, it's just very unlikely that they'd pick a Macaroni as their partner – they're so outnumbered.'

Given that both Macaroni and Southern Rockhopper numbers are in decline globally, I couldn't help wondering if in several generations there could possibly be a new species, a super hybrid immune to its ancestors' pressures.* That seemed speculative, not to mention unlikely, but for both birds the population trends were not encouraging. In the last 30 years no species had lost more penguins than the Macaroni, with a drop of almost 50 per cent across its vast territories. On subantarctic McDonald Island, a million pairs were lost to a volcanic eruption; on South Georgia, their numbers have dropped from around 5 million breeding pairs to under a million. That's still a huge amount of biomass, but a devastating proportional loss and a trend that is unsustainable.

I tried to fend off magical thinking about the possibility of a new species, but with the hybrids, an important matter needed settling. I'd heard troubling reports that these new birds had been dubbed Mackhoppers, which seemed like an awful waste considering the obviously superior alternative.

'Ah, no, it's got to be Rockeroni,' said Andy, a wise and intelligent man. 'It's just got to be.'

•

---

* Much later, an expert in taxonomy explained to me that this was virtually impossible, not least because speciation through hybridisation is almost unheard of in birds, one of the few exceptions being the Italian sparrow, which is a hybrid between Spanish and house sparrows.

War and Penguin

It took until 2020 for an estimated 13,000 landmines planted by Argentinian forces to be cleared from the islands. The removal team was led by 100 or so Zimbabwean contractors who spent 11 years digging through dunes, guided by robots to find their targets. When the final device was uncovered, officials celebrated with a ceremonial explosion, then ate sandwiches and played cricket on the white sand at Yorke Bay, the place where Argentinian troops had landed to seize Stanley.* With the islands more isolated than ever because of Covid, it was a very local affair.

It is unlikely penguins celebrated the clearing with such enthusiasm. Five species nest around the Falklands, and in places like Yorke Bay, they did so without any human interference for almost 40 years.† This had kept people, their vehicles and dogs away from the birds. Wherever they were dropped, the mines effectively created sanctuaries – the local Macaronis, Southern Rockhoppers, Gentoos and Magellanics wouldn't have been heavy enough to set one off. King penguins, of which there are a few thousand in various beaches on East Falkland, theoretically could have briefly experienced flight this way, but I could find no evidence that had ever happened.‡

Before the end of my trip, I walked to the unfortunately named Gypsy Cove outside of Stanley, then along the beach at mine-free Yorke Bay. There I watched a handful of Magellanic penguins returning from sea and, spread around high golden dunes, hundreds of Gentoos. Some had taken over little patches

---

* More mines have since washed up on beaches around the islands.

† Five and a half if you count the Rockeronis.

‡ At least one cow became burger meat having stood on a mine, however; it seems likely several of the islands' 500,000 sheep would have, too.

of grass which popped out of the sand like a teenager's uncertain beard. Down by the shore, a single King stood taller than the rest, imperious and alone. It didn't look like it had come to cross-breed so much as it had come to inspect the form of the smaller birds. In the background, a Navy patrol boat sailed into Port William.

Since 1982 Britain has maintained a huge military presence on its formerly neglected territory. The character of the islands had to be switched from agriculture to aggravation, and while some of the generational islanders grew frustrated with the permanent militarisation of their homeland, they also recognised the benefits of government no longer looking away. 'In some ways – and you have to be careful how you say this – in some ways, it was the best thing to happen to the islands,' said the local FIGAS pilot who had flown me back from Bleaker Island. There was only one other person on board, and as I was a visitor, he invited me to sit in the cockpit. Like Andy Pollard, he could trace family roots back to the original British settlement of the Falklands and knew a surprising amount about its history. 'It put us on the map,' he said. 'We've got lots of roads now. We got the airport in 1985. Even in the 1970s, folks were transporting wool with horse and cart.'

Below, the entire archipelago was visible and the pilot took time to point out dark patches of penguin colonies and crucial sites from the war. On a sunny day, with the ocean glittering, it was harder than ever to imagine 74 gruelling days of fighting in dreadful conditions here.

It was far removed from the corporate, algorithmic drone conflict of today – a traditional war with scared teenagers running into each other, bayonets drawn, bullets flying in the dark, bodies lying in the mud. For the troops the fallout was the same as ever: trauma, depression, abandonment by the government, alcoholism and, for some, suicide.

When we landed, the pilot suggested I hang out for a moment so we could watch three RAF Typhoon fighter jets fly over our heads in flawless formation. There are over 220 avian species on the Falklands, but no weirder birds than these.

In the end you live with the war on the Falkland Islands, just as you live with the penguins. Andy Pollard arrived in 1985 and the legacy dominated his childhood. When I was a kid at school, teachers would show us amateurish yet terrifying videos warning about stranger danger, unprotected sex or the raw terror of electricity pylons. 'For us we'd have people come in and show us ordinance, "This is a cluster bomb, this is a grenade, this is a landmine," and so on,' said Andy. 'They wanted us to know for when we found them lying around.'

He doesn't remember seeing his first penguin ('You get used to seeing them about') but he's very familiar with the mighty effect they can have on visitors. Birders might be as interested in an endemic Cobb's wren or Falkland steamer duck as a Macaroni, but photographers always prefer the penguins.

'Nobody is going to forget the people or the families who came here and liberated us, nor the people who are serving and providing us protection today,' he said. 'But it would be good to change the narrative a bit. When I get Google alerts for the islands, it's still almost all to do with the war. It'd be good if our wildlife could help change that.'

Did he mean the penguins? 'Well, of course,' he said. 'Naturally.'

12

Feathered, Untethered

> In these Islands we found great reliefe and plenty of good victualls, for infinite were the number of fowle, which the Welsh men named Penguin, and Magilanus tearmed geese. This fowle cannot flye, haveing but stubb wings, without feathers . . . They breed and lodge at land, and in the day tyme goe downe to the sea to feed . . . their skins cannot be taken from their bodyes without tearing off the flesh, because of their exceeding fatnes.
>
> – Francis Fletcher, aboard the *Golden Hind*, 1577

It works like this: you, a freelance travel writer, will pitch an idea to an outlet and hope that the editor sees it in the maelstrom of their inbox. If they do, they'll consider its commercial value, whether there's a timely hook, the replicability of the story as a tourist experience, the likelihood of it clashing with something already on their schedule, then whether they'd like to pinch it for themselves or a friend in the office. Assuming there's a green light, you must then work out how to actually go and do the thing.

The easiest and most cost-effective process is to throw yourself into a sort of posh bartering system with a PR company or tourist board that has something to sell. Do this and there's a good chance the flights, accommodation, most meals

Feathered, Untethered

and sometimes alcohol will be covered. If the hosts are feeling especially generous, they'll allow you to bring someone along, euphemistically referred to as a 'plus-one'. They do this because it is much cheaper than buying adverts in print or online, though it's hoped your essay will have much the same effect.*

For the freelancer, having all the costs absorbed by the people with the product is often the only way to turn a profit. I have seen much of the world like this, and it has been rewarding.† Some of the experiences were, looking back, preposterous, from competing in the British bobsleigh championship to learning Sri Lankan martial arts, from eating constellations of Michelin-starred food to driving auto-rickshaws across India, from stalking polar bears in Alaska to having my sperm tested in a Harley Street clinic.‡ Whatever the experience, if someone else was laying everything on, there was at least a chance of making a little money – £500 is a reasonable amount for most writers for each story sold.

But *is* that reasonable? Even if you managed to secure a story every week, becoming an object of perpetual motion to complete the research, you'd make £26,000 a year pre-tax, almost £10,000 below the average annual salary in Britain, and only a little over minimum wage.

If you're not careful and you aren't hosted properly, you might find yourself having to dip into your own pocket, lessening this pittance even further. While some of those costs will

---

* This obviously corrupted approach to facilitating an article is not favoured by US titles, many of which have a blanket ban on writers being hosted, instead adopting the very retro approach of simply paying expenses instead.

† Not financially, obviously.

‡ There's a great white hope joke in there but I'll not make it here.

An Inconvenience of Penguins

be tax-deductible, the scant wage can quickly drift away like ash on a windy day. The real skill with this type of work comes not in the writing but walking an incredibly narrow path between ethical conduct and solvency.

I spent years living like that, usually toeing the company lines, occasionally being lightly reprimanded for not being positive enough. Sometimes I even presented the world as it is, not how a marketing department would like it to be.* My best stories, or the ones I found most satisfying anyway, were those where I got to the edge of what was acceptable, curled my toes over the side and had a look around. I never made much money on those trips, mostly because no title in the UK pays meaningful expenses, but if the stories succeeded, they perhaps did so because there was something at risk. That's what I told myself, anyway, when the £500 came in, only for £150 to go to the tax man and national insurance, £200 on credit card debt from the trip, and the rest on whatever heavily discounted meat I could find just before the supermarkets closed in Glasgow.

I pushed PR buttons many times to facilitate researching this book, but when it came to the Magellanic penguins in Argentina, I knew selling a story to get there would be difficult. You only get support if you've got a publication onside; here there was no hook, no breaking penguin news. Chubut Province, where the majority of the population is found, is not famous for much outside of the country. Nothing had changed in recent

---

* Perhaps the most avoidable example came when I declared Vladikavkaz in Russia the least friendly place I'd ever been. The local press picked it up, the mayor was displeased, and I was invited back so he could 'change my mind'. I'm not sure if that was meant to sound as sinister as it did, but in any case I declined the opportunity.

Feathered, Untethered

years, and editors were beginning to grow weary of me endlessly pitching stories that were suspiciously penguin-adjacent.

Instead of going down the media route, I decided to ask Aurora Expeditions to fly me to Argentina before my next Antarctic guiding contract began in Ushuaia, so that I could spend some time – and money – on trying to get close to the Magellanics. Rather than accept the warm embrace of the PR industry, I would go it alone – be noble, be true to the cause, a John Muir of the penguin world. The birds are calling, and I must go.

On review, this was a mistake.

The most abundant of the banded penguins, the Magellanic is very similar in appearance to its close cousins the African, the Galapagos and the Humboldt. They also burrow, they also bray, they also have beaks which look like they've been snapped from a wizard's staff. Yet while most banded penguins are being pushed towards extinction, the Magellanic birds are comparatively thriving. If you total the penguins across the other three species, you might have around 70,000 animals; there are over 3 million Magellanics.

I'd met them in the Falklands, and briefly in the Beagle Channel while heading to Antarctica, but I wanted to see them in greater numbers. With over 2 million of the birds spread along its vast coast, Argentina was an obvious choice – there are more penguins here than in any other sovereign nation.[*] Seeing the sprawling penguin colonies would not require an epic maritime quest, yet without anyone to help me, the jigsaw still seemed complicated, and I was sure pieces were missing.

---

[*] Not including overseas territories or disputed regions of Antarctica.

An Inconvenience of Penguins

It's worth saying here that I love Argentina, one of the most beautiful and varied countries in the world, home of similarly gorgeous people, wine and the finest steaks anywhere. Yet as I began the hazy descent into Puerto Madryn on the east coast, it became clear that I was to land somewhere unfamiliar.

Chubut was very distant from the humid magnificence of Iguazu Falls, the rolling plains of Mendoza's winelands or the mountainous perfection of Patagonia. There was no large city, even. This was instead wide, dusty country shunned by meaningful vegetation, latticed with cauterised rivers and salt-baked shores. The winds were endless and desiccating. From the runway, I saw several wind turbines, burned-out and charred, presumably from overexertion. Stepping off the plane, I thought I was standing in the path of the engine, then realised that this was just how things were around here – life lived in a hairdryer. As in Marcona, where the Humboldts had taken up residence in Peru, this did not feel like a penguin region.

The trip's problems began almost immediately. I needed to collect a rental car, but despite my booking saying it was from Puerto Madryn, it was actually located in Trelew Airport, a 45-minute drive south. A tired man behind an information desk seemed surprised that I hadn't booked a transfer ahead of time but told me that it'd only be the equivalent of £20 to take a taxi, and that I shouldn't worry so long as I had pesos.

Cash? I'd spent the previous night in Buenos Aires and not had to worry about it – everywhere took card and they had Uber. Now out in the provinces, though, I needed an ATM. Sleepy Man scratched his thin grey hair and told me that the machine in this airport was empty, but he was quite sure there was one in Trelew, almost certainly.

Feathered, Untethered

When do things start to fall apart in a country? For outsiders, one of the most obvious signs is when the cash machines stop working. If you can't get your hands on paper, it's a strong signal that someone, somewhere, is holding too much while others go without.

It was early December 2023 and Argentina's economy had been in the toilet for years. The advice to visitors was to bring US dollars and negotiate a black-market rate for local pesos. This of course only exacerbated problems, but no one wanted to pay double for goods and services. I was only going to be here for five days and thought I'd just be able to put whatever I needed on a card – hard currency had seemed unnecessary.

At Trelew Airport, I left the taxi driver outside and went in to get cash. The machine said it couldn't issue me as much as £20. I tried the equivalent of £10. It still said no, which was weird because I'd been told I'd be able to get at least £15. Ah, yes, but there's a £6 charge for using the machine, and by the way, that'll come off your £15 limit, so maximum available per withdrawal is in fact £9. To get £20 of actual money, you'll need three withdrawals, which will cost £45 and leave you with £27. This was not only confusing but seemed like a very shitty deal, and when I later checked my statement, I saw that I'd also been charged at the unfavourable standard rate, not the black-market one. The £20 taxi fare ended up costing me more like £60.

Having settled up with the driver, I went over to the car hire desk. To my surprise it was staffed by a nervous young man who spoke excellent English – there would be no need for my abysmal Spanish. Mercifully I'd paid for the car in advance so wouldn't get any sliding exchange rate this time. But did I want the excess insurance for just £6 extra a day? I did not – as a

An Inconvenience of Penguins

professional and experienced travel writer, I have a comprehensive third-party policy specifically to dodge these extra charges. I took the keys to my asthmatic little car and hit the road.

I was heading almost four hours south to Bahía Bustamante, a one-time kelp farm and ranch turned eco-lodge with a healthy little population of Magellanic penguins on its property.* Ferdinand Magellan, after whom the birds are named, of course travelled a lot farther to see penguins, though admittedly he had other goals on his mind too. The Portuguese explorer had already tried his hand at violent colonialism in India before switching allegiance to Spain and becoming one of the most ambitious explorers of the day. While leading the first expedition to circumnavigate the world, he reached the southern tip of South America in 1520. In doing so, his fleet of five ships likely became the first Europeans to encounter this species of penguin.

How much enchantment they experienced is unknown but within moments they were slaughtering vast quantities of the birds. Not knowing what else they might be, they were recorded by the voyage scholar Antonio Pigafetta as geese:

> We found two islands full of geese and sea wolves. Truly, the great number of these geese is beyond words. Within one hour we filled up our five ships. These geese are black, and have the same kind of feathers everywhere, on their body as well as on their wings. They don't fly and feed on fish. They were so fat that we didn't have to pluck them, but just skin them. Their beak is similar to a horn.

---

* I was being hosted there, but not because of any pending newspaper article. The owners just really loved penguins and were happy to aid my project.

Feathered, Untethered

Months later, deep in the grips of scurvy and starvation as they slowly crossed the Pacific towards Asia, the sailors must have looked back on those gluttonous days with drooling fondness. With Death stalking the ships, eventually the men crawled ashore in Guam, resupplied and feasted before continuing to what is now the Philippines. Soon the Europeans were forcing themselves on local women while Magellan tried to convert everyone to Catholicism. Unsurprisingly peace didn't last and within a couple of months, the explorer was dead on a beach, butchered by understandably irate indigenous people who 'threw themselves upon him, and ran him through with lances and scimitars, and all the other arms which they had'.

I spent part of the tedious drive listening to a profile of Javier Milei, the newly elected leader of Argentina, a man who preferred to do business with a chainsaw rather than a scimitar. Milei's publicists have argued that he looks like Wolverine on the basis of his prodigious sideburns, but it's hard to think of a superhero when the rest of his head is so swine-eyed, weird and mean. This former economics professor ran on his strangeness, and being unhinged was part of his appeal. When he took to the campaign stage literally swinging a chainsaw around, the crowds cheered – he would slash at the old economic systems and create something new. The stuff about having telepathic conversations with his five dogs (all clones) was cute, not the sad ravings of a man with pronounced mental illness.

For all the madness, unlike other populists, Javier Milei wasn't fabricating his nation's problems – the hyperinflation and uselessness of the Argentinian peso were not being imagined to garner votes. It just seemed improbable that a man who swung

An Inconvenience of Penguins

garden tools around like a pound-shop Leatherface would be the one to fix them.

The road continued, straight and bland, hour after featureless hour. Out here, there was no phone signal, no villages, no distractions. I passed signs for Punta Tombo, home to one of the world's largest Magellanic colonies, which I planned to visit on the return journey. Eventually the route took me off the highway and on to a gravel road; with stones popping and bouncing all around, I wondered for the first time if I should have taken that extra insurance.

After an anxious hour of this I reached the gates of Bahía Bustamante. Originally a seaweed farm, it was eventually bankrupted through a combination of greed and ignorance – its valuable kelp was overharvested and ultimately disappeared. Matías Soriano is the grandson of the place's founder and today he's working to manage the land in a responsible way.

If I was writing a travel story, I'd tell you more about the place, about its ecotourism credentials, about how Matías struck a deal with a neighbouring rancher to have water plumbed from his natural spring, about their solar panels, their garden, their commitment to recycling. I'd likely emphasise that, alongside the luxe accommodation, there are 10,000 hardy sheep across the ranch's 40,000 hectares, and that dealing with them is still bloody, feral work. I'd then link this to the fact that the stock was brought by Welsh farmers in the late 1800s and let you know that Matías's family was part of that early migration. Next, I would tell you about the excellence of the food – in particular the grilled guanaco* – which had been sourced locally, and which

---

* An ungentle cousin of the alpaca, llama and vicuna.

was served to me and no one else in their quiet little restaurant. If I was writing a travel story, there'd be no way I'd neglect to tell you that I had to interrupt that meal and go outside because the sunset embroidered the whole sky with rhubarb pinks and figgish purples, becoming so intense that at one point I was sure the ranch horses were looking up at it with me. But this is a story about penguins, so you won't get any of that.

'Well, of course the penguins are super popular,' said Matías, who remembered trying to keep rescued chicks as pets as a child. 'They made a mess and they . . .' He made a grabbing gesture with a hand to signal pecking. 'Yes, very hard. I love them, but we had them in a tool shed outside. We'd let them into the house sometimes too and they'd play with the dogs. Occasionally the neighbours would call to say one had got into their house. Eventually, when they were big enough, they were released back to the sea.'

The following morning, I was taken to see a small rookery on a little peninsula, one of the pre-set activities offered around the farm. Down by the shore with few visitors, the Magellanics initially displayed the standoffishness characteristic of most banded penguins. I sat on the ground next to some low shrubs and watched the locals slowly start to ignore me as they waddled from bush to bush, arguing with their neighbours while trying to avoid the relentless wind. Soon, one felt comfortable enough to squirt some guano just past my left knee.[*]

It was an intimate morning with those birds, which eyed me with suspicion but were far bolder and friendlier than the

---

[*] And it really was a squirt, complete with a funny noise, the likes that make toddlers laugh.

An Inconvenience of Penguins

burrowers on Las Malvinas.* Those Magellanics had fled on sight, popping up and disappearing as soon as eye contact had been made, as though we were playing an endless game of Whac-A-Mole. I'd found a version of this wariness with each of the banded penguins – in South Africa, in Peru, and now here in Argentina. The only species that seemed ready to tolerate people were the tiny Galapagos penguins, and they numbered just a couple of thousand. In general, if the banded penguin has a personality type, it is that of a paranoiac or agoraphobe, ready to flee when all I wanted to do was observe them and champion their cause.

I'd planned to stay longer at Bahía Bustamante, but the weather was closing in and there was no chance I'd be able to take the boat out to their penguin island the following day. Reluctantly, I instead thanked Matías for his hospitality and in the morning started back north towards the larger colonies. The advantage of not having to fulfil PR obligations gave me this flexibility, and as I pulled back out on to the gravel road, I thought how fine an arrangement it was.

An hour later, I was back on the tarmac, immediately faced with a feverishly busy petrol station. I had just over half a tank of fuel, but the queues looked long and shouty as drivers tried to jump ahead of each other. Before my phone signal disappeared in the desert, I checked Google Maps, which told me there were two more stations between here and Trelew. Rather than join the stramash, I got back on the road.

---

* This is the term used by the majority of Argentinians for the Falklands. It is a corruption of Îles Malouines, the name assigned by French explorers in 1764, before Spain, then Argentina, started squabbling with Britain over their sovereignty.

Feathered, Untethered

Another two hours later, with growing hunger, I approached the next service station. It looked like it had been dropped in from the Mad Max universe – its food options would be grim and perhaps poisonous, assuming I could wrestle anything from the flies. I'd used less fuel than I'd anticipated, so rather than stop here I pushed on to the final option, another 40 minutes away. I'd get there without much in reserve, but it'd be a more efficient trip this way.

The haze of the windy desert dripped all over the horizon, obscuring the petrol station. It continued to do so as I sped past its marker on my digital map. I drove for 10 more minutes, then pulled over at the side of the road. Briefly concerned that I'd experienced some kind of absence at the wheel, I checked the screen then looked around the flat void. To my horror, the vital stop did not exist – there was nothing but empty scrubland, no hint that anything useful had ever existed here. The mark on Google Maps was a phantom.*

The low-fuel light was already on in the car, and I reckoned I was still an hour from Trelew. It seemed unlikely I could make that distance, but if I was careful, I could maybe get back to the previous station. With no other option, I started south once more.

I drove slowly enough that laden lorries overtook me, huge pressure changes shaking my car as they provided temporary shields from the perennial wind. In an attempt to conserve every millilitre of fuel, I turned off the air-conditioning, rolled down the window and felt immediately clammy. There was no

---

* Days later, still angry, I made a point of updating the map for this region.

dignity in this retreat, but I had to get fuel or I'd be stuck on the middle of a desert road with no signal, no contacts and no support. My shoulders hunched behind the wheel, gripped by the claws of some demonic stress creature. All of this could have been avoided with a PR handshake.

On gently descending hills, I turned the engine off to freewheel, and by the time I got back to the services, I was just about ready to push the car. Relieved and totally empty, I stepped out into the forecourt, took a deep breath and asked cheerily in my very bad Spanish for a full tank.

A severe-looking woman said there was no fuel here. There hadn't been fuel for months – hadn't I seen the state of the country? No, the next fuel was back south, down there by the turn-off to Bahía Bustamante. There was nothing else between here and Trelew, either.

I asked what I could do in that case. Surely – surely! – others had found themselves stuck at this station that refused to be a station. My hostess just shrugged. Something about her aura told me that negotiation was not an option and that she potentially had a shotgun under the till. Was there some food at least? She pointed at a sweaty meat sandwich, which I took without complaint, along with a bagful of sugary, plastic-tasting snacks. This deal done, and still showing no interest in my fate, she told me she was closing.

Back in the car I gnawed on the sad sandwich while plagues of flies danced around outside. I'd been in pickles like this during car rallies in Eastern Europe and Central Asia, but most problems there were fixed with time and bribes. There was no lateral move here – the fuel simply didn't exist. I was stuck and would remain stuck. I resolved to tackle this conundrum

Feathered, Untethered

by watching an episode of *Blue Eye Samurai*, which I'd at least downloaded ahead of my journey.*

An hour passed, then another. My planned detour to Punta Tombo withered, then died. Perhaps I could hitch back to Trelew, get some fuel, then hitch all the way back? Maybe, but that might take a couple of days. I stretched my legs and told two other luckless fools that there was nothing here when they pulled in. I tried to remember Shelley's line about the dreadful desert.† I watched some more TV. I read. I considered a nap, and then came a knock on the window.

A man with a head like a walnut shell spoke to me in fast and mostly indecipherable Spanish, but I gathered that his wife, the shopkeeper, had told him about my situation. He was here now with a jerrycan of fuel, enough to get me back to Trelew. He wanted the equivalent of £5 for this lifeline, but I insisted he take £7, all the extra pesos I'd been forced to withdraw when paying my taxi driver a couple of days earlier.

The world was once more full of amazing things.

I stayed in a shithole at the edge of town that night, a bungalow on a broken street where dogs snarled in the shadows and occasional barks echoed around the neighbourhood. It was cheap and the host was pleasant enough, but the next morning I left early to get back down to the penguins at Punta Tombo.

As its non-Spanish name suggests, Trelew was named by Welsh settlers during the same migration of European farmers

---

* Which was a fine distraction – that show is so good that if you want a break from reading to go and watch an episode right now, I will not be offended.

† 'Round the decay of that colossal Wreck, boundless and bare, the lone and level sands stretch far away.'

An Inconvenience of Penguins

that brought Matías Soriano's family to the region. Today the city has a population of just under 100,000 and a one-way road network that is dizzying to the outsider.

I learned this in brutal fashion. Trying to find a coffee shop ahead of my next long drive, I again followed Google Maps a little too closely, favouring it over looking at actual street signs. Suddenly I was driving the wrong way in a one-way system. Moments after I realised my error, an already-battered pick-up truck forced its way past me, tattooing a long, deep scrape down the side of my rubbish rental car before I could react. I got out and shouted impotent profanity after the driver as he sped away, while a woman looked at me through her curtains with irritation.

More than ever, I regretted not taking that cheap insurance at the start of the trip.* How much it would now cost me, I had no idea – the amorphous exchange rates only made it more confusing. Disgusted, head throbbing, I left the city, hoping to never return.

Two hours later I was safely back in penguin habitat. Punta Tombo's Magellanic colony is gargantuan, with an estimated 500,000 resident birds, numbers that are exceptional in part because of human interference – all the sheep farming brought the aggressive persecution of predators and pests. Pumas, foxes, feral dogs – they were all killed and chased away to protect the stock. The fact that the penguins have been able to profit too is coincidental, but they have made the most of their haven. I parked up and hoped to do the same.

---

* Without a police report or the offending driver's details, my own supposedly reassuring policy counted for nothing when I finally attempted to claim on it.

Feathered, Untethered

Joining crowds of visitors on the boardwalks to be among the birds, I felt the nauseating stress of the road begin to dissipate. The sharp tang of guano in the air, the ridiculous donkey noises coming from penguins unseen, the occasional scraps between birds out in the open – it all seemed familiar and safe compared to driving in Argentina.

While I found it relaxing, the penguins once more unearthed a particular type of mania in other visitors. A young couple laid their newborn child on the guano-blasted boardwalk as though making a sacrificial offering to some terrible avian god. A loud American father of three pontificated on the behaviour of *Spheniscus magellanicus* as though he was a wizened field researcher and not a clueless beachball in a Minnesota Vikings hat. Farther along, a young woman with cutlasses for cheekbones and a t-shirt saying I LOVE JESUS took a series of increasingly rictus selfies, only after she'd moved past a sign warning about bird flu. Everyone – including me – lost it when a lumbering guanaco seemed to bend down and have a discreet conversation with one of the Magellanics.

For their part, the penguins went about their business with remarkable calmness. Just like in Simon's Town, South Africa, they were highly habituated and protected by the boardwalks, largely ignoring all mammals, whether hominid, camelid or bovid. As our expensive boots rattled over the wooden surface above them, they didn't raise their little pink eyebrows to look at us.

At one point, I saw a chimango caracara swoop down to snatch a rodent, the raptor aiding its flightless cousins' chicks. The penguins had everything they needed here, and with their evolutionary advantages of having a varied diet, flexible nesting criteria and an ability to forage in both warm and cold water, it seemed that for now there was no existential threat to the Magellanic penguin.

Things felt less certain for me. The following day, I would skid off a road trying to avoid running over two skunks on the way out to the fantastical Península Valdés. I'd fantasised about spending a good amount of time there, but the day lost to the fuel incident meant I had no time to try and spot the globally infamous orcas which beach themselves in pursuit of young sea lions. I also didn't see a single southern right whale, nor any of the elephant seals which also call that remarkable spit of land home.

Instead, I stayed at the cheapest place in the peninsula's only town, a gloomy hovel with a mouldy, almost chewy atmosphere. Its most notable feature was a bath which looked as though it had been used by the mafia for dissolving bodies. I considered getting angry about this situation, but it was hard not to see the funny side too. So many years and so much travel, and yet without the guiding hand of a faceless PR agency, I was an incompetent boob.

Having survived the night, I drove to the 600,000-strong penguin colony at Estancia San Lorenzo and gave a ride to a Belgian hitchhiker with narrow shoulders that suggested an easy birth. The only surprise was that he turned out not to be a dangerous sociopath – unlike the nervous guy with the glasses back at the car rental place, who, when I eventually returned his rubbish car, was alright about the damage but furious when I suggested that the new president might be bad for Argentina.

That was all still to come though; first, I had time with the Magellanic penguins in Punta Tombo. I watched what appeared to be a throuple fall into a bitter physical dispute. I watched a couple sit together so peacefully that it almost looked romantic.

Feathered, Untethered

Five or six birds shared the wreckage of a dead tree, for all the world looking like they were cohabiting in a shabby-chic apartment. At the shoreline, one penguin picked up and dropped pebbles, while its colleagues expertly shot through the surf and played with surging strands of kelp.

Eventually I had to leave. Trudging back to the car, dreading whatever chaos was to come, I saw a Magellanic penguin dart out of the bushes, its face a mess of blood. A deep wound above the eye did not look like it would heal soon, pumping claret as though it had been cut in a title fight. I doubted this warrior would last the day, so I alerted the first ranger I saw and took him to the bird. Deeply unimpressed, the young man stopped just short of shrugging and said, 'He's been fighting. It happens often, he should be OK, but maybe he has learned a lesson or something. Anyway, we are not going to help him.'

There were possibly half a million birds here – of course individual care was out of the question. Anxiety surged in my brain and, panicking, I fist-bumped my own chest twice, offered a peace sign to the penguin, then walked away, embarrassed at having outed myself as another tourist in front of the ranger.

13

A Troubled Kingdom

> The penguins stood for a moment watching the tortured ship, then raised their heads and uttered a series of weird, mournful, dirgelike cries. It was all the more eerie because none of the men – not even the Antarctic veterans among them – had ever before heard penguins voice anything except the most elemental, croaking sorts of noises.
>
> – Alfred Lansing, *Endurance: Shackleton's Incredible Voyage*, 1959

For all the grand proclamations and bombastic statements made throughout his wild life, Sir Ernest Shackleton's final words came during an argument about his alcoholism. Lying aboard the *Quest* in Grytviken Harbour, South Georgia, he tried to shrug off his friend and doctor Alexander Macklin's instructions to be healthier. 'I told him, as I had told him many times before, that he had been overdoing things and that it was no good expecting any single dose of medicine to put it right,' recorded Dr Macklin.

'You're always wanting me to give up things, what is it I ought to give up?' grumbled Shackleton, jowly, exhausted and looking far older than his 47 years.* Outside, blood from Grytviken's whaling station lapped against the *Quest*'s hull.

---

* A couple of years earlier, Shackleton had been described as 'purple and bloated' by Kathleen Scott, the widow of Robert Falcon Scott.

A Troubled Kingdom

'Chiefly alcohol, Boss, I don't think it agrees with you,' answered the doctor. The expedition leader then complained of pain in his chest and expired.

Shackleton's death in 1922 effectively concluded the Heroic Age of Antarctic Exploration, though it might be reasonably argued that it had ended several years earlier, when he'd crawled back here at the end of his famously disastrous Imperial Trans-Antarctic Expedition in 1916.

That third and most calamitous of four missions south had begun in 1914 when he spent a month in Grytviken for a final resupply before a big push to Antarctica. Having missed out on the South Pole, he hoped to lead the first party to cross the continent. The grizzled Norwegians working in the South Georgian whaling station advised him against it, insisting that the ice in the Weddell Sea was particularly unforgiving that year. Shackleton, no doubt under pressure to satisfy his backers and his own ego, ignored them and charged south anyway.

What happened next is perhaps the most retold story of the Heroic Age. A few weeks after entering Antarctic waters, his ship, *Endurance*, was – as the Norwegians predicted – trapped in sea ice. There she was held for nine grinding months before being crushed and sunk. Shackleton then led the men across sea ice for over five months, marching and camping in sensational discomfort as they dragged three lifeboats with them. Eventually they were able to sail these to Elephant Island, where they made another camp at what became known as Point Wild. After some modification to its hull, Shackleton and five others sailed one of *Endurance*'s lifeboats – the *James Caird* – on what appeared to be a suicide mission all the way back to South Georgia.

An Inconvenience of Penguins

After 17 nightmarish days at sea, they crashed on to the shores of the main island where, finally, Shackleton selected the two least dead men left in the party – Tom Crean and Frank Worsley – to hike with him over mountains and glaciers to Stromness, another Norwegian whaling station. After 30 hours, this 'trio of terrible scarecrows' raised the alarm, then with the help of the whalers found the energy to rescue the three men stuck on the other side of South Georgia.* Many weeks later, on the *Yelcho*, a ship Shackleton bartered in South America, the party of 22 on Elephant Island was also saved.†

No one died under The Boss's direct command, though three were lost on the other side of Antarctica while laying depots for the crossing that never happened. Thus ended what Sir Ernest described as his 'White Warfare of the South'.

By the time of his final mission in 1922, Shackleton was in no state to be attempting another Antarctic voyage. As the writer Hugh Robert Mill put it: 'The polar regions are fitted only for the efforts of young men in the zenith of their strength, the only possible exceptions being tough old whalers who have never had time to be softened by so much as a summer at home.' By contrast, the withered Shackleton was more like a terminally ill cruise passenger who books themselves on a long voyage knowing they won't come home alive.

Today he is buried in Grytviken in a small cemetery a few hundred metres from where he died on board the *Quest*. 'Ernest

---

* Literally unrecognisable, The Boss famously reintroduced himself with the immortal line: 'My name is Shackleton.'

† The bow of the *Yelcho* is today located at the harbour in Punta Arenas, with a little plaque telling you that like many of the best ships of the day, it was made in Scotland.

A Troubled Kingdom

Henry Shackleton, Explorer' – so reads a surprisingly humble inscription on the looming granite monolith which stands above his grave, and above all his neighbours. The inferior headstones mostly belong to Norwegian whalers, men who died while going about their bloody business in this same harbour.

There are two exceptions. One is a simple white cross for the Argentinian submarine officer Felix Artuso, who was executed while a prisoner of war during the Falklands conflict by a panicking Royal Marine. The other is a plaque for Frank Wild, Shackleton's right-hand man and latterly another committed alcoholic, who died in relative obscurity in South Africa in 1939 but was reinterred here in 2011. One of just two men to have been awarded a Polar Medal with four bars, few explorers achieved or endured more than Wild, a gnarled Yorkshireman who kept the men of the *Endurance* alive on Elephant Island while Shackleton hurried around South America, searching for a ship to rescue them. Like his expedition leader, Wild's marker faces south towards Antarctica.

After the travails of Argentina, I was safely back on the *Greg Mortimer* and having spent Christmas and New Year on board in Antarctica, we had reached South Georgia in the early days of January 2024. This was my fifth time in Grytviken and so fifth time at Shackleton's plot. I had visited no other grave this many times – not even my wee gran. By contrast I was becoming a loyalty card holder in South Georgia. I wondered what I'd get for my tenth visit.

Almost every visiting tourist comes to pay respects and take selfies by the graves, then inevitably partakes in an earnest toast to Ernest, a little bit of theatre led by one of the expedition team. For some it offers a dim connection to Shackleton's deeds, but many in attendance choose not to have their nip of whisky, and instead pour it over the dead.* Poor Shackleton. Poor Wild. Even in the afterlife they can't escape the firewater.

When the cruise ships aren't in port, King penguins occasionally bumble up to the site, standing outside the little picket fence, wondering what all the fuss is about. Shackleton saw ancestors of these birds when he came to South Georgia, though it's unlikely he would have seen many around Grytviken, not during those final days in 1922, nor earlier when the *Endurance* expedition found its bookends here. At that point in the island's history, the birds, along with every species of seal and whale, were being harvested en masse.

In those years Grytviken was in full gory flow as one of South Georgia's seven whaling stations. King penguins were easily caught and killed, their oil used to start the greedy cauldrons in which blubber from elephant seals and whales were boiled down.†

Alongside the reeking machinery, there was a church, a coffee roastery and a general store which sold, among other things, perfume. While *Endurance* and other ships sailed laden with improbable quantities of booze, the Norwegians ran a dry station. There were some illegal stills, but the unhappiest whalers were known to buy and drink bottles of fragrance in the hope of feeling something – or perhaps feeling less – while the whales were being sliced up around them.

---

* Being Scottish, I am often handed unwanted drams too. Going to Shackleton's grave can sometimes feel like visiting a themed bar.

† Their killers were mostly Norwegians, including those who presumably resisted telling Shackleton, 'We told you the ice was bad,' in 1916.

A Troubled Kingdom

English-language descriptions of South Georgia at that time are as rich as they are repugnant. Writing Shackleton's obituary, the *Endurance* veteran George Marston described being plagued by the stench of dead cetaceans. 'There was no escaping it. In the bay dead whales floated, on the shore their carcasses rotted, and the beach was thick with their bleaching bones. We breathed the smell of whale day and night and fed on whale meat in company with the dogs.'

From 1904 to 1966, around 175,000 whales were caught, killed and processed around South Georgia. It's hard to fathom a massacre of that scale, especially when seeing the gallons of blood shed by just a single humpback in a recording by film-maker Charles Swithinbank from the late 1940s. The footage is grainy and monochrome, and considering its content that is a mercy. What the filmmaker calls 'the peeling' sees whales taken apart like cars during industrial disassembly. Scrap is discarded. Usable parts salvaged. Swithinbank's tone is disaffected – he shot the footage in his early 20s, then recorded some narration as a much older, wearier man. 'The stink is terrific, but after a couple of days you don't notice it,' he says at one point as a wet, suppurating mass is hooked and dragged across a deck, and bones are carved with steam-powered saws by men wearing flat-caps, dungarees and gore.

There has never been much subtlety on South Georgia, nothing gentle in its character. Lying 1,500km east of the Falklands, it is a destination for people who prefer to be beaten around the head with sensory experience, those who prefer spicy food and listen to heavy metal. It has the discretion of a headbutt, and if you forced me to choose, I'd visit South Georgia ahead of even Antarctica.

An Inconvenience of Penguins

The scenery is outrageous, appearing like a mountain range floating in the sea. Around 160km long, it stacks peaks beyond peaks and weaves glaciers with sheer-sided fjords. Millions of animals breed here, their numbers increasing, their habitat protected. It is perhaps the most hopeful place on Earth – as David Attenborough says in the South Georgia government's official visitor guide, the archipelago is 'a global rarity, an ecosystem in recovery'. From an era when several species were almost being hunted to extinction, it is now home to the greatest concentration of marine mammals and seabirds anywhere and is, for many polar travellers, the most astounding place on the planet.

During my first visit in 2015, we arrived at Salisbury Plain in a murky dawn. A ginormous King penguin colony lay ahead, hundreds of thousands of birds shimmering black, white and gold in the morning light. Some people were reduced to tears by this spectacle, while others stood stunned and unsure what to do with their cameras. There was too much information to process.

A group of birders, meanwhile, sauntered off away from the dazzling regents. I shouted after them, asking what was the matter, and they explained that they'd seen the penguins and were instead off in search of the South Georgia pipit, the world's southernmost songbird. This, they assured me, was a far rarer prize than the audience with the Kings. *How strange*, I thought, *that anyone could care so much about birds.*[*]

Two hours later, they returned having failed to spot a pipit. They hadn't even heard one.

That was before the completion of South Georgia's rat eradication project, a vast, quasi-military operation that used the island's glaciers to section off the rodents and bombard

---

[*] I know, I know.

A Troubled Kingdom

them with poison from the air. The New Zealand team in charge calculated doses that would act slowly, hopefully allowing the rats to return to burrows and die underground. If they fell in the open, birds – particularly the ever-ravenous skuas and giant petrels – would scavenge them and become collateral. The conservationists knew some of this was unavoidable, but they didn't want those newly deceased birds to also be eaten and the toxins to move another step up the food chain.

Hundreds, perhaps thousands, of scavengers died, but so did all of the rats, providing protection for the 65 million birds which breed on the island. It was declared a success in 2017. Visit today and you can see pipits at almost every landing site, their mellifluous warble sounding all the sweeter when knowing how close it came to being permanently muted.

The South Georgian pintail duck has similarly surged back since the vermin were eradicated.[*] Whales have started to return in significant numbers since their hunting stopped too. Yet nothing has rebounded with quite such force as the Antarctic fur seal, which was shot, stabbed and clubbed down to just a few thousand individuals but has come back to such an extent that they are pushing out other species. The total number of individuals is now thought to exceed 6 million, which fossil records suggest is a historic high. Such is the extent of their comeback that their abundance has closed certain landing sites to human visitation, a very small piece of revenge against their former persecutors.[†]

---

[*] In times of need the pintail will also scavenge from carcasses, making it the world's only meat-eating duck.

[†] And yet for all that, I despise the Antarctic fur seal, a snarling, snapping bully, one of which I am quite certain will someday bite me and leave me screaming on a stinking beach.

An Inconvenience of Penguins

King penguins have similarly resurged, another species showing what can happen when mankind leaves it alone, or even provides a little assistance. Today the birds are found all around South Georgia – at almost every spot where there is flat land, there are Kings. As glaciers have died away in places like St Andrews Bay, the penguins have nested on the newly open ground. The colony there could now have as many as 500,000 individuals, making it the largest in the world.

When the butchers came in the late 1800s, they seemed not to notice the mesmeric beauty of these birds, instead looking at them as nothing more than an easy-access resource. The whalers didn't fall for the turmeric colouring on their heads, nor the flawless sunset gradient on their throats, nor the intense satsuma shading of their beaks. An adult King has around 200,000 feathers, and watching them preen it seems they know the exact location of every single one. Still, none of the old murderers seemed impressed by their courtship dances, by their amazing grace.

And yet the birds did make some kind of impression. By the late 1930s, Norwegians were attempting to bring King penguins to the Lofoten Islands off their northern coast. Whalers captured them in South Georgia, then transported the poor animals over 14,000km north to the Arctic. An initial 1936 bid to make the highly adapted King penguin a European bird was always doomed, but this polar imperialism was followed by another Norwegian attempt in 1938 with a similar introduction of African and Macaroni penguins. According to the academic Peder Roberts, 'The process of becoming indigenous was culturally rather than ecologically mediated, the penguins becoming Norwegian through sponsored residency rather than birthright.'

A Troubled Kingdom

It might have been idolisation that brought the penguins north, but every one of them eventually died. Sightings continued through the 1940s, but the birds never settled. Roberts again:

> The greatest resistance to their presence seems to have come from residents of northern Norway, many of whom were entirely unaware of what a penguin was. This was worst for the Finnmark penguins, two of whom were killed by locals who in both cases apparently 'thought it was the Devil himself' they saw.

Today Norwegians have not quite abandoned their European penguin project, though mercifully they are mostly focused on a single bird in Scotland. Sir Nils Olav III, Baron of the Bouvet Islands, resides in Edinburgh Zoo and grants audiences with the public every day.* In 2023 he was promoted from brigadier to Major General of the King's Guard, giving him the third highest rank in the Norwegian forces. Nils Olav also happens to be a King penguin, the third since 1972 to be militarily honoured by the Scandinavians.†

As ridiculous as that captive animal's adoration is, it's surely understandable that ordinarily sensible modern minds have been dazzled and distracted by the King. Of all penguin species, these are the most beautiful – more abundant, accessible and colourful than even the mighty Emperors. Even when they return from sea, packed from beak to tail with lanternfish,

---

* When I visited, there were two other Kings wandering around too, largely being ignored.

† The Vikings would surely have deemed all this pantomime a maritime disgrace.

they carry themselves with dignity, marching in neat lines, their heads bobbing left and right just above their bloated bellies. Rarely covered in the guano of their neighbours, they appear to be proud birds, haughty, and only hilarious when they choose to be. Their clarion call is performed with solemn theatricality, their beautiful heads thrown back, their spines pointing perfectly skywards as they trumpet proudly across their mad avian cities.

Their chicks are less regal. While their close cousins, the Emperors, have been blessed and cursed with some of nature's most irresistible offspring, the King instead hatches a whistling brown monster. Many people compare them to an upright kiwi fruit, but to me they look like flashers in fur coats, ready to expose themselves to any unfortunate passer-by. It's a good thing this is a temporary look; their eventual transformation from disgraceful wretch to glamorous royalty is surely among the most spectacular and unlikely anywhere in the animal kingdom.

*

In late 2023, industrial death returned to South Georgia, another man-made holocaust. Highly pathogenic avian flu has ricocheted around the globe since emerging from a Chinese poultry farm in 1996. Over the decades its evolutions and mutations have periodically caught the public attention, but in a world scarred by Covid-19, it faded to be something less significant. A disease affecting birds is comparatively uninteresting compared to a planet-pausing pandemic.

And yet it has continued to do its deadly work, with an especially lethal strain tearing through bird populations in the northern hemisphere in the early 2020s. Inexorably it moved south, and by the time I started guiding in 2022, expedition

A Troubled Kingdom

cruise ships were being asked to look out for any suspected signs that the disease had jumped across the South Seas. This seemed inevitable but deeply concerning given in South America it had been transmitted from birds to mammals and was severely affecting seal populations along the Argentinian coast. In my first guiding season we saw no trace of the disease, but by the austral spring of 2023, migratory birds had brought it to South Georgia, where its tentacles slid around the island, then squeezed and squeezed.

A few months later we were searching for it everywhere. On the Antarctic Peninsula, we spent half an hour before each landing looking out for signs of illness but saw nothing beyond a couple of possibly listless penguins. Other symptoms included 'lack of coordination' and 'erratic behaviour', but picking them out from ordinary penguinisms was impossible.

On South Georgia it started slowly, first presenting in Antarctic skuas. Given their habit of rummaging in the ribcages of any dead or moribund thing, it was no surprise that these screaming brigands became vectors of disease. In November 2023, as the first cruise ships arrived, it fell to expedition staff to observe and report signs of the illness to the South Georgia government. Based on those reports, authorities started to close sites around the archipelago.

Naturalist Elena Wimberger was on those early ships and bore witness to the ravages of avian flu. We worked together on the *Greg Mortimer*, but her season had started months earlier. She was part of the first expedition teams that had to scout their landings, looking for signs of the illness. Only if it was clear could they begin taking passengers ashore.

However, while the death of birds made headlines in the northern hemisphere, on South Georgia the most harrowing and obvious fatalities were those of the pinnipeds. Elena and her team were met with mass mortality events, not with penguins but mammals, the likes of which hadn't been seen since the unforgiving days of the sealing and whaling enterprises.

'We got to Jason Harbour, fully expecting to go on shore,' she told me. 'We started our scout and I thought there were logs rolling on the beach, but we got closer and saw that there was mass mortality of elephant seal pups. There must have been 30 or 40 of them already dead and others that couldn't breathe properly and were losing energy. Essentially, we were watching them drown.'

Site by site, the island began to shut down, and as the season rolled on, visitors were given fewer and fewer options for landings. The death of the pups was upsetting, but when the adult elephant seals started dying, even experienced expedition staff had their stomachs turned. By the time we got there in January 2024, the fatalities had stopped, but the remains had only just begun their slow decomposition.

When I got back to Gold Harbour it was my first time since that transcendent pre-Covid afternoon in early 2020. It remained a beauty, even from afar, but while the glacier still hung above and the mountains stretched infinitely beyond, we were no longer permitted to land. Authorities in Grytviken had closed the site, meaning we would be restricted to Zodiac-cruising along its teeming shore.

On the northern part of the beach, close to where passengers would land in an ordinary year, a near-permanent population of elephant seals hauled out, flatulent and fabulous at all times of day. Massed together, these great foetid piles of meat have a hilarious habit of accidentally annoying each other. Sea-salt deposits in their prodigious noses cause a sort of facial farting, which in turn makes their blubbery bodies shake. However, so tightly are they grouped together that each sneeze sends a jiggle through the row like a Mexican wave, finally irritating and usually waking the last seal – which then duly savages his bedfellow for the disturbance, sending another aggravating vibration back down the line.

Watching this from a distance, I couldn't help thinking the boat tour was obviously an inferior way to experience the place, but it was better than nothing. Throughout the cruise we had briefed passengers on the dreadfulness of avian flu, about how despite the name it had been much worse for seals, and about measures to mitigate its spread.[*] Some had been sceptical about this, if not about the disease more generally. From afar, they could see the penguins were fine. This was undoubtedly a relief, we said, but it was the seals we were worried about.

What we saw that misty afternoon removed any doubt over the existence of catastrophe. The calm grey sea lapped against the beach, a gentle high tide which allowed us to push into a little-visited lagoon in our Zodiacs. Prior to navigating the narrow channels, scout boats had told us to prepare passengers and ourselves for what we'd see.

From the water, the dark shapes of the elephants were clearly visible, no longer huddled but a disparate guard of cadavers lining the shore on the way into the lagoon. Many of the carcasses were blistered and bloating, others collapsing. These giant seals, the planet's largest pinnipeds, had dragged themselves on to land to die. Now their flesh hung loose and raw, calling to mind photographs I'd seen in museums in

---

[*] Disinfecting gear, not putting anything but boots on the ground, maintaining distances from animals and so on.

An Inconvenience of Penguins

Hiroshima and Nagasaki. Other victims rolled up and down in the surf, many headless, others having lost their huge eyes to scavengers or the deep.

The southern elephant seal is the third-deepest-diving mammal, with only Cuvier's beaked whale and the sperm whale capable of reaching greater profundities. Down there, over 2,000m below the surface, the seal's body is crushed by extraordinary pressures, its massive eyes working hard to locate prey that's made the evolutionary misstep of being bioluminescent. These animals forage deep beyond the realm of reliable human study, but avian flu seems to hinder their enormous lung function just enough to be fatal. This vulnerability only reveals itself when they come back to the surface, dead or dying.

At Gold Harbour, King penguins simply marched past their fallen neighbours, occasionally stopping for some half-interested rubbernecking. An atrocious wind of putrefaction blew across my favourite place in the world, and as I swallowed my own vomit, I felt a deep relief that those beautiful regents had so far escaped this apocalypse.

At home, newspapers had spent weeks publishing articles about the disease circling Antarctica. Much of the reporting sat at an intersection of hysteria, sensationalism and inaccuracy. South Georgia was said to be in Antarctica, which it is not. King penguins were described as Antarctic birds, which they are not. Stories were illustrated with photos of Royal penguins, which reside in Oceania, the one corner of the world bird flu was yet to reach. Website after website, newspaper after newspaper misread and misreported the situation, always focusing on the unharmed penguins. While I understood as well as anyone that my beloved birds make fine clickbait, my heart was broken for

A Troubled Kingdom

the thousands and thousands of seals lying there unnoticed and unmourned.

The passengers in my Zodiac were struck dumb by what they saw. While the penguins were a welcome distraction, there was no ignoring the plight of our fellow mammals. One lady, a chatty American who'd had her heart set on seeing one of South Georgia's King penguin mega-colonies, said solemnly, 'They should close this whole island.'

In the early part of the last century, before raggedy old Shackleton came here, a young Robert Cushman Murphy was in South Georgia to conduct studies of seabirds for the American Museum of Natural History and the Brooklyn Museum. His only way of travelling to the island was aboard the *Daisy*, a rotten little whaling ship. Despite his method of transport, Murphy was able to create detailed volumes of work on the archipelago's seabirds, the first and most detailed study of the region. Throughout he also kept an extensive diary for his new wife, later published under the title *Logbook for Grace*.

Though just 25 when he sailed, the young New Yorker's writing is as poetic as it is detailed, and as insightful as it is harrowing. Everything was new to him, but he quickly saw that penguins were creatures of pure instinct:

> Devoid of the convolutions in the brain and of the gray matter by which man sets so much store, they rely, like bees or ants, upon their heritage of instinctive behaviour, and are certainly capable of very little thinking. Almost inevitably they exercise more than Chinese tenacity in clinging to the ways of their ancestors, even when repeated experience should have taught them better.

An Inconvenience of Penguins

He was also a man of empathy. Murphy suffered through an entire year with the crew on board the *Daisy* and spent long hours pleading with her crew to save him samples, or at least allow him to make measurements of their quarry before they underwent the peeling. This was true of the whales, but equally true of the elephant seals, which he watched be slaughtered with inexplicable bloodlust.*

If he were alive today, the scientist would doubtless have been as horrified by the beaches of South Georgia in 2023–24 as he was in that ugly summer of 1912–13 – at least with the awful fate of the elephant seals. And yet witnessing it, Murphy would have perhaps understood something that he'd seen during his own visit. On one of his long walks away from the *Daisy*, the naturalist seemed to discover a mass mortality event of his own, a penguin graveyard which is impossible to explain if not the result of another disease:

> By hundreds, possibly by thousands, they lay all over the bed of the cold tarn, flippers outstretched and breasts reflecting blurred gleams of white. Safe at last from sea leopards in the ocean, and from skuas ashore, they took their endless rest; for decades, perhaps for centuries, the slumberers would undergo no change in their frigid tomb.

By the end of the season, even South Georgia's most famous grave had fallen victim to bird flu. After months of allowing visitors to take the short march from the shore to the Grytviken cemetery, the local government decided there were

---

* 'I very much regret that these creatures are not likely to be there long because the gang will probably soon shed their blood and leave them as hideous stripped carcasses to undergo slow rotting in the cold.'

A Troubled Kingdom

just too many dead seals to allow people to walk through them. Shackleton, Wild, Artuso and all those Norwegians would be left to rest in peace for the first time since the last pandemic.

14

All at Sea

> I had to silently creep up on each cliché* following the sounds of their chirping, take a head count, then move on without them being aware of my presence. Several clichés were alerted by the adults and scurried off under rocks; I had to poke amongst them with a stick to get them counted.
>
> – Conrad Glass, *Rockhopper Copper*, 2005

There had been murder at Edinburgh Zoo, a lone female killed in the dark. In August 2022, during the height of the Scottish capital's tourist season, a red fox broke into the historic penguin enclosure and slaughtered an old Northern Rockhopper. Reviewing CCTV footage the following day, keepers watched in horror as the isolated penguin was beheaded.† Adding unnecessary insult to unmendable injury, the fox then triumphantly shat on the ground and left. The staff had no idea how it had got in – there was no record of anything like this happening in the 108 years penguins had been at the zoo.

Her name was Mrs Wolowitz and she was artificially ancient

---

* The collective noun for baby penguins is, in fact, a crèche.

† The fox seemed not to want to consume the bird, which considering the disgusting things foxes do eat is a damning verdict on the flavour of penguin flesh.

All at Sea

when killed.* Captive penguins are fed precisely in Edinburgh Zoo, their vitals closely monitored. If a bird shows a vitamin deficiency, it is given a supplement. Their weight, diet and fertility are carefully studied. With this upsetting exception, they are protected from predators. In short, most of the trials they face in the wild do not apply here and so Mrs Wolowitz had lived on and on.

Thatcher and Reagan were in power when she was born at the zoo. The Soviet Union still existed. You could smoke on planes. At 35, she was almost double the age she would have been expected to reach naturally. She was so old she outlived her son, so old she had cataracts. It was probably this blindness that led her away from her rookery and into the jaws of the fox.

The dozen or so surviving Northern Rockhoppers seemed not to mourn the passing of their matriarch, but then penguins rarely seem depressed about anything. The keepers, on the other hand, were distraught and embarrassed. When I spoke to them, I didn't have the heart to bring up potential negligence – they had lost a grandmother and, to some, a friend. They were quick to admit that this venerable and cherished penguin deserved better.

I wish I could say that was that: I had ticked Northern Rockhoppers off the list and no further work would be required. But captive birds of course do not count for my purposes. As the number of birds still to see decreased, the complications with getting to them rose exponentially. Most of the penguins I've described so far line Antarctic tourist routes or live near human

---

* She had been named after a character in *The Big Bang Theory* who lives with her son; Mrs Wolowitz (the penguin) and her son once raised a donor egg together.

populations. The missing ones would be novel, distant and – with the exception of the Little penguin – only reachable via rare voyages that would depend on luck as much as planning. My guiding work would no longer be helpful. Instead, I would have to lean heavily on my travel-writing crutch once more and hope it still held me up.

For the Northern Rockhoppers, I would have to make a long and profoundly inconvenient trip to Tristan da Cunha in the South Atlantic, almost 3,000km from any mainland. The most remote inhabited place on the planet, its village capital has the excellent name Edinburgh of the Seven Seas, a link that apparently justifies some of the birds being kidnapped to live in a zoo in Scotland. But this Edinburgh could not be swapped for that one, and so I began to make plans.

If you're hoping to see all the world's penguin species, there is good and bad news. The good news is that the extraordinary voyages required will take you from the glittering Galapagos to the epic shores of Patagonia, from the rough-hewn coast of South Africa to sunny cities in Australia. You must also, of course, go to Antarctica – probably more than once.

The bad news is that you will also need to visit Tristan da Cunha.

This is not to say there is something inherently dreadful about this extremely distant British Overseas Territory but rather speaks to the conundrum of just how to get there. After the African penguin, the Northern Rockhopper is the species geographically closest to the UK, but any journey to reach them is exceptionally convoluted.

Located close to the exact centre of the South Atlantic, this loosely linked archipelago lies halfway between Rio de Janeiro,

All at Sea

Brazil, and Cape Town, South Africa. There are four main islands: Gough, Nightingale, Inaccessible and the eponymous Tristan da Cunha. It has no airstrip, and though its resupply vessels offer limited berths on their slow, often brutal six-day sailings from Cape Town, they are usually taken by islanders coming and going from their community. I spent a year trying to get a space and ultimately failed.

A handful of committed maniacs sail yachts out there each year, braving the enormous unpredictability of the open ocean for weeks at a time. For normal people, the only logical option is to visit on a cruise ship. However, even if you indulge this comparative luxury, there is a 40–50 per cent chance your vessel will not be able to operate in the rough swell that commonly wraps itself around the islands.

Naturally I left this uncertainty out of pitches as I hawked a story of my trip to various newspapers. When I got a bite, I knew most cruise companies would likely host me. Only a handful visit Tristan at the end of the Antarctic seasons, briefly stopping as they reposition to the Arctic via the west coast of Africa, but like Ponant's atypical semi-circumnavigation of Antarctica, this one-way trip was unlikely to be popular with paying passengers. I knew there would be space on board if I could get a commission and generate some decent coverage.

Polar Latitudes wanted me on their ship, but they wouldn't get to Tristan until the end of March. The island's Director of Conservation, Trevor Glass, told me over email that the Northern Rockhoppers would have already left for sea by then, or would be finishing their seasonal moults.[*] The Polar Latitudes

---

[*] The Glass family have been on Tristan since it first became British in the 1800s.

An Inconvenience of Penguins

route would also take over 30 days and ultimately offer no guarantee of seeing any penguins, so I had to decline.

Leaving earlier and travelling for just 21 days, Swan Hellenic's *Vega* offered a shorter, more sensible option. The timing was right, the ship was new, and so shorn of a viable alternative, I sent the necessary emails to secure a berth.

Back in Ushuaia for the fourth time in three months, I swiftly boarded alongside just a handful of other passengers. With occupancy only around 25 per cent, Swan Hellenic would doubtless have been losing fistfuls of money, but the ship had to get to Africa anyway, so being a quarter full was perhaps better than nothing.

The itinerary would take us on a colossal detour to the Antarctic Peninsula, then South Georgia, and finally Tristan da Cunha, where the expedition's management planned to spend just two days. The Northern Rockhoppers live almost exclusively on that archipelago, with a few nesting pairs also found on a couple of subantarctic French islands.[*] Their global population is thought to have declined by 90 per cent since the 1950s, making them another species that is precipitously endangered.

My entire three-week trip would depend on successful operations at Tristan. The schedule said we planned to spend just one afternoon at Gough Island, then a morning on the main island of Tristan da Cunha. It wasn't much, but I had no other choice. In the meantime, I could simply be a passenger on the ship – I'd already spent seven weeks that season working as a

---

[*] Though not according to the 2007 animation *Surf's Up*, in which Northern Rockhoppers reside in Shiverpool, Antarctica, and take part in surfing competitions in what might be Hawaii.

All at Sea

guide on the Antarctic Peninsula and South Georgia, and had all the field research I needed with the penguins there.

In truth, it wasn't a great time to visit Antarctica anyway. Every tour company insists that late-season visits are worthwhile, but that is partly to mitigate losses before their ships reposition. When we arrived at the Peninsula after a surprisingly smooth crossing of the Drake Passage, we found it in a shabby state of disrepair. At several sites, Gentoo colonies had shat away virtually all the snow, leaving behind combinations of old guano, mud and blooming algae that resembled Jackson Pollock paintings.

The physics of their prodigious defecation have been carefully studied, with scientific papers dedicated to finding out just how much force penguins must generate to propel their shit horizontally out of their nests.* Short answer is: a lot. In the austral spring, mass excretion events are useful to the birds as they melt snow, allowing the dark rock underneath to attract more heat, a combination that provides enough bare ground on which the penguins can lay an egg. Now in autumn, the penguins had rendered the world's last pristine place a dung heap.

At the shore, juvenile birds were convincing themselves it would be a good idea to spend the next few months at sea. While they dithered, leopard seals patrolled the shallow water, offering the young birds the chance of a short, sharp swimming lesson.

Some humpbacks also lingered, but many had already turned north. Still, despite only having a couple of days on the

---

* Meyer-Rochow, V. B. & Gal, J. (2003). Pressures produced when penguins pooh – calculations on avian defaecation. *Polar Biology*, 27(1), 56–8.

An Inconvenience of Penguins

Peninsula, we spotted straggler Chinstraps and Adélies, completing the brushtailed penguin hat trick. They were all long crossed off my list, of course, but for some of the passengers on the *Vega* this was the first time they'd ever seen penguins, and there was joy to be had in watching their delight. There was happiness too in the reduced shipping traffic – like other migratory species, much of the polar armada had already left Antarctica for the season.

Two and a half days later we were in South Georgia. Things were also winding down there, and the staff at Grytviken were finally getting ready to go home after a hectic, harrowing six-month season. Access to Shackleton's grave had not long been suspended because of the number of dead seals lining the way, all killed by avian flu. For months, the staff had watched pinniped bodies pile up around them.

Three of the women working at the Grytviken Museum and post office happened to be Scottish. Two of them were happy to be leaving, but the third, a ten-year veteran, said, 'Nah, I love it here, but I'll be back in six months, so it's not so bad.' Given that her employer, the South Georgia Heritage Trust, is based in Dundee, I well understood her reluctance to head north.*

In general, though, South Georgia seemed a lot more hopeful than it had when in the tightest grips of disease. The gigantic elephant seal carcasses were gone, and over the three days we spent around the island, I didn't see a single dead bird. There were one or two rotting fur seals, but with such a huge population these days, a long list of things other than disease could have been responsible for their demise.

---

* Honestly, you should hear the daft Dundonian accent.

All at Sea

One afternoon we had a Zodiac cruise in the company of some competitive Gentoos. They played an endless king-of-the-castle game with a rolling iceberg, with no bird able to conquer it for more than a few seconds before slipping off or being pushed aside by another shooting out of the water. Their big feet gripped as best they could, but as soon as any penguin tried to stand tall, it tumbled back in. A New Zealander with smiling eyes sitting next to me laughed so much I worried she might fall in with them. Minutes later, people squealed with glee when they saw Macaronis queuing to apparently take freshwater showers in a trickling waterfall. All day minds were blown like fireworks.

On the last morning, we cruised the mighty shores of St Andrew's Bay, King penguins seeming to cover every grain of sand. The sun shone – really shone with warmth – ricocheting off a fleet of icebergs in one direction, theatrically illuminating the regents in another. The backdrop was a dreamscape of mountains and glaciers, with only a handful of unconvincing clouds above, drifting as though they'd been emitted from a delicate shisha pipe.

It was one of the most spectacular mornings I've had in the polar regions – or anywhere – and yet a horrible, squirming part of my brain whispered: *There isn't a single Northern Rockhopper here and this is all irrelevant.*

Days at sea awaited, as did a particular type of paranoia I've never previously experienced in the Southern Ocean: what if this was all a waste of time? I wanted to ignore it, but with no control over the expedition, I realised how much success mattered to me – I not so much wanted as needed to see the novel penguins. They were wild, often disgusting animals, creatures

An Inconvenience of Penguins

that I respected more than I loved, but now 14 deep into a list of 18, the completist in me was chasing victory. The time and money being sunk into the project were beginning to become unmanageable; if I missed a penguin and had to repeat any of these voyages, the chances of being able to return to any sort of old career would dwindle even further.

From South Georgia we had five days of sailing to reach Tristan, plenty of time to fret about the conditions when we got there. Like most modern cruise ships, the *Vega* had Wi-Fi; like most modern cruise ships, part of me wished it didn't. I broke every promise to myself not to check Windy, that most reliable weather app, or CruiseMapper, on which I could ogle a ship several days ahead of us, sailing in the same direction.

Nauseatingly the *Silver Cloud* hopped around the archipelago without any issues, stopping at Gough, Inaccessible, Nightingale and the main island of Tristan.* A hundred people got ashore at Edinburgh of the Seven Seas, making a mockery of the islands' truculent reputation. It was hard not to be envious from this god's-eye view, and had I been on Mount Olympus I'd have given Poseidon a nudge to make bother for them. Meanwhile, for us TDC remained very much TBC.

Away from the screens there was only water – or almost only water. A day out from South Georgia we passed the iceberg unromantically christened D28, but also known as the Molar Berg owing to its uncannily dental shape. Despite floating for five years and having travelled 4,000km from its birth site on the far side of east Antarctica, this behemoth remained one of the world's largest icebergs, over 55km long and 33km wide, weighing somewhere in the region of 150 billion tonnes. Even

---

* This was a ship on which I hadn't been able to negotiate a berth.

All at Sea

after all its time spent degrading, it still appeared as huge as land. Ice rubble bobbed around in the sea while freezing exhalations flew out from its crumbling cliffs as the South Atlantic gnawed away.

Soon the ocean warmed up and flattened out. We were at uncommon, iceless latitudes now, and while naturalists kept eyes out for rare cetaceans, I settled down to read more about our destination. One of the few resources available was a diary by Katherine Mary Barrow, written in the early 1900s when she spent three years on the island as a visiting clergyman's wife.

Being a diary, much of her prose is arid and uninteresting, but it's nonetheless an insight into the challenges and privations of life on Tristan more than a century ago. There are stories of desperate trade with passing ships, of crop blights and livestock calamities, of lunatic weather and even more dangerous gossip. It is an account of want and tedium.*

'People who have left the island still own cattle and sheep here, which ought not to be allowed, because there is not enough grazing ground for the cattle of the residents,' wrote Barrow on 23 July 1906 as milk supplies dried up. 'It is too painful to see the cattle, they are so emaciated, and their back legs seem hardly able to support their bodies.'

Inevitably, penguins get a mention in the diary too. The islanders had long harvested the eggs, meat and hides, which was understandable given how difficult life was in the world's most remote community. Still, Barrow seemed conflicted by the harvest, in one entry stating that it was a 'great help in the daily menu', while in another fretting about overconsumption.

---

* When I described this to an islander who was leaving to never return, he said, 'Truthfully, not very much has changed.'

An Inconvenience of Penguins

When on a Monday in September 1906 she was sent around 70 eggs, she recorded that she wished 'they did not take them in quite such a wholesale way'.

The Northern Rockhoppers also appear, at once delighting and disappointing the diarist:

> It is a most droll bird in appearance and has a yellow and black topknot which it raises when excited. It walks very erect – if walk it can be called – sometimes jumping like a man in a sack, and sometimes waddling like a bow-legged child . . . This is the bird from which the people extract the oil which they generally burn, but it gives a very feeble light.

Tell people you're going to Tristan da Cunha today, and you can expect looks that hover somewhere between pity and confusion. Its very Portuguese name is unhelpful, as is the enormousness of the surrounding Atlantic Ocean, which renders it invisible on many maps. For all anyone knows, islanders might still burn penguins as a light source. Ignorance is almost universal, even among experienced travel writers.

In case that also applies to you, here are some things you should know about Tristan da Cunha: it was discovered uninhabited by the similarly named Portuguese explorer Tristão da Cunha in 1506; for the next 300 years it was used mostly as a pit stop for colonial fleets from France, Holland and eventually Britain, which annexed it in 1816 and has reluctantly held on ever since. This followed a brief folly by the enterprising American Jonathan Lambert, who renamed the archipelago the Islands of Refreshment, over which he had 'absolute possession . . . solely for myself and for my heirs forever'. He spent five unhappy months there enduring miserable conditions and

All at Sea

murdering elephant seals before pathetically drowning in a fishing accident. Then, as now, everyone lived on the main island of Tristan, an active volcano appearing to float in the sea. At 2,062m, its summit is over 700m higher than Ben Nevis, the tallest mountain in the UK. In its shadow, just 250 souls live in Edinburgh of the Seven Seas, the islands' only settlement. This is trending down, though nowhere near as low as in Katherine Mary Barrow's day, when the British government pleaded with the then 80 residents to abandon the islands altogether. They refused.

On board the *Vega*, days passed slowly. With so much downtime and so few distractions, it grew hard to ignore personalities on the ship, even when I wanted to. In lieu of scheduled stimulation, gossip papered the walls of every deck. Alongside the increasingly bored passengers, the expedition team seemed disjointed, frustrated and moreover fatigued. It had been a long season, and few staff had had much time off. The expedition leader looked and sounded particularly exhausted most nights as he wearily approached the lectern for our daily recaps.

Meanwhile, the captain seemed more disillusioned than anyone, happy to anchor miles from desired shores in Antarctica and South Georgia, wasting everyone's time with extended Zodiac transfers. Unlike any other captain I've ever sailed with, he brazenly didn't bother to introduce himself to the passengers until we were five days into the trip, then had his farewell drinks three days before the end. No one appeared to want the voyage over sooner than him. Farewell, Captain! We really never knew ye.

A day out from Tristan I began to worry that this perfunctory approach to expedition cruising was going to cost me the prize. Three weeks of travel would be for nought if I couldn't see the penguins. No tourist ship would return here for six months or more – to miss now would be cataclysmic. On the upside, our first stop was to be Gough Island, home to the world's largest colony of Northern Rockhoppers.

Later in the voyage I spoke to two members of the Royal Society for the Protection of Birds (RSPB) who had been stationed out there on the most distant island of the most remote archipelago. They were being pulled from Gough six months early and unfortunately mistook me for an investigative journalist interested in finding out why. I tried to reassure them that I was much more concerned with penguins than any potential funding scandals, but they remained on alert.

The closest we came to a proper conversation was out on the back deck of the *Vega* when I asked one of these professional bird spotters if she missed the place. On the brink of crying, her mouth contorted into an uncomfortable shape as though it couldn't quite fit around the truth. Of course she did, she said with unvarnished bitterness. I asked why. 'Well, you're *living* in a seabird colony,' she replied, knowing that I didn't need much more than that – I had already told her about some of my experiences with Southern Rockhoppers and albatrosses on the Falklands.[*]

Penguins had been taken off their job list before they'd left Britain and, from their position on the island, they were always distant from the rookeries; like many crested penguin species, the Northern Rockhoppers on Gough choose to nest in preposterously vertiginous locations on cliffs unreachable for humans. I got the impression that she was more interested in

---

[*] But not about going feral on LSD there a few months earlier.

the albatross anyway – especially the endemic Tristan species. I almost understood it, the desire to surround yourself with those most airborne birds, rather than the dumpy, earthbound penguins. To paraphrase Robert Cushman Murphy, the conservationists now belonged to a higher cult of mortals, for they had studied the albatross.

During each leg of our long voyage, we had flying birds for company. The huge sky was often punctuated by wandering albatrosses and spectacled petrels which followed the ship for days. The albatrosses never looked rushed or hurried, but the unending calm didn't suit them – with so little wind, they had to occasionally beat those giant wings. It was odd to watch them flap, inappropriate somehow, like seeing a schoolteacher in jeans at the weekend.

News eventually came that we weren't going to Gough after all. Tech-savvy passengers had already seen this on Cruise-Mapper – the internet connection on the *Vega* was particularly strong and the information readily discovered. Several hours before the expedition management told us, it was plain to see that our course had changed for Nightingale, the smallest of the main islands. This felt like a bitter blow and, looking at the weather charts, I didn't understand the logic.* Instead, I frantically emailed Tristan's Director of Conservation, Trevor Glass, and asked if there even were penguins on Nightingale. After a nervous wait, he replied, 'You'll see penguins there.'

Relief flickered . . . but what if we didn't? What if the captain decided to cancel the whole thing for fear of a little discomfort? A feeling like indigestion began to grow in my chest,

---

* Though I at least respected the expedition management enough not to question it.

An Inconvenience of Penguins

a particular anxiety I hadn't felt since trying to see the Snares penguins in New Zealand almost exactly a year earlier. We were so close now – just hours away – but unhelpful weather or the bovine energy of the bridge could still leave everything in ruins.

I tried to alleviate my unease by dialling into the pre-dinner briefing that night but the whole thing felt haughty and callous. As more facts about Tristan were thrown out, the few passengers who'd come on this long journey guffawed and sneered. The islanders have holiday homes by the potato patches? Haw haw haw. Internet access only in 1999? The Neanderthals! Their only bus has broken down? Ha. Ha. Haaaa.

I suppose that's how we treat small communities all over the world: laugh, belittle, never pause to understand or imagine how life would be if you too found yourself living five days from the nearest hospital.

One thing I hadn't read before getting to the Tristan archipelago: it is also an extraordinarily beautiful place, as raw and dramatic as you'd hope such a decidedly remote outpost to be. When I looked out of my cabin and finally saw Nightingale Island, it stood bold, almost confrontational in the afternoon sun. Its gentle-sounding name is remarkably inaccurate; its topography is defined by impossible cliffs, rocky spires and Mordorian fissures in its volcanic rock. The day we saw it, the highlands wore a layer of cloud like a duvet and rampant tussock like an under sheet. Edgar Allan Poe never visited this untamed island, but he wasn't far off when he wrote in 1838's *The Narrative of Arthur Gordon Pym of Nantucket*:

> Nightingale Island [is] the smallest and most southerly . . .
> Off its southern extremity is a high ledge of rocky islets;

All at Sea

a few also of a similar appearance are seen to the northeast. The ground is irregular and sterile, and a deep valley partially separates it. The shores of these islands abound, in the proper season, with sea lions, sea elephants, the hair and fur seal, together with a great variety of oceanic birds.[*]

From the decks of the *Vega*, I strained my eyes to see penguins, but there was no ignoring the flying birds which filled the sky like a hailstorm. Yellow-nosed albatrosses, giant petrels and great shearwaters beyond count created a chaotic, fecund scene that reminded me of the Snares Islands, though with superior scenery. From the shoreline, mournful noises of seals carried out across the sea and I wanted to shout back in rapture, 'The conditions are so good! We'll get out to you soon enough!'

We'd travelled so far, and with forecasts painting a grimmer picture for the following day, I was keenly aware that this outing would possibly be my only chance to see the Northern Rockhoppers. Even the adventure-averse bridge couldn't deny us a chance to get out this time.[†]

Whereas during most operations I'd been relaxed and casual, even late to the changing room at the back of the ship, for Nightingale I was first in line, nervous and babbling while I waited. Every few seconds I looked out for Nils, a tall, possibly unhinged Norwegian who I knew to be the team's best Zodiac driver. I hardly recognised this version of myself, a ravenous,

---

[*] 'Hair' is an archaic term for the harbour seal, though they have never bred this far south. It's possible Poe was guessing here.

[†] They did, however, put arbitrary time limits on our outing, which could have lasted all day in favourable water that was no longer subject to any Antarctic restrictions.

unreasonable man presenting as some unattractive mix of birder and desperate groupie.

The sea rolled up and down the ship, rising and falling by as much as 2m, meaning passenger loading had to be carefully timed. I hoped none of the more timid decision makers were watching – most expedition leaders would prefer no passengers got an experience rather than deal with the awkwardness of only a few succeeding. But I got in, and so did seven others, and before long Nils had us bumping out into deceptively large swell.

The cloud enshrouding the centre of the island didn't want to venture far, allowing sun to dapple the coasts. Beyond Nightingale, both Tristan da Cunha and Inaccessible Island were visible on the horizon. As we pushed north, the lesser Middle Island came into view, too. It initially seemed unremarkable compared to its giant neighbours, but as we drew closer dozens of Northern Rockhopper penguins were revealed on its steep shore. In the early afternoon sun, their flamboyant crests glowed like halos, as though they knew how rare a prize they were. I unclenched my jaw for the first time in days. Swan Hellenic's unnecessary insistence that every Zodiac cruise be just 75 minutes meant this encounter would be fleeting, but nonetheless waves of relief crashed over our bow, alongside those of the South Atlantic.[*]

Red-eyed like their Southern cousins, the birds have the most outlandish crest of all penguins – garish, bouncing manes, the Spheniscidae equivalent of dreadlocks. A hundred or so

---

[*] By way of comparison, my personal Zodiac cruise record is four hours and 20 minutes. We only went back to the ship because passengers were getting hungry.

All at Sea

adults in Rastafarian plumage hung out on a rockface, casual and relaxed, with no idea of just how much effort it had taken to see them. While Nils got us as close as was safe, I machine-gunned 800 shots from my camera, grinning the whole time.

None of these adult penguins were likely to have been as old as Edinburgh Zoo's late Mrs Wolowitz, but some may have been around long enough to remember the man-made trauma caused by the wreck of the MV *Oliva* here in 2011. A little after 5am on 16 March, the 225m-long ship – sailing under a Maltese flag of convenience – crashed into the north-west coast of Nightingale at 14kt, its maximum cruising speed. In the accident report, the officers on duty said they thought their radar was mistakenly identifying storm clouds or possibly icebergs, not an island. Of the many errors that morning, a standout was that the *Oliva* also lost its lifeboat as the crew attempted to abandon ship, leaving the 22 men to be progressively rescued by Tristan islanders.[*]

As the hull failed, 1,500 tonnes of diesel and fuel oil were spilled alongside a cargo of 60,000 tonnes of soybeans being transported all the way from Brazil to China.[†] What would have already been a vast carbon expense for the beans grew exponentially as the fossil fuels poured into the ocean. The effect on the penguins was horrific. During a desperate rescue, islanders collected healthy birds, keeping them in pens on the Tristan mainland and away from the ruined sea. Video footage from a Lindblad ship which happened to visit the following week shows birds black from head to toe in oil, their magnificent

---

[*] Improbably the lifeboat washed up in Australia, two whole years after the wreck.

[†] The farmland in Brazil was likely razed rainforest, too.

crests dulled and stuck to their heads. Many urgently tried to preen themselves, swallowing toxic fuel in the process. The total number of dead couldn't be counted.

Thankfully, 13 years is a long time in penguindom. The Rockhoppers I photographed on that tense afternoon could not have looked healthier, nor more resplendent in the sunshine. The very ocean seemed clean: kelp forests swirled around the islands, and the sheer biomass of birds in front of and above me suggested this home, so far from human industry, was once more an idyllic place for them to live.

That night as we sat at anchor off Tristan, a preposterous tungsten sunset washed over Edinburgh of the Seven Seas. In the same manner as hundreds of ships over the last two centuries, we sent boats to shore, transporting fruit and vegetables in exchange for fresh seafood. We also picked up a handful of passengers, including the reclusive ladies from the RSPB. Rather than attend another lacklustre recap, I sat on my balcony watching these operations and drinking whisky to celebrate seeing the world's most inaccessible penguins.

I want to tell you more about Tristan da Cunha, about the islanders and the quirks of Edinburgh of the Seven Seas. I'd like to give you details about how life is organised on that tiny sliver of land between the volcano and the sea, about the mats they used to weave with Rockhopper crests, and the ratting days when they competitively murder vermin. I want to tell you stories about how the people interact with their penguins today, about what they remember of the *Oliva* incident, and whether they would ever consider abandoning their generational home, even now. I'd like to describe in detail the Tristanian accent, what they eat, and tell you whether or not their cattle are

All at Sea

healthier these days. I'd like to cover all that and more, but I cannot.

A robbery of polar cruising is that the people who can typically afford it are elderly, their kids grown, their mortgages paid, their bodies failing. It's robbery because many passengers cannot physically get the most out of their experience: a slick rock is a potential hip replacement; a tumultuous sea isn't a thrilling rollercoaster but a dangerous spew-ride.

While goods and people came and went from shore that night, an emergency developed: Edith, a personable 79-year-old from the US, had a fall while arriving for the recap. Maybe she passed out, maybe she just tripped. Maybe she lost consciousness, maybe she was lucid and in screaming agony. The gossip machine issued many stories over the next few days, but beyond doubt was the fact that we had to perform a medical evacuation. Her injuries were serious, if not life-threatening, and required rapid investigation that could not be done on the ship, nor at the rudimentary facilities in Edinburgh of the Seven Seas. We had to sail as fast as we could to Cape Town for proper medical care. This was an emergency in slow motion – Tristan's lonely volcano soon fell from view, but it would take almost five days to reach port.

Only when we reached the African city did clear facts emerge, along with Edith in a wheelchair, her shoulder broken, her face a little swollen. Two of her daughters had flown from California to meet her off the ship. Bending to delicately hug her mother, one became quickly emotional, her eyes filling like fishbowls.

Finally on land after 11 days – nobody made it ashore anywhere on Tristan – Edith was put on a stretcher. From the upper decks, passengers shouted well wishes and declarations of love,

An Inconvenience of Penguins

but only when everyone cheered in unison did she hear enough to respond, throwing up her working hand in a royal wave as she disappeared into a waiting ambulance. *I'm glad you're well,* I thought, *and even happier you didn't cost me my penguins.*

15

A Town Called Penguin

or

The Little Penguin That Could

> All the world loves a penguin. I think it is because in many respects they are like ourselves, and in some respects they are what we should like to be.
>
> – Apsley Cherry-Garrard,
> *The Worst Journey in the World*, 1922

Seven long months passed in the penguinless north. After the near miss at Tristan da Cunha in March, there was no viable way to see any of the remaining birds before the Antarctic spring began to break sometime around October. I instead spent most of the boreal summer working as a photo guide in the Arctic, trying not to mention penguins to guests who had come for a polar opposite experience.

This was not a simple matter, especially when surrounded by guillemots, little auks and puffins, all of which seemed an evolutionary heartbeat away from giving up their incompetent flying and settling for lives as marine animals, too. It was especially tricky not to mention penguins when discussing the extinct great auk, a flightless bird with pronounced countershading, the Welsh name for which was white head – or in their

An Inconvenience of Penguins

language, *pen gwyn*. This is very likely the origin of the name we use today.*

By the boreal autumn when the oceans began to freeze, it was finally time for me to migrate south, this time to see the Little penguin in Australia, then the Fiordland or Tawaki in New Zealand. The latter had escaped me during the previous visit 18 months earlier, and so with vengeance in my heart and a new camera in my bag, I set out to avoid further disappointment.

Seeing the Little, Little Blue or Fairy penguin would be simpler.† Their range stretches all around the wide south of Australia, encircles Tasmania and continues over the Tasman Sea to New Zealand.‡ Their population health is stable overall, though collapsing in some areas and increasing slowly in others.

I wanted to start in Tasmania, not only because the birds are abundant there, but because on its northern shore there is – irresistibly – a whole town called Penguin. To facilitate the trip, I sold a series of stories about the island to newspapers at home and had the local tourist board pay for my flights and lay

---

* Though not in French, where *pingouin* still means auk. Their word for penguin is instead *manchot*, which crudely translates as 'crippled wing'. I apologise on behalf of all of France for that – Lord knows they won't do it for themselves.

† Some ill-informed people of a certain age lament the fact that this bird is no longer called a Fairy as though they have been subjected to yet more linguistic restrictions by the despised Wokerati. In fact, the name change is unrelated to political correctness and has more to do with the evolution of language – 'fairy' was formerly the common name given to the smallest birds in several taxonomic families. There are still fairy terns, fairy wrens, fairy bluebirds and so on.

‡ There is a morph in New Zealand with distinctive wings known as the White-Flippered penguin, but it has yet to be proven as an entirely separate species. This is obviously a relief as the last thing I need on my plate is more penguins.

A Town Called Penguin

on an itinerary. Almost a year had passed since my self-made disasters in Argentina and, as though they'd heard of how much bother I'd found while driving alone, the tourist board insisted on giving me a driver rather than let me get behind the wheel again. This was annoying as it robbed me of free will, but my driver Junaidi was easy to like and something of a wildlife nerd in his own right. His company was never not a pleasure.

We ticked off the necessary stops to fulfil my tourist board obligations (A salt factory! A tulip farm!) but the organisers had at least listened to my penguin requests, arranging two viewing opportunities for the Little birds, plus some time in Penguin. We'd visit colonies of different sizes on different coasts, always at night. Viewing these near-nocturnal birds, the smallest of all penguin species, was necessarily an experience like no other.

The operation at Bicheno Penguin Tours on Tasmania's east coast was slick and efficient, a neat little tourist business that provided a home for penguins while making money for the owners. Minibuses collected our group of 15 from a surf shop in the middle of Bicheno, then transported us to some modified scrubland where we'd try and see the birds. I say 'try' not because the Little penguins were masters of subterfuge but because it was already half an hour after sunset and dark enough that we needed torches.

Our Tasmanian guide gave us a briefing on how to behave around the penguins, explaining that he'd be using a light with a heavy red filter because they 'dislike the bright white light'.* If we wanted to use our own, we'd need red filters, too. Camera flashes were strictly prohibited. Above us, the path was subtly

---

* Try saying that in a thick Aussie accent.

lit by amber fairy lights, leaving our eyes with plenty of adjustment to do. It reminded me of an approach to a posh outdoor wedding, where most of the resident guests would be wearing tuxedos and inevitably getting into fights as the night wore on. An unconvincing half-moon hung low in the sky, offering only just enough illumination to spot bats flitting across the deep blue night. As we set off towards the beach, I looked at our excitable group and wondered, *Which of these pilgrims will fuck things up with the birds first?*

We were quickly in the middle of an unseen penguin town. In bushes all around we could hear their rustling, and once in a while their dweeby calls. They sounded a little like the donkey-braying banded penguins, but with a far more asthmatic tune, their trilling noises almost wheezed during grinding inhales and truncated exhales.

Owing to its diminutive size, the Little penguin does not tarry on exposed beaches. Most penguins are only potential meals for large, specialised predators, but typically weighing just over a kilo and standing no more than 30cm tall, these birds are on the menu for a far more diverse list of diners. Large gulls can kill Little penguins, to say nothing of domestic cats and dogs. I was told of a penguin that was being tracked by GPS which seemed to move rapidly and in an uncommonly straight line inland. When the scientists retrieved the sensor, it was found in the nest of a sea eagle. Given their heightened vulnerability, they wait until darkness has fallen before congregating in the water then dashing across the beach. Only when they are safe in bushes, burrows or man-made shelters can they think about relaxing.

'Within our first 18 months of operation, a pair of boxer dogs got out from a nearby resort and almost wiped out the whole

A Town Called Penguin

colony,' Nic Wardlaw, the owner of Bicheno Penguin Tours, told me the next morning. 'We picked up 50 or 60 dead birds. The next night we saw just a single penguin come home.' The local response was to employ a dog catcher and increase fines. There are thought to be 400 penguins around Bicheno today.

As someone who loves dogs and fundamentally distrusts cats, this was hard to hear – especially as it wasn't the first time. I'd learned of terrible canine attacks in Cape Town and New Zealand, not to mention the endless examples of sled-dogs killing penguins in Antarctica. Whereas cats might take chicks for food, the hounds seemed to lose control completely, committing frenzied attacks that slaughtered dozens of birds at a time. In 2018 there were at least three such incidents in Tasmania, one of which killed 58 birds in the Low Head colony on the north shore. The government's response that time was to stiffen their laws around the island – a fatal attack on penguins in a protected area is now subject to the same penalties as an attack on a human.[*]

Back in Bicheno, half a dozen tiny penguins crested a hill in front of us. Completely unlike the tall, regal birds in South Georgia, they leaned forward, lowering their profile into an awkwardly horizontal gait, presumably in the hope of going undetected. For a second, I noticed the near-blue hue of their back feathers and remembered once being told in Japan that ninjas, if they really existed, probably wore midnight-blue outfits – not black – to increase their invisibility. I wondered if these penguins had heard the same thing.

---

[*] If this sounds excessive to you, know that in Sydney in 2009, authorities employed snipers to protect a colony of Little penguins from predatory foxes.

An Inconvenience of Penguins

Despite clear instructions not to move suddenly or approach the penguins, a lidless, red-haired child fidgeted and fussed, swinging his legs in front of a light to create a strobing effect. Understandably this freaked the birds out, leaving them unsure whether they should advance or retreat. The guide looked at the parent and, seeing that they weren't about to intervene, decided to *say something* to the child themselves. Like their guardian, the boy promptly ignored him.

I sat in the dark, trying to emanate hatred in their direction, hoping they would pick up on the bad vibrations.* We moved on, the twitching boy rushing around, scaring penguins all the way. When a nesting box was opened, his terrible arm shot forward, panicking the guide who pleaded with him to back off. All the while the parent plodded around, tuned to an entirely different frequency. I have rarely seen a more painful demonstration that – as well as all the other relentless hassles – parenthood might be fundamentally uninteresting.

Yet the boy was not the only thing being ignored that night. For the first time in my years of observing them, penguins were failing to hold human attention. Stuck on the ground, they were being upstaged in the air – the aurora australis was beginning to flow across the Tasmanian night. Later, Junaidi and I would see it much more clearly, a great pink-and-green river pulsating and shimmering in the cosmos, but at this early stage, even with light pollution and the best efforts of the doomed guide, human eyes were drawn heavenwards. He and the poor penguins never really stood a chance.

---

* This was harder to do when I heard a small Australian girl ask the beleaguered guide if the 'liddle fellas' ever got hurt and my heart immediately melted into pathetic goo.

A Town Called Penguin

A few days of government-organised itinerary later, we were driving along the north coast. As Junaidi steered us off the highway, I pointed out road signs for Penguin a few too many times. When we finally pulled into the town, it briefly seemed uninteresting – a twee, low-lying coastal settlement which, slightly out of season, felt anaesthetised. Its full strangeness was only revealed when I walked around town.

Over a 45-minute stroll I passed the Penguin News Agency, the Penguin Foodbar, the Penguin Pantry, the Penguin Community Op Shop, the Ampol Penguin petrol station, the Penguin General Practice, the Penguin Fire Station, the Penguin Vet (unclear if penguins were being treated), the Penguin Market (unclear if penguins were for sale), the Bottle-O Penguin off-licence, the Penguin House and the Penguin Café, the Penguin Senior Citizens Club Inc. (social bowls every Monday), Letterbox Penguin, the Penguin Memorial Library, the Penguin Beer Company (outside of which was a Penguinometer inexplicably not set to MAXIMUM), an ad for the Penguin Surf Life-Saving Club, the Penguin Country Bakehouse which sold 'our famous Flaming Penguin Pie – WARNING EXTREMELY HOT',[*] the Penguin Waterfront Escape, the Penguin Beachfront Apartments, the Uniting Church Penguin (We Seek to Be an Open Church), the Penguin Play Centre, the Penguin History Group Inc., the old Penguin Gaol, the Penguin Railway Station, the Penguin Men's Shed (New Members Welcome), the Penguin Caravan Park, the Penguin Skate Park, the home of the Penguin Scouts Group, the Penguin Boat Ramp, a mechanic called Penguin Auto, Reverend Helen Gleeson's Anglican church

---

[*] Which I of course bought, tried to eat, and enjoyed as much as being tear-gassed by a riot squad.

An Inconvenience of Penguins

St Stephen's Penguin, Penguin Creek, and a sign celebrating Penguin's status as Tasmania's tidiest town in 2020.

There was also the Penguin Cemetery, which hosts graves of men who travelled from this town to die in the battlefields of 1940s Europe. Some didn't make it that far, including a Penguin local, 24-year-old Sergeant Tom Fielding, who in June 1942 was celebrating a 21st birthday with comrades in the Eagle Hotel, King's Lynn, when a Luftwaffe bomb destroyed the building. 'Beyond all shadows,' reads his headstone, 'standeth God.' Next to him lies Daniel Monson, who'd instead been born in Colchester, England, and had travelled all the way down here for a very different life in the 1800s. His inscription remembers him as a 'Pioneer of Penguin'.

Long before seeing that headstone, the word 'penguin' had lost its meaning for me. Such was its ubiquity and endless repetition that the bird ceased to be a bird; there were now just two syllables bouncing around in infinity. Penguin, pen-gwin, peng-win. The idea that it may have come from Welsh or from a Latin word for fat (*pinguis*) was irrelevant – I had developed a kind of penguin dementia that only leaving this town would fix.

This was all the weirder because aside from the Big Penguin, a terrible statue which had been erected to mark the town's centenary in 1975, there didn't seem to be any actual penguins here, Little or otherwise.* They did not dash across this beach of an evening and no artificial homes had been built to encourage them to take up residence.

---

* In 2008 the Big Penguin was found to contain asbestos and was almost culled as a result. However, tests concluded that the dangerous mineral was safely contained inside the giant bird.

A Town Called Penguin

In the Penguin Visitor Information Centre, a lady selling me an 'I Just Stopped in Penguin' doorstop told me that despite the town being named after the once-abundant birds, no one alive could remember the last time they saw them on the beach. Still, she said, on the far ends of the sand, on rocks where there were bushes in which to hide, a few birds still made homes. There were no viewing platforms, and rather than trust the public to do the right thing, they chose to keep the exact locations of the hideouts secret. 'People still come from all over for our penguins,' said the lady as she wrapped my excellent souvenir. 'But I don't think they're disappointed when they get here.'

My time in Tasmania ended with a single night in Stanley, a pretty tourist village an hour's drive west from Penguin. It too had a rookery, another chance to see the Little birds before flying back to the Australian mainland. On the drive, signs warned about all kinds of extraordinary beasts being potential roadkill, from penguins to platypuses, wallabies to wombats. Local legislation lowered vehicle speeds after dark, which must have helped but didn't entirely prevent there being piles of carcasses along the roadside.*

Junaidi and I had a final dinner together. We toasted the trip – despite not wanting a driver, he'd been a fine travel companion. I'm not sure how much I'd got him to care about penguins, but he'd done a fine job of pretending. Double-checking that our wine was being billed to the tourist board, I poured myself

---

* It turned out that Junaidi had been assigned as my driver to help me avoid contributing to the bloodshed. Inevitably, then, we ended up running over a long-nosed potoroo, a small marsupial that looks like a large shrew. The incident was deeply ironic to me, but poor Junaidi felt terrible for days.

An Inconvenience of Penguins

another glass. Here's to you, Australian taxpayers, and here's to us.

Wiping the gravy from our chins, we headed out to the latest set of boardwalks. Unlike Bicheno, which had been a ticketed experience, in Stanley there was little more than a sign and some arrows pointing towards the nesting area. Feeling like old hands and perhaps volunteer guides ourselves, Junaidi and I took a spot at the far end of the path, watching in uncommon proximity as the birds passed under the boardwalk and off to their nightly accommodations. Once in a while, Junaidi shone a red torch so I could try and take photos, but it remained almost impossible in such low light.

'That light's too strong, mate,' said a man with a crevassed face and an Aussie accent that called to mind someone sharpening a fork with their teeth.

'Sorry?' said Junaidi, confused. The aggressor's criticism had come from nowhere. I was as shocked as my guide.

'It's too much, it's distracting the birds,' he blabbered on.

It wasn't. It couldn't. And the birds were walking into much brighter lights by the car park in any case. It was my turn to *say something*. In Italy four years earlier, white wine had started this penguin odyssey for me. Now the bottle of Stargazer's outstanding Chardonnay in my belly wanted it to go in another, more belligerent direction.[*] I had a very strong suspicion this dickhead would not be so bold if it were Very White me, and not my Indonesian-born friend, holding the torch.

---

[*] Ordinarily I'm not a Chardonnay fan, but Tasmania's cold-weather grapes give a much crisper, lighter character than the often overbearing, oaky stuff preferred by mainland Australians.

A Town Called Penguin

'What are you talking about? How on Earth would you know?' I asked.

'The penguins! It's bugging them,' said the baboon. 'I'm observing them.'

'You're talking shite,' I said, letting my accent drift back towards Glasgow from its more neutered international centre. 'That's what you're doing.'

'Oh, and what are you? Some kind of expert?' asked Bruce[*] grumpily, his furrowed brow giving him the look of a chimpanzee handed a smartphone. An expert? Well, funny you should ask that, my man. In my mind's eye, the unveiling of my hard-won experience would rain down on him like a dominant MMA fighter, facts as elbow strikes, my knowledge leaving him turtled on the boardwalk. Ground and pound. No referee to step in. Like all picked fights it was ridiculous, avoidable and ultimately pointless, yet here I was, free to beat a stupid man unconscious with my expertise. Before that, though, his wife stepped between us.

'Aw, look now, Bruce,' said Sheila,[†] broad-shouldered and incontestably authoritarian. She was addressing him but really talking to us both. 'I didn't come out here tonight to listen to this. Let's just enjoy the bloody penguins.'

I dared not disagree.

As I flew over the Bass Strait to Melbourne, Little penguins swam around my brain. More than any other, this species lived with people, right on the edges of towns and public beaches. There, if dogs and other pests were kept under control, they

---

[*] His name probably wasn't Bruce.
[†] And her name probably wasn't Sheila.

thrived. I wondered if this was simply because they were able to directly get people to care, to trigger an emotional, even parental, response. So small and so capable of finding trouble, they were perhaps the purest embodiment of bird-as-child.

Over the centuries, many writers have compared penguins to children – not humans generally, but very specifically infants. They are toddlers emerging from the ocean: 'this ungainly child' to Melville; a 'bow-legged child' to Katherine Mary Barrow; 'extraordinarily like children' to Cherry-Garrard. In Bicheno, Nic Wardlaw had theorised that their popularity was directly linked to their childishness: 'People look at them and see the same sort of vulnerability as a human baby, then they have this innate desire to nurture and protect them.'

There are enormous profits to be made from this emotional response. An animal with a silhouette as distinct as a giraffe or a rhino, penguins are used to promote chocolate biscuits, underwear brands, beers, a book publisher, the Linux operating system, Pittsburgh's ice hockey team,* for some reason the very notion of Christmas, and much more. The power of their image rivals any creature on Earth.

When the English philosopher John Ruskin found himself in 'states of disgust and fury' with the 19th-century world, he would 'go to the British Museum and look at penguins till I get cool'. Writing to Harvard professor Charles Eliot Norton in November 1860, he explained: 'I find at present penguins are the only comfort in life. One feels everything in the world so

---

* The Pittsburgh Penguins' name was chosen by the public, apparently because their home arena is known as the Igloo. Were ice hockey not such an inherently violent sport, I'd explain to those goons that igloos belong to the Arctic and so of course have absolutely nothing to do with penguins.

A Town Called Penguin

sympathetically ridiculous, one can't be angry when one looks at a penguin.'*

Around the world today, businesses cash in on this same feeling, and nowhere does it on a larger scale than the world's ultimate penguin commercial enterprise: Phillip Island Nature Parks. When I mentioned a plan to drive the two hours from Melbourne to visit the project, some guiding colleagues raised eyebrows and lips in sneers. It was profane, they said, like Disneyland – all t-shirts and stuffed toys, rampant capitalism masquerading as conservation. And there were thousands of people, they said, all behaving ridiculously as the Little penguins came back to shore every night. I wanted to see for myself.†

The car park was so huge it could have belonged to an airport. The tourists were yet to arrive for the evening's show, and empty the place seemed cavernous and cynical. The main building reminded me of a church built for some dreadful televangelist, a massive modern shrine where the faithful would have to pay to worship.

Before the crowds began to assemble, I spoke to the project's penguin biologist and senior scientist Andre Chiaradia.

---

* This is quite the response considering the museum's bird was presumably stuffed.

† If I'd had more time, I'd have taken a detour to Sea Life Melbourne Aquarium, which was the sudden focus of global attention thanks to a captive King penguin chick named Pesto, a hulking brown beast that had unwittingly become a social media star. Like most King chicks, it had grown larger than its parents and was continuing to follow them around begging for food. In captivity, the poor adults couldn't run far, nor escape to the ocean, but the internet gobbled this soap opera up all the same. Here was highly shareable content sitting perfectly on the intersection of a Venn diagram marked cuteness and hilarity. Personally, I thought the imprisoned baby should be mourned, not memed.

An Inconvenience of Penguins

His knowledge was broad and deep, and several times he put me back on track or dismissed faulty theories I'd developed over years of fixation on the birds. Early on I asked why the penguins here were doing so well. His long explanation started by telling me that their progress had actually halted.

The ocean around Australia was warming so fast that the penguins were breeding two months earlier than usual. Climate models ran to the year 2100, but ocean temperatures had jumped so much in 2022 and 2023 that their behaviour was already matching what had been predicted for 2070. 'It's pretty scary,' said Andre. 'The interesting thing is that the Little penguins adjust and compensate for the conditions because they can have two clutches in the same year.' This, along with the fact that they are notably promiscuous, allowed the populations to grow and grow – at least until 2022 when everything stalled as the seas boiled.

He continued, telling me that two major currents run down the east and west coasts of Australia, but that the southern part of the island continent is sheltered from both. As super-heated water is dragged down from the tropics, the penguins' food disappears. Consequently, populations in Western Australia and New South Wales were collapsing. On the south coast, however, the water in the Bass Strait was chilled as though in a lagoon or cave. The result of this was that colonies around Melbourne and on Tasmania remained stable or grew. Massive global climate change would ultimately become a challenge as it already was for other species, but for now these animals were sheltered.

This is part of the reason that Phillip Island Nature Parks's project is a runaway success, financially and ecologically. The smallest penguins in the world come here in their thousands to nest, and every night they arrive back to shore exactly on time, guaranteeing entertainment for visitors as they return to their man-maintained property. There is none of the chance that comes with penguin viewing on ships, nor the individual timekeeping of many of the other species.

I ran a theory past the scientist: it seemed to me that some penguins I'd visited benefitted from being very close to people. There were the African penguins thriving on Boulders Beach, while up and down the Argentinian coast, the abundant Magellanics living on farms were safe from predators. Now here, a short distance from sprawling Melbourne, Little penguins were profiting, too. It seemed that those living closest to urban areas prospered with cleaner waters, elimination of predators, and even tourism.

Until Phillip Island Nature Parks's colossal rewilding project, foxes had killed over 3,000 penguins here and, along with dogs, were thought to have destroyed nine of the island's ten resident colonies – the only one to survive was effectively in the middle of the Summerland housing estate. This seemed like more compelling evidence for my theory.

Andre listened patiently. 'I don't think I subscribe to that,' he replied, explaining that roadkill was an issue, as were light pollution and, of course, domestic dogs. Besides, the birds spend 80 per cent of their lives at sea. What happens on land matters much less than out in the unmanageable ocean. 'In the end,' he said, 'you need to remember that they're marine animals.'

Former human residents of Summerland insisted that they cohabited blissfully with wildlife, but by the mid-1980s the situation for Little penguins on Phillip Island was nonetheless dire. Unlike governments in so many countries, Victoria state politicians took decisive action to reverse the decline. Penguin lives would take precedence over the human ones – Summerland's 774 allotments were purchased as part of an ambitious and inevitably controversial buyback scheme. The cost, like the disgruntlement of displaced locals, was high. As recently as 2018, former residents told ABC News that the reclamation of what they felt was their land was a harrowing experience, so traumatic they couldn't return to visit. 'We were horrified and deeply shocked and incredibly saddened that all of this was going to come to an end,' said one. Even with financial compensation, they felt wronged by the loss of their homes and community, but the ecological results have been so spectacular that retrospective questioning of the policy seems ridiculous – with around 40,000 inhabitants, this is now the largest Little penguin colony anywhere, home to four times more birds than in the 1980s.

But let's imagine for a second you're a politician who doesn't care about the penguins, nor the koalas nor the eastern barred bandicoots nor the short-tailed shearwaters which have all flourished in this formerly under-used and unprofitable corner of the island; let's say you don't care about lefty policies at all, rewilding of any type, or anything other than white land ownership in Australia. Even then, there'd be something to turn your head: money, great mountains of tourist cash. Phillip Island Nature Parks takes in around $20 million a year; by the time all the hotel bookings, tour guides, transfers and so on have been calculated, its value to the Victorian economy is in the region of $500 million.

If the facility here today is indeed like a cult's church, it is at least a benevolent one. The extraordinary revenues all belong to a non-profit organisation, meaning the penguins are protected by their own iconic status. The excess money is used for marine

A Town Called Penguin

research, all those rewilding projects, and has created hundreds of jobs, both at the facility and across the island. The penguins are guarding eco and economic systems simply by existing.

That doesn't mean that visiting the main event isn't a bit weird. From the moment tourists began appearing en masse, I couldn't shake an uncanny feeling that it was too unnatural to be genuinely beneficial. By car and by bus the crowds arrived, some with translators and guides, others urgently trying to shepherd their giddy children. Inside, a polished concrete wonderland awaited, almost every inch of which was ready to collect Mummy and Daddy's money. Toys, memorabilia, clothing – all of it was for sale, all with penguin branding.[*]

I no longer cared. The chips from the onsite restaurant were $12 – so what? Buy two portions. The money here was ultimately benefitting wildlife and I couldn't interpret that as anything other than a good cause.

Ewan, a rep from the project's management, gave me a pink high-vis vest to wear over my clothes. When the penguins walked up the shore, in front of an audience of around 2,500 people in a split amphitheatre, no one would be allowed to take a photograph. The entire beach was bathed in an amber hue which had been measured to make sure it didn't discourage the penguins from returning to their nests, yet with such a massive crowd there was no way to be sure everyone's flash was turned off. Because of my own project and prior application, I would at least be able to use my flashless camera – the gaudy vest was to advertise this fact.

We walked out across the boardwalks, the grandest and

---

[*] Though with great satisfaction, I noted they didn't have any excellent doorstops.

An Inconvenience of Penguins

best maintained of any I'd seen on the trip. There were a few old concrete nests, now-archaic man-made penguin burrows dating back to the days when numbers were in decline and they needed all the help they could get. Now, just like for young humans in Melbourne a few kilometres away, housing demand had far outstripped supply.

The amphitheatre was divided in half, with a sand dune running up between the segments. This would soon become a very public penguin highway. Above us what looked like an extravagant lifeguard's tower stood sentinel. Inside, a frantic spotter would try to work out how many penguins came in that night – it was, they conceded, a bit of a guess.*

I was taken to the front row of the right-hand hemisphere. Between the privilege, the escort and the garish pink jacket, I got a lot of attention, with dozens of tourists understandably a bit miffed that I was striding out in front of them for the best seat in the venue, big camera in hand. Hindi, Mandarin, Spanish, English and many more languages said the same thing: who's this arsehole?

Ewan and I sat down and waited for public attention to switch from us to the shoreline. Nothing happened immediately and it was hard to ignore a mammalian tension in the air, the sort I've felt in football stadiums before penalty kicks. Finally, about 40 minutes after sunset, the first Little penguins emerged from the surf, a group of four, which all shook the excess water from their feathers then sprinted across the beach. Flapping and falling as they went, they clumsily made their way up the sandy

---

* In this section, 1,279 Little penguins were seen to make a full transit of the beach that night, representing just a fraction of the island's whole population.

A Town Called Penguin

hill. The crowd laughed at every stumble, oohed and ahhed in all the right places – here were their idols, performing exactly as they were supposed to, rock stars playing the hits.

Then something curious happened, something so odd and perfect that you might not believe it. It was so bizarre that even as I write these words, I'm aware that they might sound like a lie.

A second raft of penguins belly-splashed on to the sand then huddled together for the charge home. This time there were eight or even ten birds, all of which surveyed their crowd and decided along which route they'd assail the dune. They all waited for a decision maker to emerge then strode forward together.

They were not entirely united.

Just as the penguins gathered forward momentum, one fixed its eyes on me. I don't mean this in a loose, ethereal sense – it looked dead at me. I saw it through my lens, and I saw it with my naked eyes as the silly bugger sprinted towards me.

I don't know why it happened, only that it did: of all the people, the hundreds or even thousands this tiny bird could have chosen, it selected me as some kind of haven. Running as fast as its daft, lizardy feet would carry it, its wimpy wings correcting its balance every time it fell, it came straight to me, moving like a thing foretold.

The Little penguin bounced off my ankles; when I close my eyes I can still feel it now – solid and soft at the same time, clipping one medial malleolus then the other, left first, then right. An Indian man to my right watched the whole thing, giggling like he was being tickled. For a second, like the child in Bicheno, he tried to reach out to the bird and got a quick telling-off from the rep. His giggling continued all the same.

An Inconvenience of Penguins

We all sat, briefly flummoxed, while the wee hiker sought shelter before it ran up the hill to the scrub. There it was met by an impenetrable barrier, undergrowth too thick to access. In a few minutes it would work out that it had taken altogether the wrong path, after which it would recalibrate and join its brethren. For a time, though, it just stood there, as astonished as I had been moments earlier. Some tourists asked the guides to save this lost child, and they gently replied that the wild animal was just fine.

Walking back to the centre's main building half an hour later, I still thought about the penguin – left ankle, then right, soft and solid at the same time. I asked Ewan what it could have meant, and he said, half joking I think, that perhaps the penguin just wanted to be in the book.

Well, Little fella, if that's true, then congratulations: you made it.

16

Does a Penguin Shit in the Woods?

> Pengwing . . . penling . . . pengwon.
> – Benedict Cumberbatch, narrating the docuseries *South Pacific*, 2009

I was deep down the list now, rushing towards some kind of conclusion, though I couldn't picture what. I would see all the world's penguin species, or I would not, but a lack of time, money and options meant that certainty was moving beyond my control. I had no stories left to pitch, no favours left to ask. Credit cards were sliding into the red again and there were no invoices to send. A final cruise would take me into the distant territories of the Royal and Erect-Crested penguins after which I could start trying to earn my way back to solvency again, but seeing them would depend entirely on conditions at the time.

Before giving my fate back to the unpredictable ocean, there was a final penguin to see from land. From Australia, I flew across the Tasman Sea to New Zealand's South Island, hired a car in Christchurch then began a long drive to the wet west. My destination was the Wilderness Lodge Lake Moeraki, a long-standing forest haven which had led guests to see Fiordland penguins for over 30 years.

Behind only the neighbouring Hoiho and the Galapagos species on the other side of the Pacific, the Fiordland or Tawaki

An Inconvenience of Penguins

is thought to be the third rarest penguin in the world.* It is also a freak, even by penguins' eclectic standards. No other member of the sprawling family lives as they do, in the deep undergrowth of ancient forests, hidden like magical sprites.

I'd technically already seen one of these birds far from its forest home, lost on the Snares Islands 18 months earlier. However, I wasn't much interested in vagrants; at the Wilderness Lodge, I hoped for something less accidental, if not entirely guaranteed.

The drive would take seven hours, a tour so preposterously scenic that in the moment New Zealand's soaring beauty seemed to outrival anywhere in the world. I tried to think of a country with landscapes more dramatic than this, and a short list included only Tajikistan, which has an economy built on Afghan heroin, and the Faroe Islands, which isn't a true country, and even if it was, it is so permanently smeared with cetacean blood that it's hard to truly champion.

No matter how long I drove, the mountains on the horizon remained serrated and distant, like a background in an old racing video game, right there but unattainable. At Lake Tekapo, I pulled up alongside fellow tourists to take inept photos of the lovely surroundings, the ranges too distant to shoot with any skill. At Wanaka, I sat at a table opposite eight hipsters and a Dobermann. In a bid to appear as interesting individuals, they had all ended up wearing similar hats and moustaches, giving the impression that they were in a colourised photograph from the 1920s, with added hazy IPAs.

---

* Unlike the other two species, however, there is no immediate extinction threat to these penguins.

Does a Penguin Shit in the Woods?

There were still two hours to go, and I wanted to reach the lodge before sunset, mostly to reduce my chances of hitting any birds with my car. I cared not about the mammals – my Snares trip in the company of trappers and poisoners had left me unable to mourn mammalian roadkill. Whichever of my fellow milk-drinkers had been crushed, each roadside meat pile gave the birds less to worry about.

As I pushed north from Wanaka, the mountains finally arrived, acting as a gateway to the prehistoric forests of the west coast. To my happy surprise, very few cars joined me as the road curled into tight meanders and the landscape leapt skywards. Waterfalls shot from innumerable cliffs, while diamond rivers crept flawlessly along valley floors, wide and pure.

In this part of the world, annual rainfall is measured in metres, so it felt almost miraculous that I had found it dry. The flora still boomed green and 'vegetation rioted across the Earth', as Joseph Conrad had put it. Giant ferns hung over the road as though ready to fan a pharaoh, while nimble squadrons of birds darted between branches, too rapid to identify. Ravines hosted mazes of moss, incalculable plants, all striving for growth. When the late sun shone, I pulled over to smell warm pine trees.

'You're really lucky with your timing,' said Harry, a young guide taking me out the following morning to see the Fiordland penguins. I congratulated myself for not saying that luck had nothing to do with it. I'd been nervous about leaving anything to chance and this visit had been very deliberately timed to coincide with the birds' breeding season. While the chicks remained in their clandestine nests, one or both parents would be compelled to go to the ocean every day, increasing the chances of seeing them during their essential commutes.

An Inconvenience of Penguins

The Wilderness Lodge's hike to an otherwise undisturbed colony followed a public path to a public beach, yet it felt secret. The guides were concerned enough about it becoming an attraction for unsupervised tourists – in particular dog walkers – that they tended to park their minibuses in alternative locations so as not to advertise the start of the route.*

The walk took around half an hour from the drop-off. Before we got to the penguins, there were native parrots, the kea and the kaka, both sounding dreadful as pretty birds often do. They were completely out-sung by the similarly endemic tui, its call sounding elegant and operatic compared to the mad screeches of their rivals. Later, when all was dark, moth-eating morepork owls would take the stage.†

It felt as though we were walking through a huge, living thing. Along the path, all was moss or lichen or mulch or leaf. An old wooden bridge was being added to the humus, eaten and composted by the forest floor. Ghost leaves were common. Silver beech and giant fuchsias blotted out the sky. They were joined by rimu trees, slow-growing monuments which can stand for 1,000 years. Vines and stranger epiphytes scrambled over these titans in search of sunlight. The aromas of the plants danced with the songs of insects and other flying beings, all celebrating the jungle, the jungle, the jungle.

New Zealand is home to 28 species of butterfly and 25 species of bee, yet so all-smothering is the forest that these battalions of pollinators are insufficient for the ecosystem.

---

* I've decided not to name it here, either – if you want to go and visit the penguins, stay at the lodge and let their guides lead you.

† Their onomatopoeic name relates to their call, not their dietary preferences.

Does a Penguin Shit in the Woods?

Consequently, some plants have evolved to exploit the 1,700 species of moth, 206 species of birds and 124 species of reptiles, too. There was no way of telling whether all this life exists in genuine harmony, or if we were walking through a grand, green parliament, filled with deception, bitterness and death.

Even in the age of man and his vermin, so much biological weirdness remains in this country. There is a bat that runs, a fish that climbs, the heaviest insect in the world.[*] Long ago there was also the flightless moa, which was 50 per cent taller than an ostrich and weighed twice as much. Until humans arrived, it was preyed upon only by the mighty Haast's eagle, thought to be the largest eagle to have ever existed, with a wingspan over 3m and talons like crucifixion nails.[†]

Added to this outlandish cast of characters, there was – and thankfully still is – the Tawaki, the world's only forest-dwelling penguin, a little bird named after a cannibalistic, shape-shifting god of lightning, and a wee cutie to boot.

Under a mess of white hair and black beetling eyebrows, Gerry McSweeney wore a smirk. After 35 years of hard work and environmental obstinance, the owner of the Wilderness Lodge Lake Moeraki had achieved much of what he'd set out to do. 'I think this place is treasured not because of the history – of the Māori or old pioneers – but because we managed *not* to do certain things and preserved the forest instead,' he said.

---

[*] Spiders aren't insects, before you start.

[†] When the first Polynesian settlers arrived, there could have been as many as 150,000 moa, but they were hunted into extinction inside a century. Without their favourite prey, Haast's eagle soon followed suit.

An Inconvenience of Penguins

Before the lodge was built, this extraordinary land had been earmarked for clearance – known as Resource Unit 23, it was scheduled to be logged and divided into 16 dairy farms. The tui, the kea, the kaka, the morepork owls, the Fiordland penguins – all their habitat would have been razed for a land of milk and money. Instead, it was saved.

'Some of my conservation associates think it's kind of grubby because we actually charge for our penguin tours,' said Gerry when we spoke in the lodge's lounge. The Tawaki are a major focus of the experience at Lake Moeraki and their distinctive silhouette is employed as a logo on everything from wine glasses to t-shirts. Yet Gerry saw them as just one element of the whole. 'Look, I trained as a botanist. My experience is in saving high country tussock lands, so for me birds are sort of peripheral,' he said. 'But they're certainly a good hook for getting visitors here. I think people need to have charismatic megafauna to get them thinking about other elements. We've got long-finned eels here and saving them has been a big achievement, but people say, "They're not very nice." Penguins have the advantage of being cute, but both are part of the ecosystem.'

There was no road through this part of the island until 1965, so, no logging, or any significant development. Instead, there was a sense that life wasn't so different to how it might have been when the first people arrived here 800 years ago. And yet when the road came, things did begin to change: farming, mining and logging were all possible here, as they had been in so much of the rest of the country. Though the Fiordland National Park to the south had been protected in one form or another since the early 1900s, there had been a growing feeling of encroachment.

Does a Penguin Shit in the Woods?

To push back, in 1985 a movement started to have the whole region listed as a UNESCO World Heritage Site. Gerry McSweeney was at the forefront of it. Four years later, the inscription arrived. Around the same time he set up the lodge, converting an old camp which the roadbuilders had used in the 1960s. It still stands on the tranquil banks of the Moeraki River today, giving people immediate access to nature. Most nights when he's at the lodge, the boss personally leads walking tours to see great constellations of glow-worms hanging from muddy banks along the roadside, owls hooting away in the dark while he does so.

Given his lifelong dedication to protecting the wilderness, it was curious to listen to him be so evangelical about sodium fluoroacetate, the virulent poison more commonly known as compound 1080. I'd heard about its use in conservation during my visit in early 2023 and saw mention of it in Tasmania shortly before coming back to New Zealand, too. Everywhere it seems to divide opinion. One side argues that it is an incredibly effective form of pest control, an unrivalled tool in combating the devastation wrought by introduced mammals. It is also far less dangerous to people than alternative poisons.

The other side shouts back that it is inhumane, a toxin that causes convulsions and slow deaths in its victims. They also argue that it kills far more fauna than the target species. Darren Peters, the trapper and hunter I'd met while travelling to the Snares Islands, was fundamentally against its use, looking at it as somehow dishonourable and dangerous.*

---

* Though Gerry McSweeney and Darren Peters had never met, they had apparently 'locked horns' over this issue many times during their long careers.

An Inconvenience of Penguins

For Gerry it was simply a case of numbers: dead targets outweighed unplanned casualties. 'I believe the best way to get stoats is to make their prey toxic. Rats just keep eating poison or whatever is in front of them and the stoats eat them. It's not a nice death, no, but it's effective.'

He accepted that keas, New Zealand's alpine parrots, were also susceptible to the poison but far more of the birds were being slaughtered by rats and stoats, 1080's intended victims, than dying from consuming the air-dropped pellets. There had been collateral on South Georgia during their rat clearances; there was collateral here. To that end, he had no hesitation at the prospect of using 1080 on his property.

Even so, I saw him as part of New Zealand's tradition of defenders of nature, people who would once have been disparagingly called ecowarriors. There have been activists like him since the days of Richard Henry, a 19th-century conservationist who understood the threat of introduced species. He pioneered translocation of kakapo, personally rowing hundreds of the flightless parrots to pest-free Resolution Island in a bid to save them from mustelids. That particular project ultimately failed, but he never gave up trying to protect the land from animals brought here by his fellow Europeans. He so loathed the damage done to flightless birds by stoats and weasels, and spent so many years frustrated in his attempts to trap them, that I suspect he would have had no hesitation in dropping 1080 himself.

Back on the penguin trail our small group was spat out on to a pebble beach like seabirds accidentally swallowed by a whale. Finally, the great songs of the barbarian jungle gave way to a more familiar sound – the pacifying hush of the sea. Behind

Does a Penguin Shit in the Woods?

us, trees reached out, leaning across the stony shore as though trying to pull the ocean towards them.

When the first people arrived here, ending 80 million years of isolation for this land, what did they make of it all? The novel forest must have been full of terrors; the unknown calls and rustling of unfamiliar birds would have sounded alien and menacing. This was land without serpent, dangerous spider or even rodent, but they wouldn't have known that as they tiptoed deeper into the grasping dark.

Gods and other myths helped them make sense of the terrain. Savaged by *namu*, black sandflies, they told campfire stories that this biting plague had been released by Hine-nui-te-pō, the goddess of death, to keep mortals from settling in the most beautiful fjords.

Down by the unkempt shore, a lone penguin waited for us, seemingly unbothered by sandflies or much else other than the desire to preen its wet feathers. Young Harry directed us to sit on some larger rocks at the back of the beach, 20m or so from the bottom of a muddy chute used by the Fiordland birds to access the water. Through long lenses and binoculars, we watched the penguin shake saltwater from its white-gold crest, then nonchalantly navigate the beach.*

Another newly clean bird emerged from the ocean to join it. These two Tawaki used their beaks to tend to individual feathers, occasionally accessing the uropygial gland near their tails for oil to maintain their wetsuits. They seemed to luxuriate in their time on the beach, clearly not disturbed by us, but

---

* One theory about the Māori naming this penguin after their god of thunder stems from the birds' electrifying eyebrows resembling lightning bolts.

seemingly very confident that Haast's eagles and other airborne threats were things of the past. Penguin 16 brought none of the tension or stress of its recent relatives.

At the same time, another emerged from the forest, slip-sliding its way down the chute, dirtying its white front in the process. The others were coming to land, but this one's mind was made up: there was business to attend to in the water. Unlike the hyper-organised Little penguins, which came in groups at the same time every day, there was a lot more individualism here.

When it stumbled into the other two penguins, the forest bird made a couple of yelping calls, sounding distressed, almost pained. I tried to replay other calls from memory and couldn't remember a penguin with a more unappealing brogue than this, a screech that sounded like a child being kidnapped. Whatever its message, the Tawaki seemed to forget its ocean mission entirely, and rather than go to the water, it turned round and marched arduously back up the slope with the two surfers.

Five minutes later, perhaps having been reminded of the importance of food by its furious partner, the same bird came back out and sheepishly transited to the sea.

I kept back from their path with the others in my group, sniping the penguins from a distance with my longest camera lens. On my screen I saw that they looked almost indistinct from the Snares birds, crested with deep red eyes that only bloomed into rubies when the sun caught them. Its most defining characteristic was instead an unusual patch of white feathers which most mature Tawaki develop on their cheeks.

In many ways they are very similar to all the seaside birds in their genus, but as commuters they differ wildly, swimming in freshwater streams, negotiating spaghetti tangles of tree roots,

Does a Penguin Shit in the Woods?

and having to worry about introduced mammals coming for them and their eggs.*

Before long, our group had to head back to the lodge, but I was permitted to tarry for an extra couple of hours in the hope of seeing more penguins. When everyone had disappeared back into the jungle, I took a walk around the rocky bay, searching the shore for shards of jade and the waves for more Tawaki.

Finding neither, I retreated to the viewing spot and waited for more to emerge from the treeline. No doubt it would be simple enough to follow their routes through the foliage, but to do so would damage their habitats and those of many more animals besides. So much as any penguin lives in secret, then it is the Fiordland, and I was happy to leave them unseen in the forest.

Instead, I sat and I waited, the Tasman Sea crashing ashore nearby, punctuated only by the irritating call of visiting red-billed gulls. I stared along the beach, willing a Tawaki to march out of the water or the jungle, and could hardly believe it when they failed to do so.

The earliest penguins originated in New Zealand. The home of the kiwi and the kakapo and the moa is obviously a natural place to have generated something so downright weird and flightless as the penguin. For a time, they grew as big as man eventually would, measuring over 175 cm from beak to tail and weighing over 100 kg. Around 56 million years ago, these giant penguins began to disappear, an event which coincided with the

---

* Like Antarctic penguins they also have highways; however, here they follow tunnels through the undergrowth rather than melted walkways through polar snow.

An Inconvenience of Penguins

arrival of toothed whales, which either outcompeted them for food or preyed on them directly.*

Despite being earthbound, even the proto-penguins could migrate – they could fly, after all, so long as it was only ever underwater. At some point in the distant past, they used this ability to stretch their territory, pushing far and wide around the world's oceans, splitting into dozens of species, adapting to landscapes as varied as the guano-baked cliffs of Peru, the sea ice of Antarctica and the flowering shores of Africa. There were successes and failures, evolutions and extinctions. They became vital cogs in complex marine systems and then, when people arrived, became precious parts of our world, too.

The Tawaki were probably saved from annihilation by their extreme forest abodes – this land was too wild and too arduous even for the most daring Polynesian explorers. They are thought to have split from other species 8 million years ago and from an evolutionary perspective are some of the least travelled penguins in the world. In a more immediate sense, they are among the most industrious, swimming in excess of 6,000 km when the nesting season ends. This is further than any other penguin, the sort of marathon distance that may have led their ancestors to discover new fishing grounds in the first place. Penguins emerged 60 million years ago; it took another 20 million years for them to reach South America.

On the quiet beach I thought about my own travels. Almost exactly four years had passed since I'd swum with the penguins in the Galapagos; my penguin pursuit had accrued an incredible

---

* I find most whale species quite boring, but removing the terrifying prospect of a man-sized penguin roaming the Earth deserves at least a little respect.

Does a Penguin Shit in the Woods?

number of miles in the intervening period. Now there were just two birds remaining: the Royals on Australia's Macquarie Island and the Erect-Cresteds on Bounty and Antipodes Islands, east of New Zealand.

I'd travelled to absorb some of the penguins' chaotic joy, the giddy moments when they bumbled and fumbled, clowning around as though on purpose. But it had been more than that – I had travelled to see them while there were still 18 species to see. I had also been motivated by observing what they did to other people, and what we have done to them. Despite all the oohing and the ahhing, the smiles I'd seen at corners of people's mouths when I mentioned the birds, no penguin seemed entirely safe from human interference and climate change. I was likely to live long enough to see at least three species go extinct: the African, the Galapagos and the Yellow-Eyed penguins. Perhaps the Tawaki had it right by swimming far and nesting in secret, but even their numbers were not thought to be increasing.

I wanted to stay on the beach and meditate on this. The absence of penguins in that moment hardly seemed important, yet I was not entirely alone. Hine-nui-te-pō's emissaries were everywhere – swarms of biting *namu* crawled over my hands and up my sleeves. I crushed them by the dozen, but more migrated down my neck and up my nostrils. My hands became polka-dotted with bitemarks. Scratching, flailing, I stood, swore at the sky and left the beach. Tranquillity had lost. The goddess of death had won the day.

17

Macca Attacker

> I have lost myself for the time being amongst the penguins.
> – Sir Douglas Mawson, *The Home of the Blizzard*, 1915

It was late 2024 and everything was rotten in the world. War strode across borders and continents. The WWF released a report saying that the average size of wildlife populations had fallen 73 per cent in the last 50 years. Having ravaged South Georgia a year earlier, avian flu had finally arrived on the Antarctic continent. Then the United States voted Donald Trump back into office, further twisting its boot heel on the throat of the natural world.

Despite, or perhaps because of it all, penguins found themselves in the news even more than usual. In these times of crises, editors needed cheery clickbait and so turned to the birds. There was Flop the Humboldt being taught how to walk again in Dudley Zoo using a baby bouncer. There was the story of Maggie/Magnus, a male King which had been misgendered for *eight years*, its confused keepers baffled by the penguin's failure to lay an egg. And then there was Gus, an Emperor who had swum over 3,500 km from Antarctica to Western Australia, presumably by mistake.

I almost got to see that wayward bird but landed in Perth just as it was being released back to sea. I spent a week working

Macca Attacker

around the state on a couple of unrelated writing assignments, but occasionally I'd wonder if old Gus had made it home. Given the bird had arrived underweight and confused, the chances seemed vanishingly small. I suspected it'd have been better off in a decent zoo, but some alien impulse had taken the Emperor across the Southern Ocean, and authorities had decided it was better to return it to that great unknown.

After 10 days in Western Australia justifying my flights from the UK, it was time to get back to New Zealand, where I'd get on another Heritage Expeditions trip to chase down my final two penguins. For what was essentially a straight line with a single connection, the journey from Perth to Queenstown was remarkably arduous. Bad weather delayed then ultimately cancelled my original daytime route, meaning I needed to take off at midnight for a four-hour hop to Melbourne, then another three on to New Zealand. For every moment of the first flight a two-year-old boy, incoherent and insane, thrashed the back of my seat while screaming. I countered with noise-cancelling headphones and Lana Del Ray's delightfully soporific album *Norman Fucking Rockwell!** The child's distress still pierced my skull like hollow-point ammunition.

As well as the sleepless night, there was a further five-hour time difference to reckon with. When I eventually landed in Queenstown, I peeled duct tape off my eyes and looked out the window: the approach here is one of the most scenic in the world, threading through mountains towards a gleaming lake. Until I turned on my phone, I felt a little better.

---

* I find it near-impossible to get through the first three tracks of that record without falling asleep. I'd suggest you go and listen to it now, but you'd only nod off and miss the end of the book.

An Inconvenience of Penguins

Then came the emails warning me about overdraft use; I was too scared to look at my credit card balances but I knew they only offered more bad news. I hadn't been this rooked since the thin days of 2020. Money was coming in January with my next guiding contract, but I'd stepped a little too far back from travel writing in the meantime and payment for the work I'd done in Australia would take months to clear.

Money was bleeding out of me in every direction. Yet another penguin expedition awaited, and though Heritage had agreed to host me, even affording the flights to New Zealand from Australia meant leaning on another credit card. The war chest hadn't been exhausted; it had been sold, empty, to the nearest pawn shop. I was broke and, as a consequence of this brokenness, I'd booked a capsule-style bunk in a shitty hostel for that night's accommodation. One of the ironies of commercial travel writing is that you can stay in the world's finest hotels for free but will often find yourself in a fly-blown hovel if you've got to foot the bill.

Later, lying in bed listening to backpackers young enough to be my children talking nonsense, I wondered how it had come to this. I wasn't on benefits, but I had as much financial freedom as when the pandemic had haunted every hall. A cowardly part of me regretted being here, but a more obstinate part said: *You're eight-ninths of the way through and concession now would be madness.*

Earlier I'd taken a walk around Queenstown and seen that nothing had changed in the 20 months I'd been away.[*] Without money to sit in craft beer bars, I raided a supermarket

---

[*] Though presumably the people at the back of the 2023 Fergburger queue had just about got their lunch by now.

Macca Attacker

and found a bench by the lake to have a couple of warm cans. There was no feral goat curry to make here, so I gnawed on a sandwich instead.

South, some 1,250km away, the Royal penguins waited for me. With some luck, the very last species would come a couple of days after that. Every penguin had been far from home, but none were more distant than this final pair. I thought numbly about the birds that night, telling myself that everything was for them, then swallowed a handful of melatonin and immediately fell asleep.

It lasted all of 90 minutes before the extreme heat of my capsule woke me. I was being slowly cooked lying there, and the six other men in the room were only making it worse with farting and snoring, grim reminders of my unplanned time on Ascension. At 1am an eighth body drunkenly stumbled into the room. I considered murder but the exertion would only have overheated me further. Instead, I waited for him to pinball into bed, then opened my privacy curtain, hoping desperately for some cooler air. At 6.15am someone's alarm went off. At 8am the cleaner came in.

I left the hostel on the brink of tears. There had been a plan to work all day, to turn some of the research from Western Australia into money, but my brain was now a mound of scrambled egg.[*] Heritage was putting me up in a hotel at the end of town that night, so I limped up there in the hope of checking in early. This was possible, it turned out, but only because my roommate had arrived the night before.[†]

There was no way this could be good news – I was a husk,

---

[*] Specifically, the wet, undercooked kind.
[†] Roommate? Jesus.

desperate for sleep and privacy and anything that wasn't introducing myself to a stranger. Whoever he was, he wasn't here now, so I attempted a feverish sort of nap. This room was cooler than the coffin box the night before, but it was still stifling, so after some fruitless tossing and turning, I gave up and dragged myself back outside.

A stress rash had bloomed on the insides of my elbows. As far as I could tell, it was being fed by my poverty and the nervous sick feeling that came with the chance of seeing a new penguin species. I'd carried this particular nausea far and wide for four years, and now, on the eve of a final penguin voyage, it was once again resting at the back of my throat.

I spent the afternoon wandering, lingering in cafés and on park benches, tactically delaying getting back to my room until 11pm. It was still empty. This was a relief in that I didn't have to make small talk while getting undressed – with any luck he had picked someone up at a bar and gone back to their place.

I quickly got into bed but alas, my roommate arrived around 45 minutes later. A Chinese man around 60 years old, he buzzed around the kettle and said hello. I pulled my duvet up a little higher, said hello back. The man reached for his phone and spoke Mandarin into it. A female robot voice said:

'I am sorry for disturbing your rest. Is this room too hot?'

I said it was no problem and that yes, the room was very hot. Been hot all day and all night. I couldn't remember the cold. My roommate began to disrobe, first removing a cap to reveal a skull that had been shaved clean with a wet razor; standing now in just his Y-fronts, he spoke once more into the machine. I locked eyes with one of his nipples, a small, almond-shaped thing with a single black hair hanging out like a clumsy medical stitch. It seemed to be the only hair on his torso.

'Do you think the room is stuffy?' asked robot woman.

I nodded. I sure did. Christ, for some fresh air . . .

My roommate went over to a small desk fan, aimed it at the curtain, then mimed to show me how the airflow would circulate around the room, waving his arms far from his body as though he was casting a spell.

He came back over with the device again. It said:

'Please speak into the machine and then I will be able to understand you.'

Avoiding eye contact with the loose wiring on his chest, I said:

'My name is Jamie. I am from Scotland. I am very excited to see penguins on this trip.'

The woman spoke for him again while he stared at me, grinning.

'Oh yes, we are all interested in the businesses.'

Businesses! Like business geese! I knew it!

The trip that would hopefully bring my final penguins was called Birding Down Under, a two-week tour of subantarctic islands loosely dispersed below New Zealand. Not unlike South Georgia, they were home to endemic species and were in varying stages of recovery from introduced pests. Almost all of them had been bases for sealing or whaling operations in the 19th and 20th centuries, with some also selected for doomed settlement projects in the same period. Today they are all protected by conservation bodies in Australia or New Zealand, as well as UNESCO.

If things went well, we could see as many as six penguin species on this trip, maybe even seven. It was an exceptional itinerary to little-visited locations which brought birders from

An Inconvenience of Penguins

far and wide, people with binoculars and life lists, serious folk whose obsessions could drain joy from any situation. The following morning, the lobby was full of such people wearing camouflaged gear and neutral tones, as though they were about to stride off in search of an ivory-billed woodpecker, not just sit on a bus to Bluff for three hours. I couldn't decide if this was a sort of uniform or if they just hadn't bothered to pack any other clothes.

The snippets of conversation I caught were terrifying. A scruffy man with thick white hair and a bushy white beard cornered one of the guides. 'How well do you know your albatross?' barked this Stag-Do Santa like he was demanding loyalty to the crown. A slight woman with a camera lens as long as her torso was asked what she'd do with her spare hour before the bus left. Go for a walk, perhaps? Enjoy the town? 'What's the point?' she sneered. 'I've seen all the birds around here already.' A man who looked like Charles Bronson (the prisoner) with a wasting disease stared out the window with binoculars for 15 uninterrupted minutes. Meanwhile my former roommate joined the rest of his Beijing tour group, who kept themselves to themselves.*

I was to be with these people for a little over two weeks and I suspected it would feel a lot longer.

Then again, perhaps I just needed some sleep.

This trip was on the same ship as 20 months ago, and after leaving Bluff, the *Heritage Adventurer* would first visit the Snares Islands again. I wasn't *not* interested in calling in once more, but seeing the ominous swell outside of the porthole the following

---

* My friend never did tell me his name, which was a shame as I'd have liked to personally curse his endless snoring and noisy getting up for the toilet three times through the night.

Macca Attacker

morning, I didn't have the same nervous sick feeling about seeing the endemic penguins this time. Maybe this was just exhaustion, too – overnight the sea had been rough and sleep impossible as meaty waves sent big right hooks shuddering through the ship's ribcage. Not only this, but I'd been given a cabinmate – Fan, the leader of the Chinese tour group. He was friendly and spoke English, telling me that the group was called the Beijing Penguins. He also gave me a penguin passport, a little logbook to keep track of each of the species I'd seen.* I told him that I might complete the list on this trip, and he was delighted on my behalf.

The next day we sailed to Enderby Island, many people's favourite of all the subantarctic islands on this side of the world. Still sleepless, I had inexplicably spent most of the night anxious and alone in the dark, my brain a dried mushroom. I forced myself out on the excursion anyway – there was a population of Hoiho on this northernmost of the Auckland Islands; they looked healthy and that was a relief, but mostly I just wanted to stretch my legs off the ship. The birders ran around trying to record every pipit, parakeet and penguin. They got very excited about the possibility of seeing an endemic snipe. I watched on with deep disinterest.

That night I was so fatigued that I began to hallucinate. I lay in bed then found myself on a distant shore, the warm sea lapping at my feet. Ahead of me a large creature lay dying on the sand. A sad, bioluminescent thing, all around it there were clicking, creaking noises, something like a sperm whale.

---

* It really looked like an official passport, too, complete with a stiff cover and golden embossed writing. Indeed, they look so much like passports that Fan was once detained at Montevideo's airport and questioned about why he was carrying so many. He was only released when he showed them the cutesy penguin illustrations inside.

An Inconvenience of Penguins

Electric blue light shimmered hypnotically. Wait. Could it be a penguin? Some lost creature of the deep? I reached out to touch it . . . Fan flinched and asked if I was OK. He'd been reading his phone under the bedsheet.

I rolled over and finally slept for 10 tremendous hours.

Joseph Hatch was an ugly man. That's not a metaphor. I mean he was not easy on the eye. Handsomeness was alien to him. He was a rotter. A minger. Pug ugly. He was also a heartless bastard, but his horrible face probably meant he had little choice in that. A one-time mayor of Invercargill, he was the sort of cutthroat Victorian industrialist who, in a different part of the world, may have thrived like Andrew Carnegie or JP Morgan. Instead, today he lies in an unnamed grave in Hobart, which considering how he made his money is good enough for him.

For almost 30 years, Hatch was in the business of slaughtering penguins and seals on Macquarie, a lonely Australian subantarctic island a day's sail from Enderby. On an increasingly large scale, Hatch's men butchered the animals to extract their oil, a trade that became lethally efficient after he got his hands on some Norwegian-built, steam-powered digestors. He set these fiendish contraptions at five points around Macquarie, and after his gangs ran out of elephant seals, they began to fill them with penguins which were clubbed and gutted and dropped into the drums to be rendered down. There have been claims that the birds were thrown in alive, which is unlikely to be true, but even so the screams of the dying animals would only have been overpowered by the stench of the foul operation. The killing happened with such ruthless competence that by the time Hatch's license was withdrawn, over 2 million penguins had been slung into his terrible digestors.

Macca Attacker

The decision to kick him off the island was partly driven by pressure created by Sir Douglas Mawson and my old travel companion Apsley Cherry-Garrard. Both explorers were horrified by Hatch's penguin massacres and, along with H. G. Wells and others, launched an early conservation campaign to pressure the Australian government to put him out of business.* 'The penguin has won a little bit of affection from all of us because he snaps his flippers at the worst conditions in the world,' wrote Cherry in a 1919 letter to *The Times*. 'If we do not help him now, we can never look him straight in the eyes again. Poor penguin, but poorer we!'

The majority of the victims were Royals, the bird I'd come to see, my penultimate penguin. I'd heard they'd made a remarkable comeback over the last century, though their population low was never recorded by Hatch's gangs, nor is their true total known now.

If I'd been blasé about my time on Snares and Enderby, I was unsurprisingly a different person when we approached Macquarie now I'd slept. Awake but not exhausted at 5.30am, I saw it emerge through a charcoal dawn. We were sailing down the island's uncommonly calm west coast, the side usually being bludgeoned by the notorious wind and waves of the Furious Fifties.† In 30 years of operating in the subantarctic region,

---

* 'You see that these pictures of rookeries of apparently comical birds are really pictures of poor dim-minded creatures worried and strained to the very limit of their powers. That is what their lives have always been,' wrote Wells in what reads a lot like a backhanded compliment.

† The Furious Fifties are the southerly cousins of the Roaring Forties, the infamous latitudes with powerful winds that wrecked so many ships over the centuries. Get far enough south and you can also encounter the Screaming Sixties.

An Inconvenience of Penguins

Heritage had never made it down this coast before. If the reasonable swell was a rarity, the clouds were not – the island gets fewer than four clear days a year and is one of the cloudiest, rainiest places on the planet.

The land had the look of an open fracture, something you're not really supposed to see and shocking when you do. The ship's geologist excitedly told us that the long island is made of the ocean's crust, one of the only places on Earth where rock from our planet's mantle is being exposed above sea level. Consequently, the mainland looked like a huge, broken tibia with sharp sea stacks poking out of the ocean like shards of bone, their slopes stripped and infertile. As the sun rose feebly behind the island, silhouettes of birds appeared in the sky, while below us in the cold sea, penguins began to leap from the water.

From the upper decks, through the murky light, it was hard to tell which species they were. Even when the birders confirmed they were Royals, I struggled to believe them. It seemed a little too easy – I had been prepared to swim to shore if necessary. Only as we rounded the southern tip of Macquarie and floated off Hurd Point was I satisfied. The smell of the rookery carried across the gunmetal water; that sharp, familiar stench was still impossible to fully enjoy, even though I knew it meant victory.

Hundreds of birds porpoised, some then rafting together, appearing to backstroke as they cleaned the filth of the rookery off their little bodies. After half an hour, the expedition team told us that the colony here was too tightly packed to visit and the anchorage too unreliable. Instead, we'd head up the coast to Sandy Bay for a closer look at the penguins.

In the late 1800s the sovereignty of Macquarie was almost transferred to New Zealand, which, thanks to their greater protections

Macca Attacker

of wildlife, would have saved the Royal penguins from Hatch sooner. Unfortunately, late in the process the Australian government decided to keep a hold of the island. It still does today.

Macquarie was named in honour of the self-made Hebridean boy and colonial governor of New South Wales Lachlan Macquarie. Naturally the mainland Australians who have heard of their remarkable island insist on using a nickname, Macca, rather than its potentially tongue-twisting Scottish title, Macquarie.[*] Lachlan never visited this far south, and in the early 1800s he had dominion of the Australian mainland on his mind, rather than exploration of the outer reaches of the colony he was helping to violently control.[†] When eyes from the British Empire were finally laid on the island, it was deemed too inhospitable even for a penal colony.

Pity, then, the people of the Australian Antarctic Division (AAD) who call the place home today. Most come from the mainland and work year-long contracts, many having already served time on Antarctic bases.[‡] As well as scientific study – including counting how many cloudy days they have – staff

---

[*] Avoiding the possessive here is important as Macca's is Australian for McDonald's.

[†] So far as rapacious colonialists went, Macquarie seems to have been one of the better ones, though the very nature of his job would have left him with considerable blood on his hands.

[‡] The following day I interviewed one of these distant souls in the shadow of one of Hatch's old penguin digestors. Shaun was excitable and likeable, and could hardly get his words out quick enough. Like all of his colleagues, he wore a precautionary medical mask to prevent any illness getting on to the AAD base, though in his case it acted like a muzzle as much as a disease barrier. He'd been on the island for six months already and absolutely was not bored. Having spent years in Antarctica, to him Macquarie was exotic, warm and staggeringly green.

An Inconvenience of Penguins

ensure the island remains pest-free. With the final extermination of rodents and rabbits in 2014, Macca had enjoyed a decade without invasive mammals by the time we stepped off our Zodiacs on Sandy Bay. The results of this conservation were overwhelming.*

In front of a tussocky backboard, southern elephant seals and King penguins littered the beach, all amassed in numbers that inevitably reminded me of South Georgia. Blissfully, avian flu had not yet reached this corner of the world, meaning there were no rotting corpses, nor any stench beyond the usual atrocities that come with this much biomass. The lack of disease here meant that almost three years since it had last been permitted on the Antarctic Peninsula, we could get down on to our knees, improving photography for one thing, relaxing the animals for another. All around there were elephant seal weaners looking like giant, legless Shar-Peis, making stunned monkey noises as they enquired whether any of us could replace their now-absent mothers.†

Royal penguins were there from the very first moment, appearing far more interested in our movements than the three

---

* And yet as recently as 1998, the AAD field manual still had advice on what to eat if disaster struck and food ran out: 'Penguins may be killed by stunning them with a blow to the head and then breaking and cutting the neck . . . Penguin stew is palatable provided the external fat is removed before cooking, and penguin liver is excellent.'

† Ask many experienced polar guides what their favourite animal is, and they won't say penguins but elephant seal weaners. It's a funny name to say, of course, but these big babies have been weaned and abandoned by their parents, so often jiggle over, looking to suckle or at least have a bit of a cuddle with human visitors. Annoyingly, as responsible tourists, we must decline both requests. Nonetheless, with their big black eyes, silly eyelashes and ridiculous calls, these young seals make weaner-lovers of us all.

rangers who'd hiked down here from the AAD base to keep an eye on us. While those inspectors kept to the back of the beach, hidden behind face masks, the penguins gathered around our ankles, staring at us with red eyes, as though to ask: 'And you are . . .?'

I stared back. The Royal penguin is closely related to the Macaroni, so much so that for a time they were thought to be the same species. But in their looks, the regal birds are very different – while the Macaronis always have black faces, their cousins have tremendous variety. Deep golden crests sit atop their little heads, but below there are many different visages, the majority white like powdered Elizabethans, but others showing grey gradients, or even yellow patches, giving the impression that they have leaky hair dye.

Every other penguin species had shown such uniformity in their markings that these variable looks fascinated me. Peter Matthiessen had stopped at Macquarie while on his own penguin quest to see Emperors in the Ross Sea, and the appearance of these smaller birds had drawn his eye, too. 'Its glory lies in its twin spikes of golden feathers, which flare back rakishly from each brow like the wings of Mercury's helmet, only to collapse behind the eye like a fallen hairpiece.'

I walked along the beach and found a patch of ground that might be kind to my knees – despite its name, Sandy Bay was mostly rocks and pebbles, though perhaps the animals had already bagsied the most comfortable spots for themselves. Hours passed there, the little Royals coming up to nibble my lens, or simply pose for photos. Others seemed to think me some kind of civil court judge and brought cases for me to hear, squabbling with their clients, hoping for a quick ruling one way or another. Further afield, they fought with abandon,

An Inconvenience of Penguins

as cranky as any of their crested cousins, but perhaps even more persistent in their battles, some locking beaks like rutting stags.

Elsewhere seals belched and Kings trumpeted. Penguin highways were in permanent rush hours, only occasionally interrupted when a giant petrel loomed overhead. This was the Antarctic region as I remember it in the happiest reaches of my being, an experience the likes of which had upended my life when I'd first found myself surrounded by penguins years earlier. I let it wash over and around me, the bedlam, the joy.

I had a drink that night, celebrating with others during a boisterous recap. The air inside the lecture theatre carried a crackling energy that delights expedition teams, a buzz that connotes unqualified success. Some passengers compared photos, others bird lists. The latter were as delighted by the invasive redpolls as they were by the Royal penguins, but I let their obvious wrongheadedness pass without comment.

I looked at these generalists with a little disdain, but something didn't sit right. They were birders, happy with whatever came their way. How could they be so scattergun? I, on the other hand, had come with a plan, a clearly defined idea of what was important. A list. Increasingly over the last months, the idea of failure had left me uncertain, uneasy, occasionally unreasonable. The whole thing had made me a little twitchy.

I thought about this for a moment, looked around the room, then felt a spasm in my left eye.

Then, like a frightened macaque, my lips pulled back from my teeth as a realisation rushed at me.

18

Bingo Bird

> You will have seen pictures and photographs of penguins. They will have conveyed to you the sort of effect I tried to recover. They express a quaint and jolly gravity, an aldermanic contentment. But to me now the mere thought of a penguin raises a vision of distress.
>
> – H. G. Wells, *The Undying Fire*, 1919

The revelation landed like a hammer on a wooden floor. I staggered down to my cabin and looked up the definition:

'Twitcher: A birdwatcher, especially one who tries to see birds that are rare in a particular area, and is willing to travel long distances to do this.'

The example of its use was even more damning:

'Obsessive twitchers may endanger their health and their relationships as they rush around the country in search of the latest rarity.'

I'd been concerned that my penguin project would leave me with an elevated interest in birds, but now in the blistering light of day it was painfully clear: I had become a twitcher.* This, as

---

* The term apparently comes from a description of Howard Medhurst, a birder in the 1950s who would literally start twitching at the prospect of seeing a rare bird.

An Inconvenience of Penguins

everyone who is not a twitcher will tell you, is the worst kind of birder. Monomaniacal, obsessive, blinkered. I ticked every box, on this trip more than any other.

Good Christ, I was literally ticking boxes!

While birders – clear-headed and rational people for the most part – were happy to record everything nature had to offer them, I had been exclusive and ignorant. Half a dozen species of albatross had flown past the *Adventurer* in a single day, and I hadn't even picked up my camera. On the beach hours earlier, I'd ignored the King penguins – perhaps my favourite of all the 18 species – to focus only on the Royals.*

Where I once saw beauty all around, now I saw only the outline of a plump bird, its wide, reptilian feet resolutely gripping the ground, its vexatious silhouette blocking out the sun.

I sought out Phil Hansbro, one of the birding guides on Heritage's expedition team. I thought – hoped – that I'd just been doing some targeted birding, but no. 'Some people will go to see a bird, just so they can put it on their list,' he explained, a hint of scorn in his tone. 'They won't even look at the other birds around. That's not a birder. That's just a twitcher – or a lister. Most birders are also listers but not all listers are birders. What do you think you are?'

Back in the real world, the damage was now obvious – I'd let my finances fall into ruin and a career that I'd slowly built over 15 years atrophy; I'd missed weddings, endless parties and at least one funeral, all so I could chase penguins. There was no

---

* The Kings are certainly my favourite in terms of photography but I would concede that they are not the most characterful birds, their poise and lofty bearing seeming to prevent them from indulging much of the guano-spattered clowning of their contemporaries.

Bingo Bird

avoiding the truth: I was a twitcher, and I certainly felt twitchy now. I ordered a large glass of red wine from the bar and worried about how I'd pay for it later.

Leaving Macquarie, we travelled north-east for a day to reach Campbell Island, nipping out ahead of a big, mean weather system like it was a bully waiting for us after school. Other companies in the region were not so lucky – Ponant and Lindblad both had ships pinned against the side of the Auckland Islands by the same system.

It caught up with us at Campbell, the wind screaming so loudly it blew the tops off waves. I'd signed up for a long hike that day, a challenging, muddy 11km over slick roots, between giant tussock, and down wet ravines. The gales made nothing easier. In the moments we could take our hoods down, there were views across angry landscapes, raw bays and cliffs which looked as though they'd been bitten out of the land by a titan. Emerging from the mist, islands appeared like drowned pyramids. Incongruously in this elemental scene, the most notable flowers were Ross lilies, the approximate size, shape and colour of corncobs. On the New Zealand five-dollar note, they are depicted at the feet of a Hoiho. Here the flowers instead framed another bird – the southern royal albatross, exuding calm amid inclemency as always.

I'd never seen these mighty creatures up close. On the rare occasions that they trailed the ship, it was impossible to get a sense of their enormousness. With wingspans almost equal to the wandering albatross, they are among the largest extant flying birds, yet to watch them delicately preen their feathers was to witness grace. In the high wind, if they want to fly, they need only open their immense wings and let the gusts carry them

An Inconvenience of Penguins

aloft. I watched them, more elegant than angels, and knew I'd have been a lot less stressed if I'd written a book about them.*

The serious birders hadn't come on the hike, instead sticking to a long boardwalk in the centre of the island. This, they believed, was the best way to see more species, including the flightless Campbell teal, a small duck that avoided extinction thanks only to a captive breeding programme in the 1990s. Since their rerelease on to a now-rodent-free Campbell – DOC have successfully eliminated the nibbling bastards – they have once more proliferated. Elsewhere, the latest local snipe continued to elude and irritate the group, not least because midway through this latest excursion they were beset by a hailstorm. For the first time, I genuinely felt sorry for their miss.† Bad weather could easily mean the same for our final penguin.

On his famous expedition to find a snow leopard, Peter Matthiessen was seeking an animal that has evolved to be almost invisible. He spent two months trekking in western Nepal, hoping to become one of the first Westerners to ever look upon the big cat. Though it remained unseen, he found a way to accept, even embrace, the experience. The expedition may have technically been a failure, but Matthiessen's Zen outlook carried him – and us – past the miss, to something more

---

* Despite appearing to be virtual negatives of each other, taxonomically albatrosses are penguins' closest relatives. When I found this out, I thought of Danny DeVito in *Twins*. In that 1988 movie he plays the diminutive leftover parts of his superhuman twin brother Arnold Schwarzenegger. DeVito's Vincent is everything the big man is not: where Arnold is tall, handsome and albatross-strong, the wee man is cranky, dark and penguin-dumpy. And yet, if the viewer comes away loving either of those characters, it is, inevitably, the little penguin man.

† Or in birder parlance, dip: 'We dipped on the snipe.'

Bingo Bird

transcendent. 'If the snow leopard should manifest itself, then I am ready to see it,' he wrote, as though floating in the cool Himalayan air.

My quest had been much different in nature. Notions of Zen calm were long gone, and I was trying to see penguins, birds incapable of hiding. They'd become embodiments of the faraway, often making their homes in places so distant and obscure that they could only be found on the most detailed maps. Before I started looking for them along the edges of the known world, I'd never heard of the Antipodes or Bounty Islands, the only homes of the Erect-Cresteds, my 18th and ultimate penguin. The same was true for Marcona in Peru, Chubut in Argentina, the Snares Islands, Nightingale Island and virtually every place south of the Antarctic Peninsula. Reaching them all had taken months, years. Even now, there were no guarantees of a happy outcome. That's the thing about penguins: spotting them is so very easy – the trick is getting to them in the first place.

South from us our rival ships continued to be picked on by the climactic bully we'd avoided. After their ordeals at the Auckland Islands, Lindblad and Ponant made it to Macquarie, but just as one system spat them out, they were swallowed by another. They would have been able to make out the Royal penguins from the ship, but landings looked increasingly doubtful. Soon their plans to follow us to Campbell and the Antipodes were blown away in the gales. Their expeditions teams would have been comprised of experienced, knowledgeable guides; there were passengers – wealthy, dedicated and perhaps even kind people – who'd spent years building towards seeing their final penguins, only to now be juggled and dropped by a cackling ocean. By remarkable coincidence, I knew two of them: an eccentric Hawaiian couple I'd met on the farcical Swan Hellenic trip were stuck on the Lindblad ship, not having much more luck this time round.

Heritage has three decades of singular experience in this region and often operates on the exciting edge of acceptable risk in swell that would turn the stomachs of many other expedition cruise companies. They frequently find their ship more exposed than the large fleet traversing the Drake Passage on the other side of Antarctica so must meticulously plan and react as the voyages evolve and the waters churn. Yet for all that expertise, we had got lucky – the weather that was tormenting the other two ships was creating a following sea for us, strong winds and big swell that carried us directly into the realm of the Erect-Crested penguins.

The night before the attempt at the last bird, the Windy app delivered nothing but good news. The staff, meanwhile, delivered a recap and briefing, offering a potted history of the Antipodes Islands, an uninhabited archipelago which sits 750 km south-east from New Zealand's South Island. The team's historian told us that it had been pest-free since 2018, and that the last of several shipwrecks had been in the late 1990s, when the conservationist Gerry Clark's yacht *Totorore* was devoured by a storm, killing him and his crewmate Roger Sale. We heard too that it was one of two homes of the Erect-Crested penguin, the final one on my list, a bird that would offer freedom – or seal off the exit from this dank labyrinth.

I was sure it was a coincidence, but this penguin is also the one that nests farthest from my home in Glasgow, 19,300 km distant, literally half a world away. When the Antipodes Islands

Bingo Bird

were discovered in March 1800 by Captain Waterhouse and the crew of HMS *Reliant*, he named them thinking they were exactly on the opposite side of the planet to London.[*] The birds nest only here and on the nearby Bounty Islands, which had been named by Captain William Bligh on his fateful, ultimately mutinous voyage to Tahiti aboard the *Bounty* in 1788.[†] Both places were inhospitable to landing – especially the Bounties – meaning data quality on the birds was poor.

As had been the case at the protected Snares Islands, we'd be restricted to Zodiac viewings only, if they happened at all. I looked up to see how this info might land around the room, but if people were worried, they hid it well. These were experienced folk – when the expedition leader asked if anyone was hoping to finish their penguin list, five hands went up, including mine.

The least studied penguin in the world, little is known about the life cycle of the Erect-Cresteds, though there was at least enough information for the guides to tell us that these penguins are the fourth largest species overall, and that they show strong egg dimorphism, with the second normally 81 per cent larger than the first. The runtish egg is almost always doomed to be kicked out of the nest and gobbled by skuas, a sign that perhaps the birds are evolving to lay just one, though the benefits of that

---

[*] The antipode of the Antipodes Islands is actually just off the town of Barfleur, Normandy, France.

[†] A couple of days later, when Bligh's name came up in conversation on a Zodiac, some Australian passengers were quick to bash him, having been influenced by unfair, inaccurate portrayals in various bad films about the *Bounty* over the years. When I pointed out that anger might be better directed towards lead mutineer, would-be murderer, kidnapper and enslaver of Polynesians Fletcher Christian, the suggestion was not well received.

An Inconvenience of Penguins

higher-risk breeding strategy are unclear.* In any case, parents will spend three weeks guarding and feeding their chicks when they arrive, then finally go and look after themselves while the babies crèche for six weeks. Like so many penguins around the world, their numbers were in decline and had likely dropped by as much as 75 per cent in the last 50 years. Once again, no one was quite sure why.

Something that didn't come up in the recap: things would have been so much worse had British Prime Minister Anthony Eden's desire to drop a nuclear bomb on the penguins been fulfilled. In 1955 in the early days of his turbulent premiership, Eden petitioned New Zealand to request the Antipodes as a site to test Britain's new super-strength thermonuclear weapons.

OK, Eden wasn't looking to kill the penguins specifically, but Operation Grapple sought to explode a series of devices above the islands, the strongest of which was thousands of times more powerful than Little Boy, the bomb which had killed 140,000 people in Hiroshima a decade earlier. A successful programme would have irradiated the archipelago, and the fallout would very likely have also reached the Bounty Islands, just 200 km away. That would have brought a quick end for the Erect-Crested penguins, as well as tens of thousands of other birds, including two species of endemic parakeet and the Antipodes snipe.†

Mercifully, Eden's New Zealand counterpart, Sidney Holland, refused the request – as well as later pleas to use the Kermadec

---

* One theory was that the penguins were finding it harder to forage for food and that in these leaner times energy would be better used supporting a single chick.

† If someone wants to make a B-movie where this happens and the penguins instead gain superpowers, I will 100 per cent watch it.

Bingo Bird

Islands to the north. There was a chance of fallout reaching the mainland, which would have been bad at any time but especially as Holland had his own election coming up. The British government huffed and puffed but did not blow the doors down. Instead, they weighed nuking a part of Antarctica but were again deterred. Finally, they settled on Christmas Island, in what is now Kiribati.* When the tests were finally conducted in 1957, one was witnessed by the journalist William Connor, thankfully not over a penguin colony but a tropical island: 'It was a dress rehearsal for the death of the world,' he wrote. 'Ripped out of the secrets of the heart of the universe . . . it hung before us, a boiling red and yellow sun low above the horizon. It was an oil painting from hell, beautiful and dreadful, magnificent and evil.'

'Can you hear them?' asked Phil Hansbro the following morning. The bird man had left Yorkshire for Australia 33 years earlier, but his accent hadn't moved an inch. 'That's your penguins.'

A dense miasma surrounded the ship. I could indeed hear what sounded like birds, but there was nothing to be seen. We'd made it to the Antipodes and the weather was uncommonly calm. Fifty months since the Galapagos penguin, the final one was now an inevitability, though the sea fog created just a little doubt. If the birders had lent me one of their thermal scopes, would it have counted? 'Any bird that's a skulker you can find now,' Phil explained when I asked about the tech I'd heard some in the group had brought along. 'I suppose it might work in fog too though, yeah.'

---

* By the time the tests went ahead, Eden was already on his way to early retirement, chiefly because of the Suez Crisis.

An Inconvenience of Penguins

The Yorkshireman is one of the top birders in the world, with a life list that was extended to 8,432 species with the addition of Forbes' parakeet on our trip. He began taking birding notes over 50 years ago and has travelled to every continent multiple times for his passion. While we spoke, he had a habit of pausing mid-sentence to pick up his binoculars, quickly double-checking if a bird shooting past was a fairy prion.[*]

Forever unkempt, he looked and sounded like he should be managing a squad of roofers in Leeds. Instead, when he's not travelling the world to add to his extraordinary life list, he heads up a team of 50 people working on lung disease research in Sydney. When he was studying for his PhD in 1983, Peter Harrison's then new book on seabirds became Phil's bird bible, or more accurately catalogue. When we spoke, he had just eight of its 434 birds left to see – he'd finished the penguin list a long time ago – and he knew the missing ones by name, as though they were family members or sworn enemies.

I asked: do you find it hard to turn off? 'I don't wanna turn off,' he said quickly. 'I love doing this stuff, it's great, gives me a huge buzz. I just love watching them – it's mega.'[†]

When I asked if he had a favourite, he didn't hesitate: 'Light-mantled sooty albatross. Best bird in the world. Phenomenal.' It is, in fairness, a good one, a fantastically smooth-looking animal rendered in monochrome, various shades of slate covering its body and back. Airborne it looks like a piece of flying calligraphy. This would already make it a significant beauty,

---

[*] It was.

[†] He said that frequently: mega. Mega and phenomenal. When talking about birds, both words popped up a lot.

but it also has white brackets behind its eyes, which give it the interrogative look of an Adélie penguin.

Phil's knowledge of birds was incredible, his recall astonishing. He was playing a game he knew probably wouldn't – couldn't – end, but he played it every day he went outside. When taxonomists split birds into more species, his list grew. Sometimes this meant he got to add one for free, other times it meant he had yet another bird to find. In 2025 he planned to add a few more names to his gigantic list with trips to Cameroon, India and São Tomé and Príncipe. He was also heading to Alaska, where seeing McKay's bunting would mean he'd seen every bird species in North America. That would be, I had to concede, phenomenally mega.

'Unlike a lot of this stuff, trying to see every family of bird would be sensible,' he said. 'There's about 300. If you did that, you'd have a good idea of the whole world's birds.' I could see him looking at me as though it might make a decent next book for me, so I glanced away, pretending to be interested in the fairy prion.

I was almost dreading asking, but I wanted to know if penguins were exceptional in this great game, or if they were just another equal tally. 'No, they are, they're really mega,' he said to my great relief. 'There's 11,100-and-whatever species of bird in the world, but seeing a new penguin is orders of magnitude more significant than seeing some flycatcher you've never heard of before in a South American forest, then never think about ever again. One of my mates thinks you should have a multiplier to show how significant the bird would be. A penguin would be 20, say, and the flycatcher would be 0.1. They are not the same, not by a huge margin.'

An Inconvenience of Penguins

This was good news, I thought, as I went down to the Zodiac on my way to see 200 flycatcher's worth of Erect-Crested penguin.

As we puttered through the fog, the menacing shadows of the Antipodes darkened, thickened, then solidified. Soon there were cliffs, unassailable battlements which vanished into the low cloud. My Zodiac had seven other people in it, plus our driver. Among them was atrophied Charles Bronson (the prisoner), who quickly positioned himself at the front of the Zodiac, the best spot for photographs. The logic of this seemed deeply flawed: his camera was badly underpowered for the conditions, which started with poor light and soon deteriorated when heavy rain began to fall. Droplets quickly covered the face of his unguarded lens. I wondered if I could simply tell this old man to get out of my way, but some part of my fight had gone. I was here, the penguins were here. Photography was, for now, unimportant.*

The rain fell as though God thought the ocean needed a top-up. Around us, subantarctic fur seals occasionally called their sad songs to one another. The dedicated birders' Zodiacs, meanwhile, had congregated at the heel of an enormous green cliff, their binoculars trained high up its face, desperately seeking the Antipodes parakeet. Inevitably my gaze fell lower.

The hairdo is, by any measure, bombastic. Two distinct ridges lead up from its eyes, giving the impression of intense concentration. It also reminds me of a military crew cut, those

---

* This was a healthy attitude to have as the battery in my first camera failed, a slice of bad luck that would have driven me fully insane had I been as uptight as on other occasions.

Bingo Bird

lines, so precise and exact, offering a neatness unlike any other penguin. When drying, these rise like defensive dorsal fins – and that way they stay, entirely upright. The Erect-Crested penguin has not been misnamed. A nearby Eastern Rockhopper looked like it was the *before* image in an ad for a starchy hair product by comparison.* Later, looking at close-up photos of the crest, it also reminded me of regrettable 1980s hairstyles, the sort which a teenager would get to follow a trend, then spend a lifetime regretting every time they found the damned photo album again.

I perhaps thought too much about those crests.

I wondered if I'd perhaps thought too much about penguins generally. So much effort had been put in, so much time and money I didn't have, and now these final birds were strewn across another alien shore, utterly apathetic to my presence.

Two predictably fell into a fight. The Erect-Cresteds were wearing different uniforms, but I'd seen versions of this shit-stained violence 18 times around the world. Like every species, these birds were belligerent and ungentle. I admire penguins and am often entertained by them, but their frequently repugnant behaviour makes them difficult to truly love. Now, whenever I hear people say, 'Oh, I love penguins,' I suspect they simply haven't spent enough time around the birds. They hide nothing, and while they are probably no more chaotic or aggressive than any other untamed animal, their lack of discretion means everything is always on show: the tragic deaths of their babies and the vicious battles with their neighbours. Nothing is left to

---

* The Eastern Rockhopper is on the brink of being its own species, but for the purposes of this book is still regarded as a Southern Rockhopper.

An Inconvenience of Penguins

the imagination, no blank is unfilled. Forgiveness, then, is hard to come by.*

An unfamiliar mood settled inside me, a kind of apathy not dissimilar to the penguins'. Unlike Phil's impossible pursuit, my chase was over, my game won. As the rain poured and poured, an uneasy question was already beginning to form: now what?

The feeling stayed with me for days, but I couldn't put a name to it. It wasn't relief. It wasn't ecstasy. It wasn't disappointment, either. It had elements of all of these, but as time passed and we saw the penguins again at the Bounty Islands, I realised that it felt deeper, richer somehow.

I wondered if perhaps it was satisfaction.

Back on the ship that night, the general mood was again ebullient. A doctor from New York had been given a lifetime achievement award for services to public health, but she'd also completed her penguin list and said with what sounded like sincerity that the latter was the bigger deal. A joyless photographer from Norway also completed and reacted as though he'd just spotted a pigeon. Meanwhile, the more time passed, the more I settled into it. Strangers came up and shook my hand, the way they might had I been a father in a maternity waiting room in the 1960s. Glasses were clinked. Small talk made. I wasn't sure what to say, but I was happy, I knew that.

As he was leaving the dining room, Phil shouted over to me, 'Right, Jamie, c'mon.' I was being invited to the post-dinner birding club. It was open to all comers every evening at 8.45pm,

---

* I did really mean all this at the time, but two months later while guiding in Antarctica, I watched juvenile Gentoo penguins try to catch the first snowflakes they had ever seen fall from the sky. The heartbreaking naivety of the scene made me swoon again in a way that felt like love.

Bingo Bird

but now I was being asked, by name. I did not hesitate to stand, a smile cracking as I did so.

I took a seat at the bar. The lounge had the mood of a high-stakes bingo hall, the attendees all with eyes down, crossing off lists and annotating tables. One man was asleep in the corner. Two were audibly drunk, offering theories about prions and defending rumours of finally seeing an endemic snipe. The most committed birders weren't here at all because they were outside, birding. Occasionally other staff members filtered in. One notified us of an erupting sunset, a rarity at these gloomy latitudes. Phil dismissed it: 'Oh, so it's doing the same thing it does every day? Come on. This is important stuff here.'

I laughed. So many voyages taken, so many time zones crossed, all 18 penguins finally defeated. The vastness of it was starting to sink in. These people were mine now, and I was theirs – and perhaps that was OK.

Over by the coffee machine, Steve from Norfolk lurked. I nodded hello and he came over for a chat. Armed with a foot-long beard and an imposing domed forehead, more than one person had commented that he looked like a kindly Rasputin, or some kind of battle mage. He was a half-decent staff away from being able to take on a Balrog.

I'd had largely one-way conversations with him at several points through the voyage, and towards the end I'd begun to suspect his intense questioning was a form of deflection. Some people hide in this way and, for all the walking and talking I'd done with Steve, I didn't know what he did for a living – how he was able to afford all his extraordinary travel.

And it really was a baffling amount – he let slip one day that he'd long ago visited every nation on Earth and seemed almost embarrassed by it. Not only that, he'd been to every

An Inconvenience of Penguins

British Overseas Territory, including the penguin lands of South Georgia, the Falklands and Tristan da Cunha. He'd even been to the Pitcairn Islands, the resting place of Bligh's *Bounty* and her mutineers.* His travel was far more extensive than mine would ever be – and I'd spent a decade and a half as a professional traveller.†

'Y'know, Jamie, I was thinking: with this voyage and all the penguins we've seen – what is it, six species?'

It was actually seven, I said: Snares, Hoiho, Royals, Kings, a fleeting glimpse of some Littles, a lone Macaroni and now the Erect-Cresteds.

'Yes, well, I realised that thanks to this trip, I've actually seen all the world's penguin species, too,' he said with an insouciant smirk.

My jaw tightened. What had been an epic project for me – a quest that had required setting fire to my prospects, emptying my bank accounts and dislocating my life – had, for Steve, been a mere bagatelle. A happenstance. I looked at him and weighed using that beard to slam his considerable skull against the bar.

'Quite funny, really,' he said.

'Aye,' I said. Fucking hilarious.

---

* Though only the final mutineers who stole the ship and fled the Admiralty. Several others were rounded up on Tahiti, with a handful dragged all the way back to Britain for trial and execution.

† I did chase countries for a while, but the game seemed suddenly hollow when I hit 100. I decided to stop chasing numbers from then on, though only after I'd got a clichéd compass rose tattoo to commemorate the milestone.

Epilogue

1. Galapagos: South America.
   Estimated 1,200 adults in 2007. Population decreasing.
2. Gentoo: South America, subantarctic, Antarctica.
   Estimated 775,000 adults in 2013. Population increasing.
3. Chinstrap: Subantarctic islands and Antarctica.
   Estimated 8 million adults in 1999. Population decreasing.
4. Humboldt: South America.
   Estimated 24,000 adults. Population decreasing.
5. Adélie: Antarctica.
   Estimated 10 million adults in 2017. Population slightly increasing.
6. Emperor: Antarctica.
   Estimated 650,000 adults in 2009. Population stable.
7. Yellow-Eyed: New Zealand and subantarctic islands.
   Estimated 2,600 adults in 2020. Population collapsing.
8. Snares: Subantarctic islands.
   Estimated 63,000 adults in 2010. Population stable.
9. African: South Africa.
   Estimated 19,800 adults in 2023. Population collapsing.
10. Southern Rockhopper: South Atlantic and subantarctic islands.
    Estimated 2.5 million adults. Population decreasing.

Epilogue

11. Macaroni: Subantarctic islands.
    Estimated 13 million adults in 1998. Population decreasing.
12. Magellanic: South America.
    Estimated 3.2 million adults in 2020. Population slightly decreasing.
13. King: Subantarctic islands and South America.
    Estimated 6 million adults in 2009. Population increasing.
14. Northern Rockhopper: South Atlantic.
    Estimated 413,700 adults in 2020. Population decreasing.
15. Little: Australia and New Zealand.
    Estimated 470,000 adults in 2016. Population stable.
16. Fiordland: New Zealand.
    Estimated 12,500–50,000 adults in 2019. Population stable or decreasing.
17. Royal: Subantarctic islands.
    Estimated 1.66 million adults in 2016. Population stable.
18. Erect-Crested: Subantarctic islands.
    Estimated 150,000 adults in 2011. Population decreasing.

Population estimates are the most recent available from BirdLife International.

Acknowledgements

Given that I relied on being hosted by several travel companies to make this book possible, the list of gratitude is long, but before I get to that, I need to thank:

Philippa Sitters, my wonderful agent who took a book that was getting nowhere and pushed it into the light. My editor, Phil Connor, at Headline for fighting off the competition, then making sure this was an actual book rather than a collection of essays. And DeAndra Lupu for excellent final edits which were as helpful as they were precise.

Peter Ross and Monisha Rajesh for separately both refusing to allow me not to write it – for providing a kick up the arse, essentially, one boot on each cheek. This whole project may well not have happened without their interventions and encouragement.

Stephen Phelan and Graeme Virtue: editors, mentors, friends, who have sat on my shoulders for almost 20 years, one an angel, the other a devil, though after all this time I still don't know which is which.

My semi-literate friends at home known as The Wagon. In a world where I am in perpetual motion, they are my home and my beloved anchors. The photos are really for their benefit.

The magnificent Jo Davey, whose two years of patience, close readings and insights improved the book enormously. Her edits were almost always right, even when I didn't want to admit it. If the book succeeds, a huge part of it is down to her.

Acknowledgements

Oliver Smith and Henry Wismayer for reading drafts, offering thoughts and more generally striving to set some kind of standard in British travel writing when so many others settle for less.

My uncle Matt, who didn't live to read this book, but who first showed me the outdoors. He nudged a snowball that continues to roll today.

The late David Kemp, the first reader of the completed manuscript and the best neighbour I've ever had. He was frequently more enthusiastic about me seeing this through than I was.

Tom Robbins at the *Financial Times*, who often appears to be the last editor in the UK to care about genuine travel writing. Liz Edwards at the *Sunday Times* for being a pal during the dark days of Covid-19 when so many other editors had switched the lights off.

Aurora Expeditions for giving me employment and changing my life. I know you were short-staffed, but still. In particular, thanks to Howard Whelan for showing me the magic of South Georgia for the first time, and Greg Mortimer for letting me on his ship, almost but not quite killing me a couple of times, and encouraging my nonsense.

Thanks also to Cheli Larsen, Phil Hansbro and Rod Morris for supporting my project so committedly while I sailed with Heritage Expeditions.

Other companies and individuals who helped me with my penguin voyages; some, but not all, did so in exchange for coverage in travel titles: Uniquely Galapagos, the Punta San Juan Project, Journey Latin America, Ponant, the Yellow-Eyed Penguin Trust, Lou Sanson, Abercrombie and Kent, the Southern African Foundation for the Conservation of Coastal Birds, Alison Towner, Graeme 'Snowy' Snow, the Falkland Islands government, Andy Pollard, Naomi McKee, Frangelica Flook, Debra Taylor, Bahía Bustamante,

Acknowledgements

Swan Hellenic, Tourism Tasmania, Junaidi Sustantio, Phillip Island Nature Parks, Gerry McSweeney.

Also, thank you to everyone who sailed with me on these voyages, passengers and expedition teammates alike. Sorry if I got in your way on a Zodiac or bored you talking about penguins. Remember that you promised to buy a copy of this book, though – I'm holding you to that.

And lastly Jean Lafferty, who told me to say yes to everything. Christ, what a mother. What an honour to be her son.

RAISING READERS
Books Build Bright Futures

Dear Reader,

We'd love your attention for one more page to tell you about the crisis in children's reading, and what we can all do.

Studies have shown that reading for fun is the **single biggest predictor of a child's future success** – more than family circumstance, parents' educational background or income. It improves academic results, mental health, wealth, communication skills and ambition.

The number of children reading for fun is in rapid decline. Young people have a lot of competition for their time, and a worryingly high number do not have a single book at home.

Our business works extensively with schools, libraries and literacy charities, but here are some ways we can all raise more readers:

- Reading to children for just 10 minutes a day makes a difference
- Don't give up if your children aren't regular readers – there will be books for them!
- Visit bookshops and libraries to get recommendations
- Encourage them to listen to audiobooks
- Support school libraries
- Give books as gifts

Thank you for reading.
www.JoinRaisingReaders.com